CHURCH AND STATE
IN EARLY CANADA

BY

MACK EASTMAN

EDINBURGH
PRINTED AT THE UNIVERSITY PRESS
BY T. AND A. CONSTABLE
1915

CONTENTS

INTRODUCTION — PAGE ix

CHAPTER I
THE JESUITS IN ACADIA 1611-1613

CHURCH AND STATE	1
THE FACTUM	2
JESUITS AND HUGUENOTS	4
THE JESUITS AND THE FUR TRADE	4

CHAPTER II
THE FIRST CANADIAN COLONY 1608-1629

CHAMPLAIN AND THE RECOLLETS	7
THE COMING OF THE JESUITS	11
THE COMPANY OF NEW FRANCE	12

CHAPTER III
CANADA A JESUIT MISSION 1632-1659

THE EXCLUSION OF THE RECOLLETS	14
CHURCH AND STATE	16
INDIAN POLITICS	20
CHARACTER OF THE EARLY JESUITS	21
THE BRANDY TRADE	26
THE COMING OF LAVAL	31

CHAPTER IV

THE DEFEAT OF THREE REBELS (1658-1665)

	PAGE
VICOMTE D'ARGENSON (1658-61)	40
DUBOIS D'AVAUGOUR (1661-63)	44
SAFFRAY DE MÉSY (1663-65)	48
THE BRANDY TRADE	72
THE JESUITS AND THE FUR TRADE	82

CHAPTER V

THE TRIUMVIRATE 1665-1672

VICEROY DE TRACY	90
GOVERNOR DE COURCELLE	93
INTENDANT TALON	95

His Economic Policy—His Relations with the Governor—Talon and the Church—Talon and the Jesuits. First Impressions—The Three Burgs—Intendant and Bishop—Tithes—Talon and the Jesuits—The Return of the Récollets—Harmony Restored—Explorations—The Civilization of the Indians—Talon and the Sulpicians—The Brandy Trade.

CHAPTER VI

THE FIRST ADMINISTRATION OF FRONTENAC
(1672-1682)

INTRODUCTION	135
FRONTENAC AND THE JESUITS	136
THE RÉCOLLETS AND THEIR PROTECTOR	147
THE SEMINARY OF QUEBEC	150
(a) 1672-1675—(b) 1675-1682	
THE SULPICIANS OF MONTREAL	157
THE CIVILIZATION OF THE INDIANS	162
THE SOVEREIGN COUNCIL	167

CONTENTS

	PAGE
INTENDANT DUCHESNEAU	169
His Relations with Frontenac and the Church—Tithes and "Cures Fixes"—The Civilization of the Indians	
THE FUR TRADE	174
THE BRANDY TRADE	179
CONCLUSION	201

CHAPTER VII

LA BARRE AND DE MEULLES (1682-1685)

GOVERNOR AND INTENDANT	203
LAVAL AND THE CIVIL POWER	205
THE ABBÉ DE SAINT-VALLIER	209
THE JESUITS AND LA BARRE	210
THE RÉCOLLETS AND THE BISHOP	213
THE SULPICIANS AND THE POWERS	219
THE CIVILIZATION OF THE INDIANS	221
THE BRANDY TRADE	222
CONCLUSION	228

CHAPTER VIII

A THEOCRATIC REVIVAL (1685-1689)

M. DE DENONVILLE	230
PROTESTANTISM IN NEW FRANCE	230
GOVERNOR AND BISHOP	233
THE TITHES	237
SULPICIANS AND GOVERNORS	238
THE RÉCOLLETS	239
THE CIVILIZATION OF THE INDIANS	239
THE BRANDY TRADE	243
THE JESUITS AS FRENCH AMBASSADORS	254
CONCLUSION	260

CHAPTER IX

DECLINE OF THE THEOCRACY (1689-1760)

	PAGE
THE RETURN OF FRONTENAC	261
THE SUPREMACY OF THE CIVIL GOVERNMENT	263
THE JESUITS AND THE FUR TRADE	265
THE BRANDY TRADE	267

Frontenac and Champigny—The Ottawa Missions—Jesuit Memoirs—Saint-Vallier and the Traffic—The Sulpicians—Belmont's Sermon—A History of Eau-de-Vie—The Attitude of the Récollets—Mercenary Motives?—General Conclusions—The Closing Decades of French Rule

BIBLIOGRAPHY . . 295

INTRODUCTION

IN attempting a history of Church and State in Early Canada our purpose is to study the relations between the civil power and the ecclesiastical authority in matters which concerned them both. Among these matters the question of political supremacy is of outstanding importance, and in estimating the relative strength of secular and religious influences we shall follow the gradual evolution of New France from a Christian mission to a royal province, and trace the growth and the decline of theocratic tendencies.

Allied with this central issue are others of varying significance, such as the admission of Protestants to citizenship, the traffic with the Indians in brandy and furs, and Indian policy generally In our successive chapters we shall treat these topics as they present themselves Very little space will be devoted to the narrative proper, as we presuppose on the part of the reader a certain familiarity with the main events of Canadian history in the seventeenth century.

CHURCH AND STATE IN EARLY CANADA

CHAPTER I

THE JESUITS IN ACADIA

1611-1613

CHURCH AND STATE

BEFORE proceeding to the St Lawrence basin, where the real work of colonization was to begin under the guidance of the heroic Champlain, let us pause for a moment at the tiny settlement of Port Royal in Acadia. The story of the exploits of de Monts, Lescarbot, Champlain, and the Good-Time Order generally, has been told by Parkman in his own inimitable style. This first French colony in America becomes of interest for us only in 1610, when we find the Baron de Poutrincourt entrusted with its government. In their Acadian microcosm he and his son Biencourt represented the State. While good Catholics, they were of the Gallican school, and it was only financial necessity that made them accept the collaboration of two Ultramontane Jesuits, Biard and Massé. These doughty champions of the Church were destined to remain in Acadia only from 1611 to 1613. Yet in that short space of time most of the problems which were to characterize the later history of New France began to declare themselves.

First of all came the question as to which authority should dominate, the secular or the religious. For several years the Jesuits of France had cast longing eyes upon the new continent where the fields were white for the missionary harvest, and their participation in Poutrincourt's enterprise was due to successful efforts at court [1]. Biard and Massé enjoyed the protection not only of the pious and influential Marquise de Guercheville, but even of Louis XIII and Marie de Medici, and, according to their partners in the Acadian expedition, their pretensions were correspondingly extravagant. One of the most interesting documents dealing with the case, from the laymen's standpoint, is a factum drawn up in view of a lawsuit which Biencourt intended to bring against his priestly colleagues [2]

THE FACTUM

As this factum manifests a strong antipathy, not only to Biard and Massé, but also to the entire Society of Jesus, we are obliged to discount many of its assertions. Nevertheless, large parts of it appear to be worthy of credence, especially the reproductions it contains of letters and affidavits. In a letter to Poutrincourt the famous Father Coton begged him to receive the missionaries kindly, and promised in exchange to be his solicitor at court. But the Jesuits soon antagonized the baron and his friends. The factum accuses Biard of drunkenness and gluttony, and harps on the notion, prevalent at the time, that his order was devoted to Spain and disloyal to France. Worse still, he and Massé stirred up rebellion against Poutrincourt and his son, and favoured their enemies at every turn. Then, recalling their contributions to the enterprise, the monks boasted that the others were their subjects and valets because they were feeding them all. "The Jesuit fathers are haughty persons," wrote Biencourt, "who would that we were subjected to their yoke." So disagreeable did

[1] *Fds. Roche.*, Can. 13, f. 333, Letters of Coton, 1608, 1609, Carayon, p. 89.
[2] B N., 4to, Fm. 2965.

their mutual relations become that the two priests resolved to return to France Taking refuge on a ship about to sail, they locked themselves in a cabin. Biencourt's men broke open the door and induced Massé to come out, but Father Biard lay on his back behind a trunk fulminating excommunication against all who should touch him Massé declared that he had more power from the king than had Biencourt, that he acknowledged the latter's authority in nothing, and that he excommunicated him. When they finally came ashore Biencourt ordered the rebels to withdraw to their rooms, as he was resolved to prevent their wandering around like vagabonds, until he had instructions to send them back to France. After three months of silence the Jesuits feigned a reconciliation; but while Biard sent a flattering letter to Poutrincourt, Massé wrote another which destroyed the baron's credit with Madame de Guercheville Thereafter, says the factum, the Jesuits of France, Father Coton included, had recourse to "the lowest practices" to ruin Port Royal and its governor. Then they fitted out for the zealous marquise a ship which was to take possession of the vast domains which perforce de Monts had ceded her, and which the Society of Jesus evidently hoped to evangelize and govern Disaster befell the expedition at the hands of the English, and Biard was carried captive to Virginia. The balance of evidence would seem to show that the Jesuit then guided the English enemy to Port Royal,[1] a place which he, doubtless, believed to be as hateful to God as it was to him That such treachery would appear reprehensible to the responsible heads of his order is evidenced by a letter to his general in which he sought to exculpate himself.[2]

[1] Lescarbot, 1617, pp. 687-90; Carayon, p 110; Thwaites, vol iii, p 137; *ibid*, vol iv, p 45, and Biard's whole *Relation* of 1616, *cf.* also Parkman, *Pioneers*, ch. viii, and Biggar, *Early Trading Companies*, Appendix.
[2] Carayon, p. 110.

Jesuits and Huguenots

The factum accuses the Jesuits not only of ambition, hypocrisy and disloyalty, but also of aggressive intolerance. In spite of their promises, they quarrelled with the Huguenot sailors and seized their psalm-books and Testaments to throw them into the sea. Only Biencourt's intervention saved the disputants from cutting each other's throats.[1]

However, Biard and Massé had grievances against the Huguenots. When they had tried to embark at Dieppe, the Protestant ship-owners had treated them with such disdain that the phrase "Adieu, Biart," "Allons, Biart," or simply "Biart" became the formula of contemptuous dismissal.[2] Eventually they triumphed over their heretical adversaries, and Biard could write exultantly to his general: "The malice of the Demon and of his tools has turned to our advantage. At first we asked for a mere corner in this vessel, . . . and now we are the masters here."[3]

The Jesuits and the Fur Trade

This victory had been really won by Madame de Guercheville. From princes and princesses, dames and seigneurs, this pious lady had collected enough money to buy out the traders and endow the mission. As coin would be of no earthly use in the New World, the Jesuit contribution of 3800 livres was converted into merchandise amounting to half the cargo. On January 20, 1611, at "La Barbe d'Or" of Dieppe, Biard and Massé entered into a contract of equal partnership with Biencourt in the fur trade of New France.

Had the parties to this contract been good friends, perhaps the incident would have attracted little attention. But Biencourt accused the Jesuits of ruining his commerce by

---

[1] Cf. Carayon, p. 92.   [2] Asseline, vol. ii, p. 154.
[3] Carayon, pp. 7, 8.

their "hypocritical ostentation of generosity" to the Indians, and he even charged that in putting their money into the fur trade they had "frustrated the intention" of the donors These accusations appeared in the factum published in 1614, and the contract of "La Barbe d'Or" became notorious.

In his own account of the affair Biard explains that, while the missionaries were to share in the emoluments of the partnership, they had nothing to do with conducting the trade or retailing the merchandise. "There is the contract of association," he exclaims, "against which people have cried until they have made themselves hoarse. . . . God grant that they never cry against us with any more cause." [1]

Champlain, whose facts were evidently drawn from Biard's account, heartily endorses the Jesuit attitude. "It is this contract . . . which has caused such noise and complaint and outcries against the Jesuit fathers, who in that and everything else have governed themselves equitably according to God and reason, to the shame and confusion of envious persons and slanderers." [2]

In his biography of Father Coton the Jesuit d'Orléans represents Madame de Guercheville as desiring that the missionaries be furnished with merchandise in order to render the mission stable through its revenues. "No more was needed," he adds, "to make people say that the Jesuits had entered the commerce of Canada and were drawing therefrom immense treasures." [3]

A modern writer, Father de Ravignon, shows that Madame de Guercheville simply followed an established custom, which ensured a maximum return for a minimum expenditure. Thus, with the consent of Clement VIII, the kings of Portugal had decreed that of the six hundred bales of silk exported annually from Macao to Japan, fifty should be sold

---
[1] *Rel.*, 1616, p. 136.   [2] Bk. iii, ch. i, p. 768.
[3] *Vie du Père Coton*, 1688, p. 158.

by the Portuguese merchants for the benefit of the Japanese mission.[1]

At all events, while the procedure of the marquise and her Jesuit friends appears practical and proper to us, it furnished the enemies of the Society with new ammunition, and increased the bitterness of the feud between the secular and the ecclesiastical elements in the Acadian settlement.

In conclusion, we observe that this first attempt to unite a religious mission with a colonial enterprise proved abortive. The failure was due to mutual hostility of ideals and incompatibility of temperaments. The clash between the Gallican Poutrincourt and the Ultramontane Biard appears at this distance symbolical of the later political life of New France. Meanwhile another religious order was called to collaborate with Champlain in building up a new colony on the banks of the St. Lawrence.

[1] *De l'Institut des Jésuites*, 1862, p. 190.

CHAPTER II

THE FIRST CANADIAN COLONY

1608-1629

CHAMPLAIN AND THE RÉCOLLETS

BY a peculiar coincidence, in the very year that the " Father of New France " founded Quebec, Henri IV's great minister, Sully, discountenanced all effort at French colonization. On February 26, 1608, he wrote as follows : Far-off possessions are " disproportioned to the nature and to the brain of Frenchmen, who, I recognize to my great regret, have neither the perseverance nor the foresight required for such things, and who ordinarily apply their vigour, their mind, and their courage only to the conservation of what touches them nearly and is constantly present before their eyes . . . So much so, that things which remain separated from our body by foreign lands or seas will never be anything but a great charge and of slight utility to us." [1]

The concluding sentence sounds prophetic of the history of Canada, but the cause was not lack of perseverance or foresight, and these two qualities were especially conspicuous in the founder of Quebec Besides, he was a brave soldier, a dauntless explorer, an indomitable colonizer, and a fervent Christian.

His ambition was twofold the conquest of the New World for France and for the Church ; and as collaborators in the attainment of this lofty design he chose the Minor Brothers of St. Francis. In 1615 King Louis XIII accorded the Récollet province of Saint Denis a monopoly of Indian

[1] *Cinq Cents*, 203, f 236

missions. Other provinces and other orders were jealously excluded.[1]

The first superior of the Récollets was Father Denis Jamet, who for a decade faithfully aided Champlain in his efforts to colonize Canada. On July 15, 1615, about six weeks after his arrival at Quebec, this pioneer missionary addressed to Cardinal de Joyeuse a most interesting account of the country and its possibilities. He told how, in ascending the St. Lawrence, while the merchants were absorbed in their traffic, he feasted his eyes on the beauties of this new land. Nor could he avoid regretting that it should be uninhabited. Accordingly, he mapped out for the cardinal a plan of colonization, since in Canada with slight cost His Majesty could acquire greater possessions than elsewhere with heavy expenditure and effusion of blood. Here were no enemies to combat: the natives would welcome the French for their own security, and the Hurons would leave their fertile country to settle near Quebec. Continuing, with remarkable freedom from professional prejudices, this Récollet advised parents in Old France no longer to constrain their sons to become monks in order to avoid the division of their lands, but rather to give them what a religious education would cost and send them to New France, where there was good soil in abundance. The noblesse, who were consuming their substance in superfluities, would do well to retrench a little and found small settlements in the New World. This matter concerned the king as well. If he did not wish to spend of his own, let him relegate to Canada the numerous persons guilty of one or two bad deeds, but otherwise honest. " Thus in a few years one would make a second France." To the newcomers Jamet promised fine lands and excellent rivers, good hunting and better fishing. The French would advance toward the south as far as they wished ; the savages

---

[1] Sagard, pp. 10, 11 ; Le Clercq, vol. 1, pp. 32, 33, 49, 50 ; *Œuvres de Champlain*, vol. iv, pp. 5-8.

THE FIRST CANADIAN COLONY 9

would be tamed gradually; and the Récollets would minister to all [1]

Although Jamet's advice bore little fruit, he and his fellow-friars continued to support Champlain in his unwearying endeavour to build up a strong French colony in face of opposition from the fur traders. More than once Récollet delegates were sent to France to rouse the Associates of Rouen to a sense of their responsibility; but in vain: the traders wanted a trading-post and cared nought for "crowns and glory." [2]

As the rules of their order forbade the enjoyment of revenues, the Récollets were frequently left in cruel distress. Nevertheless, they toiled on bravely, and with the help of twelve skilled mechanics built themselves a monastery fortified with moat, ramparts and bastions, and ornamented with a flourishing garden.[3]

While at Quebec, by every means in their power, they were seeking to strengthen the bands of the secular authority among the Indians, the Récollets proved themselves able representatives of French interests. They broke up conspiracies, warded off attacks, and cemented alliances which encouraged commerce.[4]

They were even sent as envoys to the court of France. In 1621, when traders' quarrels were threatening the colony with ruin, an assembly consisting of Champlain, the priests, and "the best-intentioned citizens" chose as their delegate to Versailles Father Georges le Baillif. This monk was a man of high birth and personally known to the king. The Prince of Condé had commanded Champlain to undertake nothing without the participation of Father Georges. He now presented to Louis a petition which gave a glowing

---

[1] *Cinq Cents*, 483, f. 581. [2] Sagard, pp. 30-2, 40
[3] *Grand Voyage*, pp. 55-7.
[4] Le Clercq, vol. i, pp. 113-22, 161-3, 247, 259, 260, *Œuvres de Champlain*, vol. iv, pp. 122-5.

description of the "land of promise," and pointed out the dangers which menaced it. Chief among these was the conduct of the Huguenot merchants.[1]

A more sustained attack on the Huguenots in general, and on Guillaume de Caen in particular, was made in a booklet entitled *Avis au Roi*, of which the same Father Georges was probably the author. "Those who say that His Holiness is Antichrist; that, if they had the God of the Papists, they would strangle him; that, if they had hold of the last monk, they would eat him . . are not fit to execute such a design" as catholicizing the New World. Nor is colonization faring any better, for de Caen and his associates prefer to have "eux seuls part au gasteau." In short, "it is the money-demon which spoils everything."

However, the Huguenot merchant had plenty of backing, and a number of those who had navigated in New France made affidavit at the Admiralty of Dieppe that the aforesaid *Avis* was "a pure calumny and imposture devised against" de Caen.

But Father Georges was not content with open accusations. Between him and the Huguenot there seems to have been personal animosity. In his determination to destroy the royal confidence in the Protestant leader, the Récollet so far forgot his sacred character as to present to Louis XIII certain forged letters detrimental to his enemy, and purporting to be the work of Champlain and other inhabitants of Quebec. The trick was discovered; the imposture denounced; and Champlain wrote directly to Father Georges complaining of his fabrications.[2] Meanwhile, the Huguenot companies held their ground at Quebec in face of Catholic opposition.

The misdemeanour of one Récollet, though a sore disappointment to Champlain, does not seem to have altered

---

[1] Le Clercq, vol i, pp 175-99
[2] *Fds. Fr.*, 16,738, f. 143, *et seq.*

THE FIRST CANADIAN COLONY

his attitude toward the rest of the order. At any rate, he was not over-eager to welcome the Jesuits who arrived three years later.[1]

For, in 1625, the Récollets, living only upon alms from France and petty contributions from the Company of Rouen, were obliged to confess themselves vanquished They then appealed for aid to the Jesuits, whom they considered *personnes puissantes et rentées*,[2] although at this time their credit was rather low at Versailles [3]

The Coming of the Jesuits

In answer to the call came Lalemant, Brébeuf, and Massé, but not without encountering serious opposition They came in haste, without the entire approval of their Paris confrères, without adequate means of support, and without letters from the king At Quebec they found the people deeply prejudiced against the Society of Jesus and unwilling to receive them But, eventually, with Champlain's assent, the Récollets offered them the hospitality of their convent.[4]

The following year they were joined by Father Noyrot and de Noue with twenty workmen The Jesuits then set to work to cultivate the soil with an energy which excited the admiration of Champlain. Their handmill was also very useful to the colony.[5] After a time, according to Lalemant, the Jesuits succeeded in winning the hearts of all the inhabitants, while Champlain became very fond of them and took their superior as his confessor.[6] Their position was further assured by a grant of land from their protector, Ventadour, Viceroy of Canada.[7]

---

[1] Le Clercq, vol. i, pp 291, 308-14, Thwaites, vol iv, pp 216, 226
[2] Sagard, p. 862; Le Clercq, vol i, p 288-90
[3] *Vie de Coton*, pp 191-6.
[4] Thwaites, vol iv, pp 180, 210, Sagard, p 868
[5] Champlain, 1632, vol ii, pp 85, 129-31, 167
[6] Thwaites, vol iv, pp 180, 210, 216, 218, 226
[7] A N , M 242.

The Company of New France

Meanwhile the two religious orders worked harmoniously together for the welfare, spiritual and temporal, of the colony, and they seem to have been responsible in some degree for the organization of the Company of New France [1] Jesuits as well as Récollets had protested against the domination of heretical merchants, and de Caen declared that the former were "machinating" his ruin.[2] From Jesuit and Récollet envoys, as well as from Champlain, Cardinal Richelieu doubtless gathered much of his knowledge of Canadian needs.

At all events, when the Company was formed under the great minister's direction, its charter contained what the missionaries had persistently demanded. The Indians were to be evangelized through Catholic immigration, while Protestants were to be rigidly excluded. Religion was to be supported by the Company, and the religious motive was linked with the patriotic.[3]

But, although in divers ways the Church manifested her influence in the formation of this great colonial company, all progress was abruptly arrested by the coming of the Kirkes in 1628.

During the siege of Quebec the inhabitants suffered from famine. The Jesuits had sown some grain; the Récollets a good deal more. The Jesuits, says Champlain, assisted the people according to their power, but, he implies, the Récollets showed very little liberality.[4] To this suggestion the Récollet Sagard retorts: "Those who were in command at Quebec would have liked to make us suffer first and to take from our garden the little corn which remained after we had given generous alms to the most necessitous. Wit-

---

[1] Le Clercq, vol. i, p. 432; Thwaites, vol. iv, p. 218.
[2] *Fds Fr*, 16,738, f. 143 D.
[3] A E, *Am*, iv, ff 55-63; *Edits*, vol i, *Mercure*, vol. xiv, p. 233.
[4] Champlain, 1632, vol ii, pp. 211, 212, 231, 277-9.

ness the charity (of men) who wished to make us bear the suffering due to their own negligence and carelessness." Clearly the Jesuits had been rising and the Récollets falling in the esteem and confidence of the Father of New France, and this fact doubtless affected the subsequent history of Canada.

When negotiations with David Kirke had failed, the priests were in favour of holding the fort, but Champlain won them to approval of an honourable capitulation [1] Though his conduct was afterwards blamed by M. de Caen,[2] it was evidently approved by Richelieu and the Company, who gave him their confidence again in 1633.

[1] Champlain, 1632, vol ii, pp 218, 220, Le Clercq, vol i, pp 400-3
[2] *Fds Fr*, 16,738

CHAPTER III

CANADA A JESUIT MISSION

1632-1659

THE EXCLUSION OF THE RÉCOLLETS

IT was only by chance that in 1632 Canada became a Jesuit mission, for the all-powerful Richelieu had assigned this colony to the Capuchins

This order enjoyed his especial protection, and to all appearance the cardinal had intended to reserve the missions of America for them He placed Capuchins in Acadia and bequeathed a fund to their seminary [1] From Razilly he received eulogistic accounts of their work in New Guiana.[2]

Finally, when France was about to resume possession of Canada, Guillaume de Caen was charged to transport to Quebec three Capuchins.[3] For some years the prestige of the Society of Jesus had suffered diminution in France,[4] and it was only when the Capuchins delicately refused to reap where others had sown,[5] that the court judged it " necessary

---

[1] Dom. Arch , M 123

[2] A E , *Am.*, IV, f 106. Razilly's language recalls that of the Jesuit *Relations*, e g " The great number of people in France whom necessity forces to commit many sins will find in this land of benediction an assured asylum for the repose of their souls."

[3] A E , *Angleterre*, IV, f 31

[4] *Vie de Coton*, pp 191-6 Father d'Orléans tells us that in 1625 the Assembly of the Clergy was hostile to the Jesuits , Cardinal Richelieu was displeased with them , the Parlement of Paris was once more unfriendly ; the court itself, heretofore an unfailing refuge for the order in its adversities, was no longer well disposed However, after a time, king and cardinal came to see that they were mistaken.

[5] Bressani, p 295

to restore the Jesuits to the place belonging to them near the fort of Quebec."[1] Not until the spring of 1632 did Fathers Le Jeune and de Noue receive a written assurance that Richelieu approved of their return to Canada.[2]

Whatever they really felt about the cardinal's intention to supplant them, the Canadian Jesuits showed no sign of resentment. The *Relations* sang his praises, and in 1635 Father Le Jeune wrote him. "You are the heart and soul of this Company and of all New France. You can give the life of the body to an infinity of poor French artisans who go begging it in foreign parts through lack of land."[3] In time Richelieu became cordially interested in the Jesuit mission, and established a fund in its favour.[4]

Meanwhile, what had become of the Récollets? In spite of their ardent desire to return, they had found themselves excluded from their beloved mission. Not unnaturally, they suspected the Jesuits of secretly exerting their influence against them; but in Jean de Lauson, president of the Company of New France, they found a declared opponent. Lauson claimed that the Récollets would not be able to live in peace with the Jesuits, and that their vow of poverty rendered their order unfit for work in an infant colony. "In our century," he said, "they have reformed ethics, and they have even found that to establish the spiritual, one must employ the temporal; thus a country is better governed."[5] Probably Lauson was enunciating the views of Richelieu as well as his own. Besides this, the cardinal's policy seems to have been to entrust the spiritual government of each colony to a single religious order, with the object of avoiding "the harm which might arise from the mixture of persons of divers conditions", and this was the reason he gave for withdrawing the Récollets from

---

[1] A E, *Angleterre*, IV, f 31   [2] *Rel*, 1632, p. 1.
[3] A E, *Am*, IV, f. 138   [4] A E, France, 835, ff 64, 65.
[5] *Mémoire de 1637* (Margry), Le Clercq, vol 1, ch xiv, Sagard, end.

Acadia when in 1633 he entrusted that mission to the Capuchins.[1] Hence, when the minister became convinced that Canada would profit more from the activity of Jesuits than from the ministrations of Récollets, he doubtless favoured a complete monopoly for the former.

In choosing between the two orders Richelieu would surely be influenced by the opinions of Champlain. The governor of Quebec was charmed with the personality of his confessor, Charles Lalemant, and filled with admiration for the superior energy, industry, and helpfulness of the Jesuits in general. The new edition of his *Voyages*, dated 1632, tended to give prominence to the Jesuits and place the Récollets unduly in the background. What part Champlain himself actually had in this revision is matter for speculation,[2] but the new volume was calculated to influence the court in favour of the sons of Loyola, and doubtless helped to secure them undivided control of the religious administration of New France.

Church and State

For a quarter of a century after the restoration of Canada to France, Church and State were practically one. The Church was represented exclusively by the Jesuits, while the official State consisted at first of the Company, the governors, and then, after 1647, of a Council in which the habitants had two representatives. However, even in the Council the superior of the Jesuits had a seat. So that, when the governor appointed by the Company of New France was sufficiently docile, the monks would be the real rulers of New France. And this is what usually happened.

During the last two years of his government Champlain

---

[1] A E., *Am.*, iv, f 100 , Champlain, 1632, vol ii, p 282.

[2] *Œuvres de Champlain*, vol v, preface, Kingsford, vol i, p 15; Biggar, *Early Companies*, p 279.

was coming ever more completely under the domination of his spiritual advisers, until by his testament, drawn up five weeks before his death, in violation of his marriage-contract, he bequeathed most of his property to the Church of Canada Though in Paris the will was declared null and void, in the meantime the Jesuit chapel of Quebec had benefited to the extent of nine hundred livres from the sale of Champlain's furniture.[1]

That Canada was already a theocracy is evidenced by the fact that the commission of Champlain's successor, M de Chasteaufort, had been for some time in the hands of the Jesuit superior, Paul le Jeune.[2]

Under Chasteaufort and Montmagny (1636-48) irreligion was repressed by the secular arm. Blasphemy, drunkenness, and absence from mass cost the delinquents the stocks or the wooden horse[3] On one occasion, when two men became intoxicated while awaiting the midnight mass, "on prescha fortment contre," says the private *Journal* of the Jesuits, and Montmagny had the culprits placed on the wooden horse exposed to a "frightful north-east wind."[4] Montmagny was a knight of Malta, a monk as well as a soldier, and his purpose was to make religion preponderate in Canadian life [5] With the governor of Canada, the president of the Company the Ursulines, and the Sisters of Charity all working in harmony under the guidance of the Jesuits, the Canadian State became absorbed into the Canadian Church.

The merchants alone held aloof, but in 1645 the Jesuits eized an opportunity to secure the goodwill of their leaders. Canada was being utterly neglected by the Company of New France, and the principal families of Quebec were clamouring for the right to control the fur trade themselves.

---

[1] Gosselin, *Bernières*, p 153, Faillon, vol i, p. 287
[2] Thwaites, vol viii, p 308, note 53
[3] *Rel.*, 1636, p 43   [4] *Journal*, pp 35, 53, 106
[5] Dom. Arch., N 128, f. 52.

With the aid of the dowager-queen the Jesuits intervened successfully on their behalf, and the new Community of Habitants was bound to contribute 5000 livres annually to Canadian missions and to transport free of charge thirty tons of supplies each year for the Jesuits of Quebec.[1] However, the merchants were not willing to sacrifice themselves for the sake of the Jesuits. The Community did not prosper, and in 1654 the Council of Quebec refused any longer to pay freight for the religious orders or for the governors. The governor at the time was Jean de Lauson (1651-56), whose rapacity exceeded even his piety, and though he could not prevent the enforcement of the Council's decree against " those who were not in authority," he exacted compensation for himself.[2] Nevertheless, for three or four years the Community of Habitants asserted its influence very strongly. Finding Montmagny too disinterested to play into the hands of " their little republic," its members caballed against him and intrigued for the appointment of one of themselves, M. d'Ailleboust (1648-51).[3] Though a friend of the Church, Ailleboust showed a more independent spirit than the other governors of this period.[4]

His successor, the aged Jean de Lauson,[5] as president of the " Great Company " had long befriended Jesuits, and, declared Jérome Lalemant, merited every gratification from their Society.[6] But, though they hailed his arrival with joy, the Jesuits were soon obliged to confess that, in spite of his piety, Lauson lacked the experience, decision, and strength essential to the salvation of the colony. Besides he was too aged, too much embarrassed in his finances, and

[1] *Lettres*, p. 72, *Journal*, p. 3, C.G., I, f. 239
[2] C.G., II, f. 22
[3] " Mémoire de La Chesnaye,' F 3, II, f 3
[4] E.g. *Journal*, pp 138, 233
[5] For further references to Lauson cf. Dom. Arch., N 128, f. 69, Fds. Fr, 17,871, f 136.
[6] Rochemonteix, vol. i, p. 195, note 5.

too anxious to enrich his sons.[1] This sentiment was voiced by Father Ragueneau The superior had the reputation of attempting to dominate the political and social life of Quebec by inquisitorial methods [2] His power was increased by the fact that his position made him *ex-officio* member of the Council. Not only outsiders, but even his fellow-Jesuits disapproved of his domineering ways Father Poncet repeatedly wrote the general complaining of his superior's habit of meddling *circa publica pariter et privata* : he monopolized M de Lauson, directed him, made him enact laws and issue ordinances , the situation was full of danger and the superior should be recalled.[3]

Ragueneau was not recalled, but in 1656, by order of General Nickel, he was removed from Quebec. It is possible that this good father has been made something of a scapegoat. In any case, it is interesting to learn what qualities he considered essential for successful work in New France "Industrios ac strenuos operarios hic noster exposcit labor "[4] Himself an industrious and strenuous worker, Ragueneau aroused especial indignation and animosity because his natural love of power and his zeal for the Church and his order were untempered by gentleness and prudence.

Meanwhile, the antipathies he was exciting against their Society made the Jesuits regret that their superior was a member of the Council of Quebec [5] They had been doubtful about the wisdom of entering the Council in the first place,[6] but they were obliged to do so by regulation of the Council of State Now, in 1656, they requested that in future the Canadian missionaries might be relieved of this care in order to be freer to pursue the conversion of the Indians [7]

---

[1] Rochemonteix, vol ii, p 135.
[2] E g Œuvres d'Arnauld, vol xxxiv, p 733.
[3] Fds. Roche , 22, f 29.
[4] Ibid , f 17.
[5] Rochemonteix, vol ii, pp 183, 198.
[6] Journal, p. 93.
[7] Nouvelle France, p 104

Indian Politics

Not only were the Jesuits a potent force in the domestic life of the colony, they were the indispensable agents of its external policies. As their *Relations* clearly show, the conversion of the Indians was the " be-all and end-all " of the Jesuits in Canada. The early governors encouraged their work, while they in turn served the governors as interpreters and political agents. Champlain gave the keynote of subsequent French policy when he exhorted the Hurons to embrace Christianity in order thereby to cement their alliance with the French [1] Following his example, Montmagny declared : " If they (the Indians) range themselves within the pale of the Church, I will protect them " [2] When in 1647 the English colonies proposed an eternal alliance with Canada, independent of any rupture between the two crowns, the Jesuit Druillettes was the French ambassador to the governors of New England. Unhappily his efforts proved futile, because, as a complement to the proposed commercial treaty, Druillettes stipulated that the English should join the French in wiping out the Iroquois, the plague of Canada [3] Meanwhile, Fathers Ragueneau, Jogues, and Bressani were Montmagny's fearless and self-sacrificing envoys to the Five Nations [4] The septuagenarian Lauson, timorous and vacillating, relied upon the missionaries in all the delicate and dangerous negotiations with the Iroquois enemy. In the abortive and nearly disastrous mission to Gannentaha, he allowed the Jesuits to shape his policy, shoulder the responsibility, and face the peril. Father Ragueneau was reproached with having forced the hand of Lauson and having induced him to commit this deplorable diplomatic error.[5] Even a Jesuit could blunder. On one

[1] *Rel.*, 1635, p. 19.   [2] *Ibid.*, 1641, p. 21.
[3] *Coll. MSS.*, vol. i, p. 127
[4] *Vie du P. Jogues*, p. 179 ; *Relations, Journal, Lettres de Marie*, passim.
[5] Arnauld, vol. xxxiv, p. 734.

occasion a superior presumed too much upon his influence. That was in 1657 when Father du Quen neglected to transmit to Ailleboust, interim governor, certain presents and messages from the Onondagas. Ailleboust protested, and the superior gave way [1] This incident sounded perhaps the first jarring note in the harmony which had reigned between the temporal and the spiritual powers for twenty-five years

CHARACTER OF THE EARLY JESUITS

But more discords were soon to follow Argenson, Avaugour, Mésy were all to war against the theocracy as represented by the Society of Jesus, or by M. de Laval, who came to Quebec in 1659 as Apostolic Vicar and titular Bishop of Petræa The last named of these governors stated that the inhabitants of Canada were in " servile subjection beneath the clerical yoke," in " captivity enchained by the conduct of their directors of conscience " Before we leave the Jesuit period proper, it may be well to sum up the causes of their great authority over the conscience of the people.

In the beginning the Jesuits had powerful protectors and generous supporters in France, and their *Relations* constantly acknowledge their indebtedness to them. Among others may be mentioned the Marquise de Guercheville, the Duc de Ventadour, the Duchesse d'Aiguillon, the Marquis de Gamache, and the Commandeur de Sillery As time passed, these benefactors dropped off one by one, and the Canadian missionaries had to look elsewhere for aid. Their influence upon the Associates of New France was very great, but when they saw the Company declining, they supported the more substantial merchants in the formation of the Community of Habitants, most of whose principal members

[1] *Journal*, p. 233.

22   CHURCH AND STATE IN EARLY CANADA

were their firm friends. As we have seen, the Jesuits we
in the confidence of all the governors up to Argenson, an,
their superior was, rather against his will, a member of the
Council of Quebec. The Hospitalières and the Ursulines
were important factors in the life of the colony, and the
Jesuits were their spiritual guides Even at Montreal for
fifteen years they alone performed the functions of curés.
So that Jesuit influence permeated all the important organs
of colonial life But this was not all

The character of the missionaries and the nature of their
environment increased their hold on the popular mind.
Mother Marie, the Ursuline superior, speaks continually of
their phenomenal courage, devotion, disinterestedness, and
freedom from every " sentiment of nature "[1] In sickness
or pestilence they shrank from no sacrifice   when the Sisters
of Charity were ill during a scourge of smallpox, they took
charge of the hospital[2] When the Iroquois beset Montreal,
they gave heart and hope to the valiant colonists[3]   The
governor of Three Rivers, Pierre Boucher, a man devout
but independent, praised them highly   they instructed all
the inhabitants in their religious duties , the people were
very devout ; libertinage was repressed.[4] Bishop Laval,
who placed himself at their head, was their consistent
eulogist · they were saintly, disinterested, and as atten-
tive to the common people as to the chief citizens[5]
The Jesuits themselves declared · " We live here in an
age of gold."[6]

The embarkation of intending settlers was carefully super-
vised, and women of immoral habits were eliminated or else
deported. As for scapegraces who slipped into the colony,
they were obliged to live there honestly : " car on sait

---

[1] *Lettres, passim.*   [2] *Rel* , 1634, 1647, etc   [3] *Rel* , 1653, p. 3.
[4] *Hist. Vér* , pp 154, 159, preface
[5] *Doc. inéd* , vol xii, p 258 , *Mandements*, vol i, pp 24, 25
[6] *Rel* , 1640, p. 5

pendre aussi bien au Canada qu'en France." [1] The result of this selection and repression under Jesuit auspices was an almost complete absence of irregularities in social life One evidence of this is contained in the fact that out of 674 children baptized between 1621 and 1661 only one was illegitimate.[2]

Then, too, this was the heroic age of Canadian history, and amidst the general bravery and tenacity of the colonists the consecrated audacity of the Jesuits commanded especial admiration In negotiations with the Indians and with the English they were the governors' trusted ambassadors. In the tragic Huron missions they had won the prestige of the saint with the crown of the martyr And by their words and example the hideous and tedious struggle against the Iroquois was elevated into a holy war, a crusade of Christianity against paganism. For, although at the risk of their lives the Jesuits sought to secure for New France the blessings of peace, they did not advocate peace at any price. In 1644 Father Vimont pointed out the Iroquois as the " real tyrants and persecutors of this new Church "[3] A lay brother was killed at Sillery while directing the neophytes in the construction of a fort Other Jesuits accompanied the war-parties of the allies[4] The *Relation* of 1650 [5] affirms that it was almost a holy war, for " the greater part of our Christians take arms only to conserve Christianity in their new churches." In other words, they responded to the appeals of the missionaries The neophytes of Three Rivers said : " It is to combat the enemies of prayer that we expose our lives voluntarily."[6] A letter to the king, ostensibly from the Abenakis themselves, invited the French to settle and fortify themselves in the Abenaki country, since the Catholic religion united the two

[1] *Hist Vér*, p 155.
[2] *Notes sur les registres*, p. 39
[3] *Rel.*, 1644, p. 19.
[4] *Journal*, pp. 196, 245, *et seq*
[5] Pp 29, 30
[6] *Rel.*, 1651, p. 8.

peoples. Then the Abenakis would care little for the secret hatred of the English.¹

Not only did the Jesuits endeavour to rally to the defence of the colony all the Indian allies, Christian and pagan, but they made stirring appeals for help to the mother country. The *Relation* of 1660 recalls the glory of the French name, which never shone more brightly than in the Crusades against the Infidel ; and for the honour of the Very Christian Kingdom, the prosperity of commerce, the safety of the colonists, and the salvation of souls, begs the king for regular troops. " The majority of our people, more accustomed to handle the hoe than the sword, have not the resolution of the soldier." " The Iroquois live only on blood and carnage . . . certainly they deserve to be scattered . . ."² The same year Le Jeune returned to France to ask the king for the necessary succours.³ In 1661 Ragueneau begged the Prince de Condé to use his influence with the king in favour of sending a regiment to Canada.⁴ And once again the *Relation* urges a " happy crusade " against " this little Turk of New France."⁵ As for the Apostolic Vicar, at first he deprecated a war on the Iroquois as repugnant to the spirit of the Gospel and the Apostles, but with fuller knowledge of the situation he came to recognize in these perfidious barbarians an insuperable obstacle to the extension of the faith " He changed his sentiments entirely, and agreed with all the wise persons of the country that it is necessary either to exterminate them (the Iroquois), or to let all the Christians and Christianity of Canada perish."⁶ Under the pressure of circumstances the Jesuits came to regard with equanimity the burning of prisoners as an evil inseparable from Indian warfare, even when the perpetrators of this horror were their own neophytes,⁷ and " fort bons chrétiens."⁸

---

¹ *C.G*, I, f. 266.   ² *Rel*, 1660, pp 2-5, 13, 38.   ³ *Lettres*, p. 557.
⁴ *Fds Roche*, Can 13.   ⁵ *Rel*., 1661, p 21   ⁶ *Lettres*, p 558.
⁷ *E g. Journal*, pp 95, 173   ⁸ *Lettres*, p 558.

Thus, then, we see that in every sphere, civil, religious, and even military, the influence and power of the Jesuits was immense.

Nevertheless, their dominance was by no means absolute As early as 1644, delegates were sent by some of the habitants to procure, among other things, the return of the Récollets to Canada to serve as curés, on the ground that the special work of the Jesuits was the evangelization of the Indians.[1] This was probably a symptom of the unrest which was already felt in some quarters in face of the religious monopoly exercised by the Jesuits The words of the *Relation* of 1651 [2] reveal a consciousness of the discontent of a minority "The majority of those who are in this country avow that in no place in the world have they found more instruction or aids to salvation, or a gentler and easier care of their conscience." A few years later Mother Marie comes to the defence of her spiritual advisers: "These people who say that the Jesuits constrain the consciences in this country, deceive themselves, I assure you, for people live here in a holy liberty of mind. It is true that they alone have the conduct of souls, but they constrain nobody; and those who seek God, and who wish to live according to His maxims, have peace in their hearts."[3] Evidently those who have peace in their hearts are the docile penitents who submissively follow their spiritual guides in questions of belief and of conduct and in matters which, like the "firewater" trade, hover between the two jurisdictions, temporal and spiritual

In 1658 Father Ragueneau, in a letter to the general, claims that, even during the presence at Quebec of the Sulpician de Queylus, everybody came to the church of the Jesuits —a fact which showed the falseness of the accusation that consciences are oppressed by their intolerable yoke. He

---

[1] Thwaites, vol. viii, p 309, note 57   [2] P. 2
[3] *Lettres*, p. 198.

sums up the situation thus: at Montreal they are loved by all, at Three Rivers by nearly all, and at Quebec by the greater number.[1]

The lesser number was described by Bishop Laval as being unfriendly to the Company of Jesus, either through jealousy, or because the fathers showed no favour to those who were "too much attached to temporal goods."[2] He was thinking chiefly of the brandy traders and of those who accused the Jesuits of engaging in the fur trade.

THE BRANDY TRADE

A subject of ceaseless controversy in the seventeenth century was the traffic in brandy between Frenchman and Indian. This commerce had its obscure beginnings in the first part of our period, and its gradual development may be traced almost year by year from the foundation of Port Royal to the death of Frontenac. The "fire-water" question evolved from a missionaries' quarrel with traders to a grave national problem, and throughout the Old Régime it pitted against each other the party of commerce and the party of religion. In successive chapters we shall endeavour to trace the evolution of this struggle from its genesis to its culmination.

In the *Mercure François*[3] we read that the English who occupied Quebec from 1629 to 1632 were accused of introducing the sale of brandy to the Indians. Even on the face of it this accusation would appear open to suspicion, for Basque and Breton fishermen must long have carried with them supplies of *eau-de-vie*, which they would doubtless employ in commerce with the natives. However, as we have earlier sources than the *Mercure* of 1633, we are not reduced to mere conjecture.

[1] Rochemonteix, vol ii, pp 176, 180. [2] *Doc. inéd.*, vol. xii, p 259.
[3] Vol. xix, p. 841.

In the first Acadian settlement, according to Lescarbot, the French had already accustomed their Micmac hosts to wine and brandy. On one occasion Poutrincourt presented the aged Membertou with a bottle of wine, "whereof he is very fond, because," says he, "when he has drunk thereof, he sleeps sound, and has no further care or anxiety." [1]

Soon after, in 1611, Father Biard ascribed the increase of disease and mortality among the Acadian natives largely to gluttony and drunkenness : they were over-fond of the unaccustomed foods and drinks imported from France.[2]

At Tadoussac, as early as 1608, the traders kept on hand supplies of wine, while at Quebec in 1623 Champlain took the precaution to suppress a trap-door through which people were in the habit of passing drink—"nos boissons sans aucune considération." [3]

Another source from which we may glean information for this period is the work of the Récollet friar Gabriel Sagard According to him, in 1617 Father Joseph le Caron wintered with a Montagnais named Chaimin or Grape "because," volunteers Le Clercq, "he loved liquor." [4] But this guess of Le Clercq's is not a happy one, for, although the Indians ate the wild grape, they neither cultivated the vine nor made wine.[5]

On one occasion Father Paul Huet aided some half-dozen travellers with "a little brandy and wine that we (the Récollets) keep expressly for similar necessities." In fact, Sagard considers that in long journeys in Canada "one or two bottles of brandy are very necessary to strengthen the stomach on the road You ought to give some to the Indians, but with such care that it may last to the end of the voyage. Without this refreshment, one suffers greatly from debility

---

[1] *History of New France*, Toronto, 1911, p. 336.
[2] *Rel.*, 1611, pp. 14, 15
[3] *Œuvres de Champlain*, vol iii, p. 153 ; iii (2), p. 67
[4] *Histoire*, p 52 ; Le Clercq (Shea), vol. i, p. 32.
[5] Sagard, *Grand Voyage*, pp. 103, 329.

and sickening of the stomach." Further on, the missionary thanks God for the absence of wine, beer, and cider from the feasts of the Hurons, and for their consequent exemption from drunkenness. "For it is credible that, if they had the usage of wine, they would become intemperate like us and then act like madmen, as has been seen in the case of certain Montagnais tipsy with brandy which the sailors trade them." Again, he relates how some Indians, intoxicated with brandy obtained from Frenchmen in exchange for moose-meat, roasted one of their own companions almost to death over the fire.[1]

When David Kirke approached Tadoussac, he seized a young neophyte, Antoine, whom he needed as interpreter. Antoine agreed to ascend the St. Lawrence and bring the Indians down to Tadoussac for the fur trade. As his boat was stocked with biscuits, peas, a barrel of brandy and another of wine,[2] it is obvious that these liquors were already familiar to Indian traders

During the English occupation of Quebec the consumption of strong drink assumed alarming proportions. The Protestant minister sought to save some Iroquois prisoners, but their keeper, drunk with brandy which the English bartered him for beaver-skins, incited his own brother to stab one of the captives. This outrage exposed Quebec to Iroquois vengeance, but to the minister's reproaches the guard retorted: "It is you and yours who have killed him, for if you gave us no brandy, we should not do that."

Upon his return, in 1632, Father Le Jeune found intemperance rampant: the Indians yelled and fought and slaughtered the animals of Madame Hébert. Afterwards they would protest to each other "... It is not I who wounded you, but liquor which made use of my arm." So frightful were its effects upon the temperament of these children of the wilderness, that several of their chiefs

[1] *Histoire*, pp. 105, 179, 295, 677   [2] *Ibid.*, p. 937.

implored the interdiction of the traffic. Otherwise, they asserted, the French would prove the ruination of them.[1] Accordingly, Champlain forbade all Frenchmen, upon pain of fines and bodily punishment, to furnish the Indians with intoxicating liquors,[2] but, notwithstanding his prohibition, there was always some one ready to sell them a bottle in secret, and then the victims themselves would urge " Keep your wine and your brandy in prison. It is your drinks which do all the ill, and not we Indians "[3]

As Le Jeune remarks, the Indians had always been gluttons. Now the same propensity showed itself in their inordinate appetite for the new " fire-water " which was depopulating their country. " Give a couple of Indians two or three bottles of brandy," continued the same writer, " and they will sit down and drink them empty, one after the other." The Company of New France was " marvellously praiseworthy " for prohibiting this trade, while Champlain and General du Plessis did wisely in enforcing its prohibition at Quebec and Tadoussac respectively.[4]

However, their enforcement of the law was not complete, for, two years later, Le Jeune tells us that during Champlain's illness M. Gand visited the Indian cabins with the object of checking a traffic which was not only killing off the natives, but was threatening to break the peace and so ruin the trade between them and the French. Gand laid down the rule that intoxicated Indians must tell from whom they secured liquor, upon pain of exclusion from French houses. By punishing some of the French culprits he won the confidence of the Indians, who observed that the authorities had passed from words to acts.[5]

Under Champlain's successor, Chasteaufort, drunkenness was a civil offence punishable with exposure on the wooden

---
[1] *Rel.*, 1632, pp. 9, 10.
[2] *Mercure*, vol. xix, p 841, *cf* vol xviii, p 67
[3] *Rel.*, 1633, p. 32   [4] *Ibid.*, 1634   [5] *Ibid.*, 1636, p. 55

horse.[1] But though Frenchmen were punished for drunkenness, there was no opposition to their drinking. With the red men it was different. If they take one drink, says Mother Marie, they become "mad and furious. Perhaps it is because they do not know the use of salt. Liquor kills them ordinarily, and that is why Montmagny has forbidden its sale. However, the sailors sell it to them secretly. Even some of the neophytes have gone to excess, and have been condemned by their old men and the Jesuit superior to pay a great number of skins for the decoration of the chapel, as well as to say prayers and do acts of penance."[2]

The Community of Habitants was organized in 1645, and to acquit itself of its heavy debts to merchants of France it levied a duty of 10 francs on each cask of wine, 20 francs on each barrel of *eau-de-vie*, and 5 sous on each pound of tobacco entering Canada. This levy was to cease when the debts were paid; but even after the king took over the colony, although the debts were never paid, a levy continued.[3] But though the Jesuits had helped in the formation of this Community of the principal habitants which was now responsible for the maintenance of the colony and of religion, they consistently combated one of its sources of revenue —whether wisely or unwisely will appear as we continue our narrative. At Sillery they tried to save their neophytes from what they considered a plague.[4] Among the Abenakis Druillettes made war on English brandy.[5] At Tadoussac no one could trade in wines or brandy without the written order of the missionary [6]

From 1651 to 1656 Jean de Lauson was governor. If we may trust the memory of the famous merchant, La Chesnaye, most of the quarrels of the period centred about this for-

---

[1] *Rel.*, 1636, p. 43. [2] *Lettres*, p. 382.
[3] *C G*, xxxiv, f. 193, "Mémoire de Ruette d'Auteuil, 1715"
[4] *Lettres*, p. 432 (1647).
[5] *Rel.*, 1647, p. 53; 1652, p. 30. [6] *Ibid.*, 1650, p. 40.

bidden traffic. The Jesuits had " much power over the mind of the governor," and the Council of Quebec was under their control. Certain habitants, however, received permits to sell in moderation. Those of the opposite faction raised the cry of favouritism, then shared in the spoils. The rabble, too, joined in, and great disturbances followed [1] But during these few years contemporaries said little of the question, the Iroquois wars absorbed the attention of every one. Then in 1657 we find Major Closse consulting the people of Villemarie as to the best means of keeping out this traffic. As the first Associates of Montreal [2] had renounced all commerce, the liquor trade had not invaded the colony earlier. The colonists now agreed to prohibit it entirely [3]

In 1658 at Three Rivers a certain Potene opened a cabaret where they sold the Indians two jugs of wine for winter beaver, and one for summer beaver. As disorders arose, M. d'Ailleboust, acting-governor, ordered the complete suppression of this commerce, but without result [4]

This brings us to the close of the period during which Canada was a Jesuit mission. Thus far the civil authorities had supported the missionaries in their efforts to root out a traffic which injured their missions. Now the forces of the Church are to be strengthened by the arrival of a bishop who, in this question as in others, will prove himself the faithful ally of the Jesuits.

The Coming of Laval

Canada was long a bone of contention between Gallicans and Ultramontanes. The former, led by Monseigneur Harlay, claimed New France as part of the diocese of Rouen;

[1] *C G*, xii, f. 380.
[2] In 1642 a mission-colony had been established on the island of Montreal under the leadership of Maisonneuve
[3] Faillon, vol. iii, p. 27 [4] *Journal*, p. 228

and, finally, in spite of their general's disapproval, the Jesuits of Quebec admitted this claim.[1]

Meanwhile, the Associates of Montreal were planning to establish a secular clergy in Canada, with one of themselves as bishop. In 1646 their project was approved by Cardinal Mazarin and the General Assembly of the Clergy.[2] However, the Canadian Jesuits felt that the time was not yet ripe for a bishopric; the scant population and the Iroquois wars were reason enough. Moreover, they foresaw the danger which would menace their religious monopoly were a secular clergy introduced along with a bishop who might prove unsympathetic.[3]

On the other hand, the Associates of Montreal feared the domination of Quebec. Ever since the foundation of their mission-colony in 1642 an undercurrent of rivalry had existed between the younger and the older settlements. Montmagny, Lauson, and the Company of New France were all unfriendly to a community so jealous of its independence. Nor did the Jesuits heartily endorse it. Although for fifteen years two of their number served as curates of Villemarie, yet the *Relations* gave this romantic enterprise but scant attention.[4]

Hence we can readily comprehend the vigour with which each of the rival communities endeavoured to secure the nomination of a prelate in sympathy with its own aspirations. Not that the Jesuits wished a mitre for one of themselves. They refused the request of the Great Company that Charles Lalemant be made bishop.[5] From 1650 to 1653 Charles Lalemant was superior of the Maison Professe in

---

[1] *Journal*, pp. 93, 115, 185-7; Rochemonteix, vol. ii, pp. 189-91, 207. Daval says of François de Harlay "Esprit entreprenant et énergique, et peut-être d'un caractère ardent et despotique... Il combattit les doctrines des Jésuites" (*La Réformation à Dieppe*, vol. ii, p. 191).

[2] *Procès-Verbaux*, vol. iii, pp. 379, 389.   [3] Cf. *Lettres*, p. 80.

[4] *Vide Hist. Mont.*, p. 37; *Véritable Motifs*, p. 203.

[5] *Doc. inéd.*, vol. xii, p. 255; Rochemonteix, vol. ii, p. 195.

Paris. Anne of Austria suspected him of favouring the Fronde, and Mazarin placed him under espionage, but a reconciliation followed [1] In November 1651 Mazarin faced the possibility of a "relegation to Canada," though he does not say in what capacity.[2]

But while the Associates of Montreal were winning Mazarin and the General Assembly to approval of their new candidate, the Abbé de Queylus,[3] the Jesuits were putting forward a competitor in the person of François de Laval, Abbé de Montigny. Mazarin yielded, and Laval's name was presented to Rome.[4] In deference perhaps to Jesuit opinion, he was made merely an apostolic vicar, a bishop *in partibus*, dependent solely upon the Pope As the Archbishop of Rouen, the bishops of France, the parlements of Rouen and of Paris—the entire Gallican party—all raised objections, the Papal Nuncio consecrated Laval secretly in the church of St. Germain-des-Prés.[5] The contest continued with varying fortune, but eventually the Ultramontanes triumphed, and in 1659, accompanied by Charles Lalemant, M. de Laval sailed for Quebec [6]

But though Laval had been successful in the contest for the bishopric, his defeated rival had preceded him to Canada. In 1657 the Abbé de Queylus and three other Sulpicians had come to Montreal, of which their order was soon to assume the seigneury As vicar-general of the Archbishop of Rouen,

[1] *Fds Roche*, Can 13, Letter of Chéron
[2] Chernel, *Lettres de Mazarin*, vol. iv, p 511
[3] *Procès-Verbaux*, vol iv, pp 368-70; Arnauld, vol xxxiv, p 725 Rochemonteix, vol. ii, p 278.
[4] A E, Rome, supp 195, f 122
[5] *Mélanges*, iii, f 464; A E., Rome, 133, ff 596-9, 609, 612. The Archbishop of Rouen wrote Mazarin, December 10, 1658, that his reasons for claiming New France as part of his own diocese were "joined to the interests of the Gallican Church." A week later the Parlement of Paris discussed enterprises (Laval's included) "against and to the prejudice of the rights of the Gallican Church of this kingdom" The Nuncio considered the Parlement's action an insult to himself and to the Holy See.
[6] *Lettres*, p. 541

Queylus soon came into violent collision with the Jesuits of Quebec.[1]

Fatigued by their quarrels, every one felt the need of a superior ecclesiastical authority. Mother Marie now favoured the erection of a bishopric, provided the incumbent were united with the Jesuits in zeal for religion.[2] As we have seen, M. de Laval satisfied this condition completely, and, upon the advice of "the most enlightened," the Ursulines and Sisters of Charity turned from the representative of Rouen and yielded obedience to the Apostolic Vicar.[3]

However, the Abbé de Queylus proved an indefatigable and irrepressible champion of Montreal, St. Sulpice, and Rouen. Only after being twice expelled from Canada by order of the king did this incorrigible Gallican acknowledge himself vanquished.

Now that the defeat of M. de Queylus has left François de Laval undisputed master of the ecclesiastical field, it behooves us to inquire into the antecedents of this man with whom we shall have to deal through successive governorships, and also to note the impression he made upon contemporaries when first he landed at Quebec.

When a student at Paris, Laval was one of the "Amis de la Rose Blanche," a religious society founded by the famous Jesuit, Bagot.[4] Years later we shall hear Frontenac speak scornfully of "Bagotisme," whose adepts differed from Jesuits only in that the latter wore bands and the former did not.[5]

Leaving Paris, Laval retired for four years to the famous Hermitage of Caen, that "school of perfection" presided over by Bernières, author of the "Chrétien Intérieur,"[6] the

---

[1] E.g. Parkman, Old Régime, ch. vii.
[2] Lettres, p. 197.
[3] Juchereau, p. 117.
[4] Allier, p. 150.
[5] Clair., 1016, f. 45; A E, Am, v, f. 319.
[6] Eloge funèbre, Fds Fr., 12,226, f. 3.

" angel " of Madame de la Pelterie and counsellor of Mother Marie. This Hermitage was as the cradle of the Church of Canada. Laval and his principal collaborators were all trained there : Maizerets, Dudouyt, Morel, Henri de Bernières. The presbytery of Quebec was the Hermitage transported to the banks of the St. Lawrence.[1]

The director of the Hermitage and his friends were always closely united with the Jesuits and aided them in their war on Jansenism. Enthusiasm ran high. On one occasion four of Bernières' young disciples, more fanatical than the rest, took refuge in a forest. With a few kindred spirits they marched through the streets of Argentan, crying : " Follow Jesus Christ , the faith is leaving France , let us go to Canada ! " They had heard of the good works of their countrywoman, Madame de la Pelterie, who founded the Ursuline Convent at Quebec Next day they recommenced their litanies against the Jansenists, but were checked by the civil authority and the ecclesiastical court. After further indulgence in the wildest extravagances and the most severe mortification of the flesh, they finally submitted [2]

This outburst of noisy fanaticism was not typical of the activities of the Hermitage At first the friends of Bernières consecrated themselves to the poor. Then they endeavoured to suppress all the evil within their ken, from family troubles to Jansenism, of which latter they accused every one who felt the least coolness toward the Jesuits.[3]

Founded in 1642, the Hermitage was a branch of the influential Company of the Holy Sacrament. In December 1659 this Company received from M. de Laval a letter assuring them of his constant affection, and declaring that though separated from them by over twelve hundred leagues, he

---
[1] Gosselin, *Bernières*, pp 8, 15, 16, 111.
[2] La Sicotière, *L'Emigration percheronne*, p 35
[3] Allier, pp. 347-9.

would never be absent in spirit.[1] Shortly after this persecution obliged the Hermits to disband, and some of them finally appeared among the founders of the Seminary of Foreign Missions,[2] with which Laval was later to unite his Seminary of Quebec.

Meanwhile congregations and brotherhoods were springing up in Canada after the pattern of those to which the new bishop had belonged in France. At Quebec we find several: the Brotherhood of St. Anne, a religious and benefit society for workmen; a Congregation of the Holy Virgin, for men; and a Society of the Holy Family, for women. By 1664 divers congregations had been formed with Laval's approval.[3]

Having now considered some of the factors in his early environment, let us see how the character of the Abbé de Montigny impressed observers. Latour, his first biographer, dwells upon his hero's pre-eminence in the exercises of self-mortification. "They used to see him in the hospitals dressing the most disgusting wounds and rendering the lowest services, and by a mortification like that of St. Francis Xavier, carry to his mouth, press with his lips, and slowly suck the pins and bandages full of pus, making believe, by humility, to do so unintentionally . . . He has been seen to make several long pilgrimages on foot, without money, begging his bread, and purposely hiding his name, in order to lose none of the confusion, the scorn, and the ill-treatment customary upon such occasions."

A pupil of Bernières could not help being imbued with mystical theology, and it must have afforded Laval great satisfaction to find a congenial religious temperament among the Jesuits, Ursulines, and Hospitalières of Quebec.

---

[1] "Annales . . . Argenson," *Fds. Fr.*, 14,489, f. 1102.
[2] Latour, pp. 8, 32.
[3] *Journal*, p. 329; *Vie du P. Chaumonot*, pp. 74-84; Gosselin, *Bernières*, p. 272; *cf. C S*, vol. iii, pp. 599, 601, 647; H D Q, 344; C G., *passim*.

An anecdote related by the Ursuline superior illustrates one aspect of the religious mentality prevalent at Quebec. A converted Huguenot, a rejected suitor, resolving to attain his purpose " by the ruses of his diabolical art," evoked demons and spectres which affrighted the young lady. The bishop sent the Jesuits there and went himself to " chase away the demons with the prayers of the Church," but in vain People continued to see phantoms, to hear drums and flutes, and to see stones detach themselves from the walls and fly hither and thither The place was distant from Quebec, and it was extremely fatiguing for the fathers " to go so far to practise their exorcism." Consequently "Monseigneur, seeing that the devils were trying to fatigue them by this labour and to weary them with their buffoonery," ordered that the man be imprisoned and the girl shut up in the Ursulines' convent.[1] This mingling of mysticism with practical energy was characteristic of our prelate. On another occasion, when he had carried the Host to a conflagration in Quebec, several " remarked that the flames subsided " [2]

But mystical piety was only one of the bishop's virtues. He had been the Jesuits' choice, and from the very first they lauded his qualities : modesty coupled with firmness, saintliness, disinterestedness, zeal, and capacity [3] They received him as an " angel of consolation," and lodged him in their convent [4] In 1665 they joined in an " act of association " with the priests of Laval's new Seminary—a remarkable pact, since elsewhere the secular and the regular clergy were inclined to distrust each other [5] Two years later the Ursuline superior declared that the Jesuits and the Seminarists seemed but one [6]

[1] *Lettres*, p. 563 After this hunt for sorcerers the whole country was afflicted with a universal malady, and people had " great reason to believe that these wretches had poisoned the air "
[2] *Journal*, p 290   [3] Rochemonteix, vol ii, p 287
[4] *Rel*, 1659, p. 2, *Journal*, p. 303.   [5] Latour, p 41   [6] *Lettres*, p 251.

Nevertheless, although the bishop fitted in so perfectly with the Jesuit scheme of things, he very shortly came into conflict with the communities of women. He thought it his duty to interfere with the Sisters of Charity at Montreal and Quebec as well as with the Ursulines. The nuns resisted, but Monseigneur would not listen to their reasons. Mother Marie declared that Laval was a prelate of very great piety, who, when once persuaded that the glory of God was concerned, would never turn back. He feared their singing might make the Ursulines vain. They ceased to chant at mass because, said the bishop, that distracted the officiating priest. " I attribute all this," concluded their superior, " to the zeal of this very worthy prelate, but experience should outweigh all speculations."[1]

Even before this Mother Marie had observed that Laval was no respecter of persons, but believed in speaking the truth freely to everybody. This was all the more natural for him that he was a scion of an ancient and illustrious family. Though inflexible toward others, he was severe with himself. Continually at the hospital, waiting upon those stricken with pestilence, no eloquence could turn him aside from acts of humility.[2] His private life was excessively austere. Unlike the Abbé de Queylus, who won popularity through liberality, Mgr. de Laval had renounced his patrimony before leaving France.[3] He was not a man who would ever make friends to advance his own interests; he was dead to all that. Perhaps, opined the practical mother superior, if he were not so much so, things would go better. The country was in a chronic state of poverty, and nothing could be accomplished without material aid. " My own opinion is that if we suffer in our persons, it will be through poverty rather than by the sword of the Iroquois."[4] According to Governor Boucher, of Three Rivers, Laval made him-

---

[1] *Lettres*, pp. 212-17.
[2] *Ibid*, pp. 541, 544
[3] Latour, p. 11.
[4] *Lettres*, pp. 203, 544.

self poor to enrich the poor ; he resembled the bishops of the primitive Church.[1]

What we have just attempted is not a complete character sketch of the Bishop of Petræa, but rather a presentation of certain characteristics which impressed contemporaries upon first acquaintance. Thus we shall be enabled the more easily to understand his relations with the representatives of the State Mgr de Laval, a convinced and thorough Ultramontane, had now superseded the Jesuit superior as head of the Church in Canada. With his arrival and with the strengthening of the civil power New France ceased to be a Jesuit mission.

[1] *Hist Vér*, avant-propos.

CHAPTER IV

THE DEFEAT OF THREE REBELS

1658-1665

VICOMTE D'ARGENSON (1658-61)

For twenty-five years the governors of Canada had been devoted servants of the Church, and with scarcely a murmur they had borne the mild yoke of their Jesuit guides. With the coming of Bishop Laval and the Vicomte d'Argenson the harmony was broken In the clash of opposing ideas and ideals Argenson was defeated. His two successors, Avaugour and Mésy, likewise revolted against clerical control, and were likewise vanquished

The famous merchant, La Chesnaye, remembered M d'Argenson as a young man of from thirty to thirty-two years of age, wise and God-fearing [1] Endued with a strongly religious nature, he lent his moral support and sometimes his official authority to the cause of religion and good conduct among laymen and priests For instance, upon the petition of the inhabitants of Beaupré, Argenson appointed a commissioner to inquire into the life and morals of the priest, Vaillant The commissioner heard eighty-three witnesses, and condemned the priest to pay the costs Some time later the Jesuit superior made a secret inquiry himself " for the acquittal of his conscience," and at the first opportunity Father Vaillant left the country.[2]

Yet while his conduct and correspondence prove him a fervent Catholic,[3] the viscount had a strong animus against

[1] F 3, II, f 4.
[2] *Rel.*, 1658, p. 17; *Journal*, pp 250, 251, 262.
[3] *Vide* Faillon, vol II, Parkman, *Old Régime*, ch viii, app C.

THE DEFEAT OF THREE REBELS

the Society of Jesus. One would hardly draw this inference from the *Journal*, much less from the *Relations*. They tell how the new governor was received " in three tongues " at the Jesuit College, and how he and the Abbé de Queylus dined at the Jesuit convent Later they exalted his Christian virtues and valorous conduct [1] But beneath this pleasant surface flowed dark currents of mutual dissatisfaction, and in their private letters the Jesuits of Quebec complained of the governor's aloofness from them, while Father Ragueneau even despaired of the colony [2]

Within a short time after his arrival at Quebec, in " divers public assemblies," Bishop Laval had seen Argenson's hostility toward the Jesuits manifest itself. Having been forewarned of this by the governor's own brother, the prelate gave him " a caution important for the welfare of the Church " Proud and sensitive, the viscount resented the advice, and Laval became thenceforth an object of suspicion as an ally of the Jesuits.

Needless to say, their mutual relations were not uniformly disagreeable Not only did they observe the conventional politenesses,[3] but they acknowledged each other's virtues To Argenson the bishop appeared a " true man of prayer," while Laval claimed to be the young governor's " most veritable friend." Nevertheless, the public encounters of these two dignitaries were far from edifying, and most of their squabbles pivoted on questions of precedence in public ceremonies

The struggle over precedence was not as petty and as personal as it seems on the surface, for the relative position of governor and bishop was symbolical of the relative authority of Church and State Throughout the rest of the century the protagonists of the two powers were to contest this issue vigorously Between Laval and Argenson

[1] *Journal*, p 237, *Relations, passim*.   [2] Rochemonteix, vol II
[3] E.g *Journal*, p 272

incident followed incident Bishop and governor disputed for precedence at church, at festivals, and at public assemblies. So unceasing was their rivalry that the Jesuits resolved to invite neither of them to dinner Albeit, on St. Ignatius' Day they presented them each with a salmon [1]

Thus in the struggle between the civil and ecclesiastical powers the Jesuits strove to maintain at least an appearance of neutrality—the more so because Jérome Lalemant was the confidant of the governor and Father Ragueneau. Argenson said that in all these disputes he had made Lalemant mediator, for this priest was a man of "great merit" and "complete good sense," [2] who, unlike his confrères, never interfered with the civil government. However, if at heart the other Jesuits were hostile to the secular authority, they endeavoured to keep up a show of impartiality. But, steer their course as skilfully as they might, they could not clear every reef. In 1661 occurred an incident insignificant enough in itself, which, nevertheless, gives us the Quebec atmosphere wonderfully well. At the solemn catechism, over which the Jesuits presided, the head of the Church and the head of the State each wished to be saluted first by the pupils. To escape from this dilemma the good fathers had recourse to an innocent stratagem they bade the children keep both hands occupied and salute neither the one nor the other. Unhappily, two boys "poussés et séduits par leurs parents" did just the opposite, and saluted M d'Argenson first. This "offensa puissamment Mons. l'Evesque que nous taschames d'appaiser, et les deux enfants eurent le foit le lendemain pour avoir désobéi " [3]

Sometimes the governor appeared indisputably the aggressor, but as the contest took place in his adversary's

---

[1] *Journal*, pp. 269, 285.
[2] Rochemonteix (ii, 288) says: "Nul ne possédait au même degré le don du commandement et de l'administration, la valeur intellectuelle et morale." [3] *Journal*, p. 291.

domain, he was foredoomed to defeat Thus in a religious procession, his "self-styled gentry" having been placed next the governor and ahead of the churchwardens, there was a commotion, which resulted in the interdiction of processions and like ceremonies [1]

More frequently the bishop assumed the offensive, as when he brought a death-sentence against a contemner of Holy Church—a sentence which caused a "grande brouillerie entre les puissances," and against which the viscount revolted [2] In fact, the governor was confronted with but two alternatives : docile submission or perpetual resistance ; and of the two evils he chose the latter.

But although constantly at loggerheads with the Church, Argenson was by no means a total failure. According to Mother Marie, who seems to have agreed with Lalemant rather than with Ragueneau and the rest, the governor sought to render justice to every one. When the people heard that he was to remain for a third year, "the joy was universal and public." They would have liked him to be continued in office the rest of his days, and if the Company of New France realized his merit they would procure this benefit for themselves and for the whole country.[3]

Yet, in spite of his general popularity, Argenson's situation was becoming rapidly untenable Entrusted with the welfare of Canada, abandoned by the Great Company, unaided by the royal government, harassed by the Iroquois and powerless to repulse them, he desired his own recall, and, according to La Chesnaye, Laval for once aided the governor toward the fulfilment of his desire [4] He had neither the robust health, the mature strength of character, the high birth, nor the fortune demanded by his responsible position Vanquished by the combined pressure of foes without and adversaries within, M d'Argenson abandoned the struggle.

[1] *Journal*, pp 291, 293
[2] *Ibid*, p 292.
[3] *Lettres*, p 204
[4] *Ibid*, p 567

Proud and susceptible, he had wished to enjoy the same prestige, the same deference as his predecessors, and to discharge the duties of civil government without let or hindrance from the clergy. Opposing him stood the Apostolic Vicar, who claimed that a bishop can do what he will, and who asserted principles which, once triumphant, would have made of New France a theocracy in form as well as in fact. Against his pretensions Argenson rebelled, but the rebel himself was broken

Dubois d'Avaugour (1661-63)

The next governor was the Baron d'Avaugour, a veteran soldier, unceremonious, stubborn, stern, and perhaps over-confident [1] Louis XIV's great minister, Colbert, characterized his temper as rather "bizarre and incompatible" [2]

But the baron was a devout man, and a friend of the Jesuits,[3] who, he assured the great Condé, were the ones that had laboured most for the country.[4] The Jesuits, in turn, approved of the governor, and, in a letter to Rome, Jérôme Lalemant styled him a *homo cordatus*. Although, from what we know of his career, we should hardly have selected *cordatus* as the most appropriate epithet, yet the phrase is apt enough in its context. For, in obedience to royal command, Avaugour's first act was to render a service to the Apostolic Vicar by the expulsion of the "emulous Abbé" de Queylus, whose "tenacity of purpose *contra jus fasque*" was so great, and who, added the Jesuit, "served all good men ill." [5] A month later, in prudent compliance with episcopal demands, the baron executed upon Daniel Will and another brandy trader the death-sentence which had made Argenson recoil.[6] At the Corpus Christi of 1662, with pious submissiveness, the king's representative allowed

[1] E g A E, *Am*, v, f 6
[2] C G, II, f 102
[3] *Journal*, pp 302, 304
[4] Fds Roche, E 20, f 348 bis.
[5] *Ibid.*, E 23, vol. 19, f. 60
[6] *Journal*, p 303

THE DEFEAT OF THREE REBELS 45

his soldiers to kneel bareheaded with the muzzles of their muskets against the ground.[1] Doubtless Argenson's struggles and defeat had been held up to Avaugour as an example for him to shun, and the aged warrior was resolved upon peace at all costs.

In the preceding chapter we observed that in 1656 the Jesuits sought to have their superior excused from attending the Council of Quebec. Shortly before Avaugour's arrival a royal edict remarked upon the Jesuit's absence from the said Council, and awarded his seat to the Bishop of Petræa.[2] However, the new governor seems to have ignored the king's ordinance. He preferred the Jesuits to Laval, and insisted that Superior Lalemant should be present at the Council. He would accept no excuse, but set aside a place for him or his substitute.[3]

Evidently Father Lalemant was averse to assuming political responsibility, for we find the strenuous Ragueneau acting in his stead. Twelve days later Avaugour wrote the Prince of Condé: "I put at the head of a general council for the service of the king and the welfare of the country the Rev. Father Ragueneau, who has the honour to be known to your Highness. With three others he deliberates every day upon public affairs. Because of his merit I thought I could do nothing better."[4]

Official connection with the Council not only prevented the Jesuits from consecrating all their time to Indian missions, it also exposed them needlessly to attack, and really diminished their influence while seeming to increase it. But Father Ragueneau did not agree with his brethren on this point. His love of authority remained unabated, and in spite of past unpleasantness he was ready enough to re-enter the arena of colonial politics as head of the Council.

Thus far all had gone smoothly; but in spite of auspicious

[1] *Journal*, p. 309.
[2] A E., *Am*, v, f. 15.
[3] *Journal*, p. 302.
[4] *Fds. Roche.*, Can 13, f 3486.

beginnings M. d'Avaugour was destined to collide with the forces which had defeated his predecessor. A new era had begun, and Canada was in transition from the state of a mission to that of a royal province. No matter how conciliatory they might show themselves, the governors would find the spiritual power so strongly entrenched that they must either abdicate or fight. Yet Avaugour first came into collision not with the clergy but with the lay officers of the Church, and under such circumstances as to place him unmistakably in the wrong. Carelessly or arbitrarily, he authorized his soldiers to cultivate a plot of ground belonging to the *fabrique* and rented to an habitant. The Council of Quebec excused the habitant from payment of rental, and permitted the churchwardens to recoup themselves with any grain they might find on the land in question.[1]

Soon the governor and the Council declared war on each other. The origins of the feud are obscure. However, we know that the Company of New France, suspicious of the Community of Habitants, had sent out its confidential agent, Dumesnil, to investigate and report. Dumesnil set boldly to work, and soon accumulated against the principal habitants so many charges of wholesale fraud and embezzlement that the little colony was in a welter of excitement and wrath. As one of Dumesnil's sons was Avaugour's secretary, it is probable that the governor's sympathies were with the commissioner in his dauntless fight against influential foes.[2] At all events, he dismissed the members of the Council of Quebec, which was practically a committee of the Habitants, and appointed others on his own authority.[3] As the principal members of the Community were staunch friends of the Jesuits, whose missions they were bound to subsidize,[4] we may surmise that in any grave difference with the

---

[1] *C S*, vol. 1, p. 62.   [2] *Vide* Dumesnil's memoir, *C G*, II, f. 106.
[3] *C G*, II, f. 22; *Journal*, p. 307.
[4] *Edits*, vol. 1, p. 28; *Journal*, pp. 9, 67.

THE DEFEAT OF THREE REBELS 47

governor they could count on the support of the Jesuit delegate At any rate, although Father Ragueneau had occupied the seat of honour in the old Council, Avaugour omitted him entirely in the new The most fertile cause of discord, the one which utterly estranged the governor from both Jesuits and bishop, was the traffic in brandy with the Indians. Avaugour's protection of the brandy traders finally drove Laval to temporarily abandon the struggle and seek redress from the king.[1]

Meanwhile, like his predecessors, M. d'Avaugour had shown an inclination to take umbrage at the quasi-independence of Montreal; and this brought him into conflict with another religious body, the Sulpicians For example, in 1662 he proposed to levy a sort of customs duty on their imports, but the bishop protested against this measure as contrary to the rights and privileges of the Church, and the following year a royal edict protected both clergy and laity of Montreal against the imposition of such taxes.[2]

But strong influences were at work for the governor's undoing Within a year of landing at Quebec the blunt and naturally vehement old soldier had tossed aside his mantle of meekness and thrown down the gauntlet to his former friends Their response was quick and effective. In August 1662 Laval sailed for France to plead his cause at court. Supported by Jesuit influence, he insisted upon the removal of Avaugour, and the king, desirous of restoring peace to New France, recalled the alleged fomenter of trouble in 1663.[3]

In the defeat of Avaugour the clerical forces had triumphed for a second time over the secular foe which was assaulting their citadel, and in 1663, at the very moment of the establishment in Canada of royal government, the

---

[1] *Lettres*, p. 571 [2] *C S.*, vol 1, pp 414, 444; Faillon, vol ii, pp 35, 36
[3] "Mém. de La Chesnaye," *C.G.*, ii, f. 102v, Col to Tracy; A.E., *Am*, v, f. 34

Gallican court, with notable generosity, allowed the Ultramontane bishop to choose him out a governor after his own heart.

SAFFRAY DE MÉSY (1663-65)

Not only did Laval, supported by the Jesuits, triumph over a governor who had become an adversary, but at the invitation of Louis XIV he chose for the colony a new head, from whom he hoped for complete satisfaction. As the documents relating to this governorship are exceptionally numerous and little known, we shall discuss the period more minutely than its intrinsic interest seems to warrant.

Saffray de Mésy had been " very debauched," but had later experienced a signal conversion and become one of the most considerable personages of the Hermitage of Caen. With more zeal than knowledge he aided Bernières in his war on Jansenism;[1] and such was his humility and charity that he would carry poor people on his shoulders publicly in the streets of a great city. In this old friend Laval thought he had found his ideal governor, and when Mésy urged his debts as one obstacle in the way of his going to Canada, the Bishop of Petræa got the king to pay them[2]

But even before the choice of M. de Mésy as governor, the disorders which had marked the administrative life of New France had determined the court to effect important changes in the organization of the colony. A royal edict of 1662 recognized the impossibility of efficiently governing Canada across an intervening ocean, and established, in place of the Council of Quebec, a Sovereign Council, to be composed of Avaugour, Laval, and seven others.[3]

The Great Company had been in distress for a score of years. In 1645 it was obliged to relinquish the fur trade to

---

[1] Parkman, *Old Régime*, p 196
[2] C.G., II, f. 102v; A.E., *Am.*, v, f 59 , Allier, p 352
[3] *Ancien Fds*, 5581, f 41

THE DEFEAT OF THREE REBELS 49

the Community of Habitants, and in 1662, its strength being further diminished, it abandoned to the king the forty-five shares which remained out of the hundred.[1] Colbert was convinced that the feebleness of the Company, together with its surrender of the fur trade to a clique of Canadians, was the cause of the languishing state of the colony;[2] and for years the government had been flooded with memoirs concerning the losses of the Company and the fraudulent dealings of the principal habitants,[3] which proved to the great minister the necessity of a commercial reorganization on a large and generous scale. In other words, the Company of New France was to give way to the Company of the *Indes Occidentales*, and the commercial as well as the political régime was to be radically altered. Mgr. de Laval had arrived at the psychological moment. Under his direction the new Sovereign Council, decided upon in 1662, was to be created the following year. The members were to be Mésy (instead of Avaugour), Laval, Robert (the intendant), and four others whom they should choose, and whom they should continue or replace at the end of each year as they should judge expedient. They should also nominate an attorney-general and a clerk. This Council, much more powerful than its predecessor, should judge sovereignly and finally of all causes, civil or criminal, according to the form and manner of the Parlement of Paris.[4]

The intendant Robert never went to Canada, and so the privilege of choosing the new Council rested with the governor and bishop. But as Mésy was totally ignorant of the situation, His Majesty entrusted the blank commissions to Laval.[5] Highly pleased with his success, the bishop embarked for Canada, accompanied by the governor

---
[1] A.E., *Am*, v, f. 139.   [2] *C.G.*, II, f. 200.
[3] *E.g Fds. Fr.*, 17,871, f. 136; "Mémoire de Dumesnil," *C.G*, II, f. 106; *ibid*, f. 58.
[4] *C.G.*, II, f. 10 (March 1663).   [5] B, I, f. 97.

and by Gaudais-Dupont, whom Colbert was sending to report on the financial affairs of Quebec.

Arrived at his destination, Laval lost no time in selecting the members of the Sovereign Council. Marie de l'Incarnation remarked among them all a complete union. M. de Mésy was very pious and wise.[1] This "great union" is not surprising when we know the personnel of the Council: Bourdon, Villeray, La Ferté, Auteuil, Tilly, Damours, with Gaudais in place of the absent intendant. Had the Company of New France remained in control, the first three councillors would presumably have been brought to trial on the charges of commercial dishonesty formulated against them by Dumesnil. Gaudais was related by marriage to another habitant responsible for a huge sum. Dumesnil had been sent out to judge these men, and he now found the tables turned upon him. It was evidently with the approval of Laval and Mésy that the new councillors violently seized his papers and ultimately caused their disappearance. Escaping from their clutches, he made a full report to Colbert—a report which Gaudais' reply does not radically contradict.[2] The affair seems to have been allowed to drop soon after. The Great Company was claiming a general indemnity from the government, and probably thought it useless under the circumstances to prosecute individuals so far away. Moreover, a new régime had been instituted at Quebec, and the king was doubtless unwilling to disturb it by prying into the past misdemeanours of its principal magistrates. The accounts of these men were in all likelihood hopelessly confused; their ally, Gaudais,[3] says they were uneducated and inexperienced and incapable of resolving an affair of consequence. The Community of Habitants had not prospered in spite of all its manœuvres, and its leaders were evidently tempted to recoup themselves

[1] *Lettres*, p 589.   [2] *C G*, II, f 88 and ff. 106-18.
[3] *Ibid*, II, f 89

by irregular methods. Their liabilities to the Great Company could hardly have reached the enormous total at which Dumesnil places them, but their own books were in no condition to defend them satisfactorily against his charges. Had he succeeded in pressing his accusations and in inflicting adequate punishment upon the offenders, the most influential citizens of Quebec would have been ruined. And this is where the Church, too, would have suffered.

For, as we have seen, the Jesuits had helped to win for the Habitants the monopoly of the fur trade; and in return the Community was to be responsible for the support of religion. Now, the men most heavily involved in Dumesnil's charges were precisely the two men who had supported the Jesuits and their bishop most loyally. If Villeray and Bourdon were ruined, and certain of their colleagues crippled, it would spell disaster for the Church of Canada. Thus, to Laval and his Jesuit counsellors, Dumesnil would appear the evil genius of the colony. His claims were grossly exaggerated, perhaps quite false. The Company which gave him authority was now defunct. Assuredly the staunchest allies of the Church must not be sacrificed to no purpose. Moreover, though relatively illiterate, two or three of these men were the most capable merchants of Quebec, and enjoyed the confidence of most of the inhabitants. Obviously the only course of action which seemed likely to avert a scandal and avoid ruin was to place them beyond the reach of their malignant foe, and to join with them in office men who were likewise thought to be devout and submissive sons of the Church, even though still more ignorant.[1]

[1] Of all these new councillors, Villeray was probably the most capable According to Dumesnil, he came to Quebec as valet to Lauson. About twenty-three years later Colbert referred to him as the wealthiest of the inhabitants of Canada, adding that the good which he could do infinitely exceeded the ill, and that Frontenac had no right to depose him on the pretext that he was attached to the Jesuits (B, VI, f. 28). Frontenac

Now, though Laval's new councillors left much to be desired in point of ability, it would be unfair to tax the bishop with a bad choice in that respect, for the same Gaudais who rated so low the intelligence of his colleagues added that outside of the councillors it was equally difficult

indeed repeated this accusation time and again. Villeray was the principal emissary of the bishop and the Jesuits, and the most dangerous (C G., IV, f. 64v), he was a mischief-maker; moreover, he had taken the vows of the Society of Jesus, without wearing their robes, and through him they could indirectly regain control of affairs, for he had understanding and knowledge (C.G., III, f. 249). Nine years later Frontenac's opinion had not changed, but Villeray, he alleged, was guaranteed against all punishment by "certain people" to whose great interest it was to protect him (C G., v, f. 270v (1681)). Even before Frontenac's time, Courcelle had expelled Villeray from the Council because of his liaisons with Laval and the Jesuits, but Talon's secretary, Patoulet, styles him "the only man capable of judicature" (C G., III, f. 275v, IV, f. 66).

The intendant Duchesneau naturally differs from Frontenac in his delineation of Villeray's character. While Frontenac dwells upon the charges of commercial dishonesty brought against Villeray by the merchants of La Rochelle and even by other habitants, Duchesneau describes him as a capable man, of known probity, who did honour to the colony by his noble birth and other good qualities (C.G., f. 37 (1679)). He was the most talented man there, and the most capable of rendering service to the king, a very honest man, who lived honourably on the product of his land, which he cultivated with great economy (C G., v, f. 166).

In 1685 Denonville testified to the "universal esteem he had acquired as a man of integrity and a judge incorruptible, who had always conducted himself with complete disinterestedness" (C G., VII, f. 113). From all this it will be seen that Villeray was praised or blamed according to the party to which his critic belonged, but it is also evident that his abilities grew with exercise.

Of Bourdon we do not hear so much. His rôle was less important. But Mother Marie (*Lettres*, p. 635), speaking of Madame as well, said "It is a family which I love and cherish more than any other in this country." She lauded the probity and merit of Bourdon, his piety, courage, charity, he consumed himself in good works.

Of Auteuil we know little which would indicate much personality. In 1674 Frontenac said he was like a *frère donné* of the Jesuits, and that you might as well place in the Council the superior and minister of the Jesuits as Villeray and Auteuil (C G., IV, f. 67).

As to Tilly and Damours, the author of the *Etat Général* du Canada for 1669 characterized the former as "good," the latter as "good but ignorant." Mésy often called them "just men" and "good servants of the king."

to find persons capable of administering public funds. Nevertheless, Laval is open to one serious charge: he placed his friends out of the reach of justice by assigning them places as sovereign judges.

Although the new governor acquiesced in all these extraordinary proceedings, his moral responsibility was not great, as the king placed him, one might almost say, in the bishop's tutelage. The two dignitaries co-operated in another line of activity—one along which the warring factions in Quebec could usually work harmoniously—viz. the restriction of the liberties of Montreal. A few days after their arrival they used the power accorded them by the edict creating the Sovereign Council to impose upon Montreal a royal seneschalship. This action was, of course, resented by the Seminary of St. Sulpice, which in 1663 had received from the Associates of Montreal the seigneury of the island with all seigneurial rights and duties. The acts of transfer recognized the great services rendered by Maisonneuve, who was to remain local governor for life.[1]

To enforce their authority, bishop and governor visited the Island in 1664, and deposed and installed as they saw fit. Even Maisonneuve was formally deposed and reinstated by Mésy, who claimed the right to appoint the lieutenant-governors. Boucher, of Three Rivers, was treated similarly.[2] So far, then, we should hardly be prepared for La Chesnaye's description of Mésy as having done " nothing more considerably than to accentuate all the difficulties sprung from the subject of the powers of the bishop and of the governor." [3]

Nevertheless, within a short time of his arrival the governor had come into collision with Villeray, and had perhaps begun to conceive grievances against Laval. A document of December 5, 1663, is marked " One of the

[1] F, II, f. 32.   [2] Faillon, vol. iii, pp. 73-80.
[3] "Mem.," F 3, II, f. 5.

papers sent by M de Mésy against the Bishop of Petræa and some officers of the Sovereign Council of Quebec, to convince His Majesty of the cabals which go on in Canada against the welfare of his service." In this paper he attacks only Villeray, accusing him of having stated that the Quebec councillors did not always receive the decrees of the king's Council. Mésy replied that His Majesty must be obeyed. Villeray recited a sonnet concerning the wars of Paris, which said that everybody loved peace, and everybody declared himself servant of the king, but nobody did his duty. Then the other councillors denied that they had heard this discourse, and withdrew.[1]

At this time Mésy was, outwardly at least, still on good terms with the clergy He dined with the bishop at the Jesuits'; and on New Year's Day 1664 the bishop dined with him. Moreover, his confessor was a Jesuit.[2] However, on February 5 he caused a notice to be posted with sound of the drum, warning people that for matters regarding the royal service they must address themselves to the governor, and not to the councillors [3]

On February 13 an ordinance signed by Mésy, Tilly, La Ferté, and Damours suspended Villeray and Auteuil from their functions as councillors. The governor declared that Bourdon, Villeray, and Auteuil owed their positions to the bishop, who had known them "entirely his creatures" They had tried to make themselves masters of the Council, in the interests of individuals and not of the public [4]

---

[1] F 3, III, f. 297   [2] *Journal*, pp. 321, 322   [3] F 3, III, f. 298.
[4] It is to this situation that the anonymous "Réponse au mémoire" (C G, II, f 93v (1664)) refers when it says the merchants must be accountable to the king for the expenditure of his money, because "if they were accountable to the Council of Quebec, which is entirely under the thumb of the bishop and of the Jesuits, this would be putting all the interests of the king in the hands of the ecclesiastics, who would not fail to apply His Majesty's money to the establishment of their authority and the augmentation of their revenue." The "Mémoire" itself had recommended (C G, II, f. 96) that the imported labourers should be distributed by the Council

Therefore they had been commanded to absent themselves from the Council until they should answer for the cabals they had fomented in violation of their oath of fidelity to the king, and until His Majesty's pleasure in the matter was known

Mésy now invited Laval to acquiesce in this interdiction for the good of the service, and to proceed to the election of new councillors by a public assembly. For Mésy himself could not consent to nominate any one after the manner in which he had been surprised the first time by his *facilité*, due to imperfect knowledge. Moreover, if any of the interdicted councillors disregarded this warning, they would be treated as fomenters of rebellion.

However, Laval refused to endorse Mésy's action. So the governor, with his three supporters, caused the ordinance to be published with the accompaniment of the drum.[1]

Mésy seems to have been endowed with a violently emotional nature guided by two ideals the service of the king and the pursuit of personal salvation. Presumably the former had made him Major of Caen; the latter had brought him to the Hermitage. In Canada he tried to keep both before his eyes. But the same impetuosity which had been ever ready to scent Jansenism in sermons and to denounce it was equally quick to discover rebellions, cabals, and treasons in the speeches of councillors [2]

"for the greatest good of the country," but the anonymous reply remarked "This Council being particularly under the control of the bishop, and, after him, of the Jesuits, the distribution of the men will take place as suits their particular interest." It is hard to say in how far this "Reponse" agreed with Colbert's views at the time. Usually he attributed the chief activity and the dominant influence to the Jesuits rather than to Laval.

[1] F 3, III, f. 299; C.S., vol i, p. 121.

[2] A memorial upon the abuses introduced by the governors (C G, II, f. 22) bears the date of 1663, but refers to events of 1664. Though anonymous, it is written in the interest of the Council "But M de Mésy, not having found that the said Council followed blindly all his desires, and,

The suspected plotters were summarily dealt with; but when his wrath had cooled Mésy found to his distress that the pursuit of the one ideal was in danger of placing the other beyond his reach. His spiritual guides were the allies of his political adversaries.

So a fortnight after the last rupture in the Council the governor felt constrained to ask advice of Jérome Lalemant, Superior of the Jesuits. In the opening lines of his letter he acknowledged the personal merit of Laval and his own indebtedness to him. However, these considerations must not allow him to "betray the interests" of the king. Duty compelled him to publish his declaration of the 13th in order to stop "certain practices." His notice involved the bishop, and this had made him appear to all the ecclesiastics as a calumniator, a bad judge, an ungrateful person, and a man of wrong conscience. These and other injurious terms tending to sedition were published daily, against the authority of the king. One of the principal ecclesiastics had warned him that he might be refused the sacraments unless he made reparation for his offence, and this had disturbed his soul. For enlightenment he was reduced to appealing to his declared adversaries, who judged of the fact without knowing its cause. He was doing so because there is nothing so important as salvation and loyalty (which he considered inseparable), nothing so certain as death or so uncertain as the hour thereof, and because a soul, though it knows itself innocent, is always in fear. He begged the "father casuists" to advise him how to clear his conscience

wishing to have more than all his predecessors had had, overturned the Council, interdicting all who did not enter into his interests, but pointed out the injustice of them." The memorial concludes by recommending that the governor's power be moderated in such sort "that he cannot change and interdict any member of the Council, but that he shall understand that it is not a crime of *lèse-majesté*, or the spirit of sedition and cabal, not to enter into all his sentiments", also that free speech ought to be allowed the councillors in the things which the king has willed that they should regulate.

and at the same time preserve his fidelity to the king He wished their reply to be written below his inquiry, to serve him as a guarantee before His Majesty.

Lalemant's answer was that the affair belonged to the civil tribunals as well as to the tribunal of conscience. As for the latter, Mésy would be safe in following the sentiments of his confessor. As for the former, it was not for men of religion to decide, as the words and example of our Lord give us clearly to understand.

Then, regarding the injurious terms imputed to the ecclesiastics, a personal inquiry had proven that they were not used by any of the Jesuits who had spoken in public, for they declaimed only against vice in general.

Finally, the allusions Lalemant himself had made to the possibility of excommunication and refusal of sacraments were intended not as threats, but as respectful and charitable warnings of what a bishop might ultimately do. Far from being the governor's opponents, the Jesuits prayed for him daily, and would gladly give their lives a thousand times over to avert such disasters. They were striving to conserve everywhere and in everything the authority of His Majesty.[1]

Now in the time of Mésy, as in the time of Argenson, the Jesuits of Quebec sought to maintain an attitude of neutrality between the contending authorities,[2] but Mésy knew that, in spite of their prudence and tact, they must necessarily, in the ultimate analysis, belong to the hostile camp. As might be expected, the Jesuits were too wary to fall into the trap the governor had half consciously set for them. Suppose their written opinion had favoured Mésy, it would have broken their union with Laval. But, as a matter of fact, their judgment would certainly have supported Laval, and Mésy would have used it to arouse against them the displeasure of Colbert. So the wise and tactful

[1] F 3, III, f. 300. [2] Rochemonteix, vol. ii, p. 337.

Jérome Lalemant smoothed matters over and sent Mésy to his Jesuit confessor. It is difficult to see how this spiritual adviser could in the present case maintain Lalemant's conventional distinction between the two tribunals In the secrecy of the confessional he would hardly do otherwise than urge his penitent to reconcile himself with the head of the Church, and with Laval reconciliation would imply submission. Of this Mésy had little thought

On March 5 he endeavoured to induce Laval to agree to a substitute for Bourdon, the attorney-general, whom he had interdicted also. But neither the bishop's "conscience nor his honour nor his fidelity to the king's service" would allow him to do so until the officers thus interdicted were proven guilty of the crimes charged against them Nevertheless, he did not wish to prevent the governor from doing as he thought best, on his own authority.[1]

On March 10 Mésy and his supporters signed a resolution installing the Sieur Chartier as attorney-general They gave their motives for so doing : they must defend themselves against malicious and secret calumnies circulated by persons who wished thereby to bury accusations against themselves These enemies were the most subtle and crafty people in New France, and as Mésy was ignorant of chicane, he wanted the public to be witness of all his actions. The bishop had refused to respond when summoned by the governor to aid in choosing a substitute for the interdicted attorney-general Thus justice was blocked But, in accordance with the prayers of the habitants and in their presence, the councillors had appointed M Chartier substitute for Bourdon[2]

Three days later Bourdon protested against this nomination in "an assembly of a few habitants." He was willing only that a substitute be appointed to try him for the crimes of which he was accused in the proclamation of February 13.

[1] C S., vol i, p. 127. [2] F 3, III, f. 302, C S., vol i, p. 129

THE DEFEAT OF THREE REBELS

or to replace him in case of sickness Apart from that, he protested against all the substitute might do as null and void

Possibly La Ferté, Tilly, and Damours felt that they had followed the governor too far already, for this time they said the petition concerned only him. Accordingly Mésy replied, stigmatizing Bourdon's language as "full of scorn and tending to sedition." Once more he forbade him to participate in public affairs until he had explained to His Majesty.[1]

A month later Mésy seems to have felt that his bellicose enthusiasm for the maintenance of the royal authority had overleaped itself, for on April 16 he erased certain words from his ordinance of February 13, declaring it null and void. The Sieur Chartier then resigned.[2]

For a few months a calm seems to have settled down upon the troubled waters of colonial politics, and in June we find Mésy, Laval, Le Jeune, and Ragueneau collaborating in explaining to the king the land policy of the Sovereign Council.[3] However, in August Mésy again reprimanded Villeray for forming cabals, and forbade him to give his opinions except in his rank.[4] On the 25th of the same month he "humbly supplicated" the bishop to agree with him to change the members of the Council at the end of their year of office, as they had power to do. To facilitate an agreement, he proposed that either of them should nominate twelve persons, and that from these nominees the other should choose the requisite number of councillors. Mésy had always recognized Tilly and Damours as gentlemen intent upon the service of the king and upon justice, but if they were suspected by the bishop he would let them be replaced also.

But Mésy had already lost influence with the home

[1] F 3, III, f. 303
[3] A.E., Am., V, f. 120
[2] C.S., vol. i, p. 170.
[4] C.S., vol. i, p. 255.

government, and was ignorant of its plans. Laval was better informed: Colbert had told him that the Marquis de Tracy would effect a general reorganization the following spring. So the prelate refused his consent to any change in the Council before that time.[1] Clearly the governor was fighting a losing battle. Nevertheless, he kept on the offensive, and in September he came once again into conflict with the bishop over the election of a syndic. Both parties give us their interpretation of this affair, and they agree in essentials.

Mésy accuses the cabals in the Council of hindering the election of a syndic by the inhabitants of Quebec; for a popular representative might be in the way of the councillors. Seeing that the people dared not come to the assemblies convoked for this purpose, he sent notes to all the inhabitants above suspicion, summoning them to meet in the council-chamber the following day, Sunday, September 14. For fear of the cabal he kept the object of the meeting secret, but when they were assembled he "exhorted" the people to elect an independent syndic. Their choice fell upon M. Lemire, but M. de Charny (Laval's representative) and his brother-in-law La Ferté, together with Auteuil, opposed his election, and thus produced a deadlock.[2]

The bishop's comments claim to correct the governor's assertions. His accusation that a cabal was opposed to the election of a syndic is false, as M. de Charny had asked for such an election several times. Notices were sent to only about sixty persons, who were ordered to be present under penalty of a fine of ten livres. At the Sunday meeting the governor controlled the whole election. On the 17th he wished to administer the oath to Lemire, brother-in-law of Damours, but the alleged cabal prevented him. Speaking of the governor's defeat at this point, the bishop remarks

[1] F 3, III, ff. 310, 311.   [2] C.S., vol. i, p. 278.

that God blinds those who do not walk in the path of truth.
He charges Mésy with using invectives and menaces against
the Council, declaring that he was master. In spite of his
agreement to nullify Lemire's election, on September 19
Mésy brought him to the Council, and on his own authority administered to him the oath. Afterwards, concludes
Laval, he refused Charny's request that the deliberations
of the 17th be recorded [1]

Then Mésy, according to his own account, seeing how
opinionated was the cabal, and believing it necessary for
the king's interests that the Council should be changed,
made another appeal to the bishop. The latter retorted in his
marginal notes (probably made after Mésy's illness or death)
that the change was so little necessary that the governor
had offered to let the Council stand, providing Laval would
give him a written pledge that Villeray would neither do
nor say anything against him in France. When Charny
heard this proposal he said: "People do, then, what they
like with the interests of the king?" Mésy replied that
a man defends himself as he can. He also affirmed that
Laval was seeking his own advantage when he refused to
renew the Council before the arrival of Tracy. The bishop's
rejoinder was that he was seeking only justice

Here we may venture the opinion that the prelate's view
of justice coincided with his own interests and those of the
Church. The royal edict provided for a renewal of councillors at the end of the year if the spiritual and secular
chiefs judged it expedient. Laval, on the contrary, was
more than satisfied with most of the councillors he had
appointed. How could he justly abandon such allies as
Villeray, Bourdon, Auteuil, and even La Ferté, brother-in-
law of Charny, who had now come over to the clerical side?
These men, if office-holders when Tracy arrived, would give
a better account of themselves than if they were reduced to

[1] *Colonies*, F 78, Factum of Laval, F 3, III, f. 312.

the status of private citizens. Besides, Laval might have found it somewhat difficult to nominate even twelve other eligible candidates who could be depended upon to support the Church against the civil power, for Mésy's appeals to the citizens had probably made him popular,[1] while the prelate's insistence upon the *dîmes* and his war upon the liquor trade had caused much excitement and irritation among the habitants.[2]

Exasperated at the obstinacy of his opponents, Mésy flew into a passion and, baton in hand, cried out to the councillors: " Je vous chasse Sortez d'icy ! " But when he used the same words to Bourdon, the attorney-general refused to consider himself dismissed, and demanded that the royal edict be read. Mésy resented this as " manifest sedition " " Sur quoy," says Laval, " il se leva de sa chaize, prist Monsr. Bourdon à la gorge, et le tira par force hors de sa place, le maltraitta à coups de baston sur la teste ; tira son espée ; lui en donna plusieurs coups," then followed him outside, struck him several times more, and cried " Je vous tueray." Bourdon withdrew in silence, and got a surgeon to dress his wounded hand. Charny was also warned to keep quiet unless he wanted to be treated as a rebel.

In concluding his factum Laval claims to have used all possible diligence in discovering and recording the truth of the matter. He had every opportunity of learning the facts, and his account is much fuller than Mésy's, which sins too much by omission In concluding his narrative Mésy admits that it is not in the form of a practitioner ; he is not supposed to represent His Majesty as an orator ; and

---

[1] Moreover, they do not seem to have attracted unfavourable notice from the home government

[2] A E., *Am.*, v, f. 145 ; Faillon, vol. iii, pp 72, 73 ; Latour, pp 157-68 " La révolte fut générale." " . . . à la côte de Beaupré . . . il fallut en retirer le missionaire, qui n'y était pas en sûreté." Latour represents this controversy as a quarrel between clergy and laymen Mésy supported the opposition to the *dîmes.*

THE DEFEAT OF THREE REBELS 63

against all this chicanery he is defending himself in cavalier fashion.[1]

On September 23 Bourdon sailed for France.[2] On September 24 the Council met again. Mésy, Tilly, and Damours were present. Laval had been notified, but excused himself as indisposed. Denis, Tessene, and Demazé (son of Dumesnil) were made councillors in place of those whom the governor had dismissed. Chartier was again accorded the position of attorney-general, and Fillion that of registrar and secretary.[3] Laval signified his opposition, but as this was ignored in the public announcement posted at the church door, he caused it to be mentioned in the pulpit the next Sunday.[4]

On September 29 Mésy was absent at Ste. Anne de Beaupré. On his return he heard that in his sermon Pommier, a priest of the Seminary, had published " several things against the service of the king." Tilly was appointed to investigate,[5] but we have not found his report. Moreover, this entry was afterwards crossed out, Mésy probably saw that rumour had exaggerated the incident.

Nevertheless, the following Saturday, according to the private *Journal* of the Jesuits,[6] the governor published, to the roll of the drum, a placard of insults to the bishop and others. He complained loudly and everywhere that he was refused confession and absolution ; but the Jesuits' response was that God knows everything.

On November 19 the governor took a most extraordinary step : he opposed the receipt of any funds by the ecclesiastics until he had declared his reasons to His Majesty.[7]

---

[1] F 3, III, f 312 ; *Colonies*, F 78 : " Factum de ce qui s'est passé dans la Dissolution du Conseil l'an 1664, le 19 septembre " ; C S , vol 1, p 278.
[2] *Journal*, p 328
[3] C S , vol. 1, p 280. All this entry, pp. 278-80, struck out by Tracy, etc , May 31, 1666
[4] *Journal*, p 328
[5] C S , vol 1, p. 283
[6] P 329, October 5.
[7] C S , vol 1, p 300

However, on New Year's Day 1665 the Jesuits went to salute him as usual, although, says the *Journal*,¹ " he was on bad terms with us and with all the ecclesiastics." This was too much for the governor ; that evening he sent his major to them and to Laval with an order for the payment of their pensions.

On December 16 previous the Council had authorized the syndic to obtain a monitory with the object of revealing the identity of those who sequestered the goods of the merchants, but the bishop refused absolutely to grant it, saying that it was not à propos, and that the syndic had abundant means of justice.² Though this request of the Council was signed by Mésy's nominees, the prelate's refusal was probably due not to personal antagonisms, but to a general attitude which was to cause some friction with future officers of the crown.³

A few lines from the *Vie de la Mère Marie Catherine*⁴ will enable us to see how the governor's conduct was regarded by the religious element of Quebec. This biography is written by Father Ragueneau, who for eighteen years was the nun's director of conscience. As her knowledge of these political troubles was doubtless drawn from ecclesiastical sources, her visions must reflect to some extent the views of her spiritual advisers Early in 1664 she sees the demons in festival over the disturbances they have excited with regard both to the *dîmes* and to other matters Having the spirit of Mésy on their side, they are sure of victory The governor's soul is in an unhappy state ; he purposely smothers his good impulses ; he is guilty of calumnies

---

¹ P. 330.   ² *C S* , vol. i, p. 309.
³ A royal declaration of 1657 provided that the bishops should cause to be announced from the pulpits only the orders received direct from the king. The parlements and judges could not constrain the clergy to make these announcements (*Mémoires du Clergé*, vol. vi, p. 220). However, this declaration does not seem to have become operative, as we shall see later.
⁴ Pp. 250-61.

THE DEFEAT OF THREE REBELS 65

against the Church, of disobedience, of his own sins and those of others His heart is hardened, and the visionary nun beholds him as if " stifled in a horrible thickness of shadows." At another time he is " frightful to see ; . around him is a great troop of demons " After his death the Judge is in anger against him, for his contrition has not been sincere. In spite of the intercession of saints, and of the souls of those who have lately died at the hospital (the latter asked that since their bodies were to rest in the same place, their souls might also be united), Mésy is condemned to as many years of Purgatory as he has lived hours in Canada.[1] Finally, however, before his death the rebellious governor recognized the great mercy which God showed him by putting him in a place like Canada, where he had had such strong aids to his salvation " Les Prières de M. l'Evêque l'ont puissamment aidé." Nevertheless, concludes the mystic sister, his torments in Purgatory were frightful

Early in 1665 the unhappy Mésy had fallen grievously ill The Jesuits sought to facilitate his reconciliation with the Church. This was effected at the beginning of March, when he confessed and communed On St Joseph's Day and at Easter mass was said in his chamber. But the old major was not utterly vanquished even yet, as we feel when reading his letter to the Marquis de Tracy, dated April 26, 1665.[2] This letter, composed on his death-bed, reveals a pathetic doubt as to whether, after all, he or his opponents were mainly in the wrong He has requested Councillor Tilly to give the viceroy his papers containing records of what has passed between the Bishop of Petræa, the Jesuits, and himself "You will explain far better than I the things I might have made known to the king touching their conduct in temporal affairs. Nevertheless, I do not know

[1] "Item, veut et désire ledict seigneur que son corps soit inhumé dans le cimetière des pauvres de l'Hospital de Quebecq " (" Testament de Mésy," Dom Arch)
[2] Dom. Arch.

whether I may not have made the mistake of allowing myself to be rather too lightly persuaded by the report of it I received." He died on May 5, the third successive governor to suffer defeat in a struggle against ecclesiastical dominance.

But Mésy's death did not instantly solve the difficulties he had raised. Colbert was ever ready to sympathize with a representative of the king in difficulties with the Church, and especially with the Jesuits,[1] and his judgment of Mésy was not very harsh. Nevertheless, it was quite impossible to protect him further, and in the year preceding his death the minister was arranging for his trial. This did not prevent him from criticizing the governor's adversaries. His instructions to Tracy (autumn, 1664) acknowledge the zeal and fervour of the Jesuits, but add that they have not restricted themselves to things spiritual: they have sought to fill all positions, ecclesiastical or civil, with men attached to their interest—if they have any, apart from the service of God and the propagation of the faith. Colbert wrongly attributes the choice of Mésy to the Jesuits — which probably indicates that they lent Laval their vigorous support in his nomination. Continuing, he alludes to the strife which has broken out between them, and adds that Mésy, "who seems to have plenty of good sense," has been obliged to send the attorney-general to France to render account of his conduct.[2] So, although the governor's action in giving Bourdon the opportunity of working against him at court would appear at first sight most imprudent, it does not seem to have injured him with Colbert.

In his instructions to Talon, dated March 27, 1664, the

[1] On September 7, 1665, Father Raguencau, now at the College of Clermont, writes rather dryly to Colbert. He had gone to present the minister with two letters from the Bishop of Petræa, but was not able to find entrance. He mentions that under Mésy the disorders had become insupportable (*Mélanges*, 106, f. 617). [2] *C G.*, II, f. 102v.

minister again ignores Laval's part in the selection of Mésy. The Jesuits "found themselves short in their measures" when he was in command. According to them, not only did divers passions of anger and avarice, which he had hidden at the commencement, break out, to the disadvantage of the colony,[1] but, on his own authority, within twenty-four hours he made Bourdon and Villeray embark for France. This violent conduct cannot be approved by the king, and Tracy, Courcelle, and Talon are to inquire into the truth of these charges. If they find them well founded, let them arrest him, and, after conviction, send him prisoner to France. His Majesty owes this satisfaction to justice and to the repose of his subjects.[2]

Unfortunately for our knowledge of the entire truth, "several papers of consequence" which Mésy was keeping, with a view to presenting them to Tracy, were "sequestrated, torn, and burnt." After his death those who were

[1] To Tracy also Colbert says the Jesuits accused Mésy of avarice and violence (C G , II, f 102v) In the anonymous memorial already cited he is charged with retaining for himself part of the lands allotted to the garrison of Quebec, and with demanding that the Council furnish his soldiers with utensils which his predecessors had always supplied themselves Then, too, he appropriated goods worth 600 livres left by Avaugour's lieutenant, as well as presents worth 1300 livres given by the Indians to the French The Council was accustomed to use the proceeds of Indian presents to defray the expenses of their negotiations with the different tribes Again, although the king had borne all the cost of his voyage, he had obliged the Council to give him 1000 livres for his alleged expenses. In view of these facts, the memorial urges that the salary of the governors be regulated so that they be no longer free under any pretext to misuse the public funds in this way (C G , II, ff 22, 23)

It is difficult to appreciate the exact measure of truth which these charges contain, but we notice that Mésy's testament shows that besides his personal effects he could dispose of over 8000 livres. As His Majesty had been obliged to pay his debts in Caen and his passage to Canada, we may assume that he landed at Quebec well-nigh penniless, so that his 8000 livres were accumulated in less than twenty months. As all the governors found their salaries inadequate, Mésy must have given considerable attention to the business of making money. His testament shows that he had commercial relations with the prominent merchant La Chesnaye.

[2] A E , Am , v, f 130 ; cf also F 3, III, f 321

entrusted with them boasted that the matter could go no further, as that would be contrary to royal orders. Nevertheless, the Council commanded that the affair be investigated.[1]

Evidently the guilty parties were enemies of the governor, but it is impossible to conjecture what influence the lost papers might have had on Tracy's opinion. Our narrative has shown that Mésy's mind was obsessed with cabals, seditions, and rebellions. Nevertheless, he was making secret accusations against the Jesuits, which we shall deal with later, and it is possible that the missing documents were intended to substantiate the charges contained in his letters to the king.

On the 30th of August 1665 Marie de l'Incarnation wrote her son that the king had discovered the knavery of the numerous calumniators and the innocence of the servants of God. The viceroy, Tracy, had seen clearly into the question, and now those whom envy had sought to abase were more esteemed than ever, while their enemies were humiliated by being deprived of office.[2] We learn from the records that on July 6 the former councillors resumed their places,[3] although it was not until September 23 that the old Council was formally re-established and the new one dissolved.[4]

On October 4, 1665, the new intendant, Talon, wrote to Colbert that the viceroy, the governor, and he had not judged it expedient to inform against Mésy after his death, as the bishop and other aggrieved persons no longer insisted upon it, and they thought that His Majesty would not be displeased if they buried the fault of the deceased with his memory. But this would not prevent their settling just claims for damages.[5] His Majesty approved this attitude.[6]

---

[1] *C.S.*, vol i, p. 346.
[2] *Lettres*, p. 239
[3] *C S*, vol i, p. 365
[4] *Journal*, p. 355
[5] *C G*, II, f. 147v
[6] *Ibid.*, f. 206v.

THE DEFEAT OF THREE REBELS

A year later the Jesuits seem to have changed their minds in this matter It was because they had obtained knowledge of accusations formulated against them by the late governor and sent to Louis XIV. Their superior, François le Mercier, presented to Tracy, Courcelle, and Talon a petition dated May 8, 1666, the object of which was not to complain of Mésy, but " to entreat them very humbly to ascertain the truth of the things which have been written to the disadvantage " of their Society by the said Sieur de Mésy, in order that, the truth once known, they might be purged of blame .

1 Is it true that the clergy enrich themselves by trading in liquors and furs with the Indians, to the detriment of the colony ? Are people afraid to speak of this because of their servile subjection beneath the clerical yoke ? Elsewhere Mésy " speaks of this captivity as if the people of this country were enchained by the conduct of their directors of conscience."

2 At Easter 1664 did the Jesuit preacher try to make Mésy pass for a " calomniateur, ingrat, bourreau, conscience erronée, reprouvé, etc." ?

3. What lawsuit is there between His Majesty and the Jesuits, of which people are awaiting the result in this country with fear ?

4 Are the Jesuits unwilling to suffer the Indians to be governed according to the laws of His Majesty ? In what way do they find this so much to their advantage ?

5. Is the religion of the Indians quite imaginary ? Are they Christians only through policy, and because of the gratifications which are given them ? And, apart from that, are they all in their error as before—which one may see them practising every day ?

Le Mercier continues that the foregoing appear to the Jesuits the most important charges the late Sieur de Mésy has made to the king against their Society. Mésy sent copies of his letters to France, to be communicated to his friends, and several were sent back to Canada. The Jesuits, therefore, demand that the truth of the aforesaid be judicially proven, or that Mésy be declared a calumniator in the highest degree, both because the defamatory letters were addressed to the king, upon whose displeasure or goodwill depend the results of the Society's work, and because they contain matter (especially the last article) from which most injurious conclusions may be drawn, as if for more than thirty years the Jesuits had made falsehoods pass for truth

Yet, although they have every right to demand all this, they do not ask for any judicial rigour against M. de Mésy, but only that the representatives of His Majesty take such steps as shall make known the truth and purge the Company of Jesus in Canada and in France of the calumnies with which the pen of the said Sieur de Mésy has loaded it.

Upon receipt of this petition Tracy, Courcelle, and Talon appointed the Sieur Chartier attorney for the late governor, whose interests he was to defend

Beneath this, on the same document, we find a note of the Jesuits . " After he had conferred with these gentlemen, M de Tracy has counselled us not to pursue this affair. The reason he has given us is that these articles are in a letter written to the king, which is supposed to be secret, and which cannot be lacerated , and, secondly, that they have written advantageously to His Majesty for our justification and *ita est   Ainsi tout va bien*." [1]

[1] A N , Carton M 242. As we have seen, Tracy, etc., judging the new Council illegal, had simply replaced it by the old. But at the next renewal, December 6, 1666, a compromise was effected : Villeray and Bourdon represented Laval's party , Tilly, Damours, and Tesserie, Mésy's ; Gorribon was a new member.

As Le Mercier said, the Jesuits of Quebec considered the five charges we have enumerated as the most important of Mésy's accusations against them. However, there was still another count in the indictment, the only one which attracted Colbert's attention at all. From the minister's instructions to Tracy we learn that the deceased governor had complained of the Jesuits' tendency to encroach upon the authority which the king had committed to him, their creatures long being in the Sovereign Council, all its resolutions were taken in harmony with their sentiments[1] In reality Mésy could hardly have ignored Laval's influence so completely, and Colbert's interpretation of his complaint is probably rather free. At any rate, the Jesuits avoided asking for any investigation of this charge, partly perhaps because of its vague and general character, and partly because they could fight to better advantage upon the ground they had chosen

Whatever may have been the exigencies of a policy of pacification, the historian cannot but regret the refusal of Tracy and his colleagues to inquire into the questions raised in the Jesuit petition With two judges as able and as different as Tracy and Talon, the examination of witnesses and the sifting of evidence would have thrown a searching light upon the relatively obscure history of the previous two or three decades As it is, we can form our opinion of the justice of Mésy's attack only by our knowledge of antecedent and of subsequent events. The fourth and fifth counts can be better treated later on when other witnesses have added their testimony The meaning of the third is not clear. The second has been answered already by Jérome Lalemant The first brings us back to the controversies over the brandy trade and the fur trade

[1] C G, II, f 102v

THE BRANDY TRADE

In the preceding chapter we saw how from the very beginning the Jesuits had denounced the traffic in liquor, which was the chief enemy of Indian missions. Although the Sulpician Abbé de Queylus had fought them on other grounds, he joined forces with them on this issue, and declared it a mortal sin to sell brandy to the natives [1] But the Jesuits received a greater accession of strength from the new bishop

Shortly after his arrival Mgr de Laval held an assembly of the clergy to decide whether this commerce was a sin The assembly must have decided in the affirmative, for in the spring of 1660 the bishop published a decree of excommunication against the traders, and reserved to himself alone the right to absolve the excommunicated [2] This is the "reserved case" which was to involve endless discussion in the Sorbonne as well as at Quebec Its immediate effects were diverse One brandy dealer, "excommunicated on nomination and also pursued from all sides, returned to the Faith and submitted to public penance"[3] Another, less docile, refused a public absolution. "Entreated by the bishop to repent in God's name, he mocked at God and the Church," and refused to see the bishop again. He was therefore declared excommunicate [4] As far as possible the traders sought to avoid contact with the ecclesiastics, and when two Jesuits set out to Tadoussac with "the gentlemen of the fur trade," the latter "did their best, underhand, to avoid taking them on board "[5] Only the farmer of the Tadoussac domain was duly authorized to sell liquors, and out of the revenues of this farm were paid the salaries of governor and councillors Yet, if the memory of La

[1] *Journal*, p 233.
[2] *Mandements*, p 15
[3] *Journal*, pp 268, 282, 295
[4] *Mandements*, p 30
[5] *Journal*, p 285.

Chesnaye may be trusted, "in those unpleasant days, on the pretext of poverty, certain people had permission to trade," with the proviso that they should not intoxicate the Indians [1]

Governor Argenson fell out with the clergy on the "firewater" question, as on others Though a "God-fearing man" he had his own opinions, and questioned the bishop's right to "hurl excommunication" against the citizens for doing what the civil government allowed for the public good.[2]

Argenson's idea of public good was largely commercial prosperity for the French colony, but the churchmen thought of the natives The Jesuit *Relation* describes the effects of alcohol upon them Drunkenness, it says, is a demon which so impassions the savages, that after their hunt, finding themselves rich in beaver, instead of furnishing their family with food and clothes, they drink everything in a day, and are then constrained to pass the winter quite naked, in famine and poverty Sometimes the mania drives them to sell their own children in order to get drunk The youths use it as a philtre to corrupt the maidens Men who have a quarrel pretend to be drunk in order to revenge themselves with impunity So, in view of the inefficacy of the orders of king and governors, the prelate has "smitten with excommunication" all Frenchmen who intoxicate the Indians. His vigorous action has fully succeeded, and the best of the natives have thanked him on behalf of their tribes. Drunkenness is "almost altogether exterminated from among them, and Laval has ended an evil which long seemed irremediable." [3] As we shall see, the *Relation* was much too optimistic.

When Avaugour succeeded Argenson as governor-general of New France, he at first strengthened the hands of the

[1] C.G., xii, f 380. [2] F 3, ii, f 4 ; Faillon, vol. iii, p 28
[3] *Rel*, 1660, p 34

clergy in their struggle against this traffic. Stern old soldier as he was, he did not shrink from executing the death-penalty upon two men who had despised the ecclesiastical prohibitions. Daniel Will and La Violette were " hung," or rather " shot," for having supplied the Indians with brandy, while a third trader was whipped for the same offence. In the margin of the *Journal* of the Jesuits—in which these facts are noted without comment—is the phrase : " Exécutions pour la traite " [1] Will and Violette were the first and last victims of clerical severity in Early Canada.

But Avaugour was not long content to play the executioner for the clerical party. His views may have been influenced by the economic argument, for he seems to have watched for an opportunity of breaking up the system of repression which he at first supported. According to Latour, Jérome Lalemant was the unwilling occasion of the governor's change of attitude. A woman was imprisoned for participation in the liquor trade. Father Lalemant interceded for her release. Latour suggests that his action was dictated merely by friendship for her family, and not by a real desire to prevent her punishment In any case, Avaugour roughly declared that he would no longer be the plaything of Jesuit contradictions; since the trade was not a crime for this woman, neither should it be for anybody.[2]

The clergy raised an outcry against the governor's decision. " We forget nothing in our opposition to it save excommunication," wrote Jérome Lalemant.[3] On February 1 a deliberation in the Sorbonne resulted in a conclusion favourable to Laval, and, almost as if he had an intuition of his victory, three weeks later he launched again his decree of excommunication.[4] It was all to no purpose : Avaugour stood firm, and the people rebelled against ecclesiastical severity.

[1] *Journal*, p. 303 (Oct. 7, 1661).
[2] Latour, p. 79
[3] *Journal*, p. 305
[4] *Mandements*, pp 41, 42.

THE DEFEAT OF THREE REBELS 75

The same day, or the next, the bishop was obliged to revoke his decree "because of extraordinary disturbances and disorders." [1] However, when the storm had passed over, Laval again assumed the offensive by re-enforcing the former decree and widening its scope.[2] Meanwhile, far from Quebec, alcohol was doing deadly work among the tribes. In 1662 the Iroquois surprised a whole village of Abenakis drunk with liquors obtained from the Dutch. The *bourgade* was simply a great tavern full of drunkards, and, says the *Relation*, the Iroquois made the blood flow like wine. But the Iroquois themselves carried home from New Holland such quantities of liquor as to be able to hold tavern at Onondaga, and, when a drunkard came near killing a Jesuit, the other Iroquois threw the blame upon the Dutch who had given him "a certain drink which maddens the wisest."[3] According to the Ursuline superior, Mother Marie, an Algonquin chief protested in vain to Avaugour against countenancing the traffic. Even the Indian girls were affected, and when the nuns pointed out to them the sin of following their parents' example, these girls never darkened the doors of the convent again. Notwithstanding all this, the colonists, because they were sustained by "a secular power who has a strong hand," despised the remonstrances of Laval. They said that liquors were allowed everywhere. The bishop's reply was that in a new church and among uncivilized peoples they ought not to be tolerated, because experience showed them to be contrary to the propagation of the Faith and to the good morals of new converts. But his gentleness and his reasons were alike vain. Zeal for the glory of God obliged him to excommunicate the traders. However, "this thunderbolt has not astonished them more than the rest." They took no account of it, saying the Church had no power

[1] *Journal*, p. 305 (Feb. 24 or 25)   [2] *Mandements*, p. 43.
[3] *Rel.*, 1662, pp. 2, 10.

over affairs of this nature. In his extremity Laval was going to embark for France. " He has almost died of grief over this question, and we see him withering away " If he could not achieve his design, concluded the Ursuline, he might not return, and that would be an irreparable loss.[1]

But when we read of the tireless zeal of the clergy in their battle against the liquor trade with the Indians, we must be on our guard against confounding them with the temperance workers of our day. To the moderate usage of brandy by Frenchmen bishop and Jesuits made no objection, and as for wine—it was the normal beverage of the priests themselves. An insertion in the *Journal*[2] informs us that even to the children of their Seminary the Jesuits ordinarily gave beer, while a jug of wine was given sometimes on holidays. Since, then, the priests had no aversion to liquor in itself, for themselves or other white men, we must consider all the more seriously their hostility to its use by Indians. Some of their arguments have already been given. Others will be added from time to time as the question develops in range and importance, together with the arguments of the liquor party and their occasional criticism of priestly motives.

But the clerical group was not alone in its denunciation of the traffic. So independent a man as Pierre Boucher says that all the savages near European settlements became drunkards, and that they would give any price whatsoever for a bottle of *eau-de-vie*. Since they had been given brandy evils occurred among them of which people had never heard previously. " For the savages are not naturally capable of great maliciousness as are Europeans." Boucher heartily sympathized with the bishop and Jesuits in their zealous opposition to the traders of *eau-de-vie*.[3]

In spite of everything the plague of intemperance kept

[1] *Lettres*, p 571 [2] P. 315 [3] *Hist Vér*, pp 93-6, 116

THE DEFEAT OF THREE REBELS

spreading ever more widely. The *Relation* of 1663 [1] has lost the optimism of its predecessor of 1660. The Demon, it declares, has raised up a domestic enemy more cruel than the external foe, viz the mania of some Indians and some French for taking and selling strong drink. "At first all the Americans have a horror of our wines,[2] but when they have once tasted them they hunt them with passion. This plague extends from Gaspé to the country of the Iroquois At the former point, a missionary writes, it has entirely ruined Christianity among the natives "I do not wish to describe the miseries that these disorders have caused this infant church. My ink is not black enough to paint them in their true colours, it would need a dragon's gall to set down here the bitterness we have experienced from it To sum it all up, we lost in a month the sweat and labour of ten or twenty years." At Sillery and the Madeleine the Christian Indians are grouped together within four walls to protect them "rather against this demon than against the Iroquois."

In the autumn of 1663 Laval returned from France, accompanied by Saffray de Mésy, the governor of his choice People said he had had great contestations on the subject of the liquor trade [3] Early in this same year, in face of the general contempt shown for the authority of the Church in this matter, the excommunication had been renewed. Little amendment followed, and God appeared to intend to ward off these insults [4] For the skies began to blaze with meteors and terrify the people with portents of the divine wrath, while the earth was convulsed with recurring earthquakes [5] A frightful spectre appeared to a youth setting out with

[1] P 7.
[2] Le Clercq tells us that the Gaspesians at first mistook wine for blood They were convinced that the French were cruel and inhuman, since in their amusements they drank blood without repugnance (*New Relation of Gaspesia*, vol 1, p 108).
[3] *Lettres*, p 589 [4] *Journal*, p 316 [5] *Rel*, 1663, pp. 2, 6.

eau-de-vie for the Indians. He and his comrades accepted this as a sign of God's displeasure at their scorn of the decrees of the Church. They abandoned their trip, and that night they just escaped being engulfed by the earthquake.[1] All these evidences of Heaven's anger smote the guilty consciences and caused a sudden revival of piety and sobriety at Quebec. When Laval had chosen the members of the new Sovereign Council, it met under Mésy's presidency on September 28, 1663. Bourdon, the attorney-general, pointed out that since the foundation of the colony the drink traffic with the Indians had always been forbidden because they drank only to become intoxicated, and because of the fury into which drunkenness threw them. In spite of the punishment of offenders the disorder had grown until His Majesty's Council of State, on March 7, 1657, forbade the trade upon pain of corporal punishment. In contempt, said Bourdon, of these prohibitions and of the censures of the Church this unhappy commerce had continued, and notably during the last two years (Avaugour's administration), when several had vied with each other therein because of the relaxation in the punishment of delinquents. The Indians inclined to intemperance, despising the laws of Christianity, had given themselves up to all sorts of vices and abandoned the chase, by which alone the colony had subsisted up to this day.

In consideration of these facts, and upon the advice of the Reverend Father Jesuits, it was forbidden to all sorts of persons, of whatever quality or condition, to trade or give directly or indirectly any intoxicating drink to the Indians—not even a draught—upon pain, for the first time, of a fine of 300 livres, applicable, a third to the informer, a third to the Hôtel-Dieu, and the remaining third to the fisc; and, upon pain, in case of a second offence, of the whip or of banishment. This ordinance was to be read, published, and

[1] *Lettres*, Aug. 20, 1663.

posted up in the accustomed places at Quebec, Three Rivers, and Montreal, so that none could plead ignorance.¹

In connection with this document we note three facts : it is the official pronouncement of the bishop's party, given upon the advice of the Jesuits ; its statement concerning the abandonment of the chase introduces an economic argument to buttress the religious motive ; it records the non-enforcement of a royal decree by two successive governors

During the first months of Mésy's administration repression was sincere and effective Even a non-resident, ignorant of the law, was fined fifty livres for selling liquor to the Indians ² Among Frenchmen also drunkenness was punished For instance, a domestic who had indulged too freely was fined ten livres and compelled to pay his master four livres for every day he had lost ³

But Mésy soon broke with the bishop's party, and drunken disorders recommenced For the protection of French women the Sovereign Council was obliged to decree that henceforth for the crimes of rape and murder the Indians should be judged by the laws of France ⁴ By the middle of April 1664 law-breaking had reached such a point that nearly all the habitants had contravened the ordinance of the preceding year Though the Council felt compelled to make some show of repression, yet " for good reasons " it remitted the transgressors' fines, and, following the lines of least resistance, contented itself with enacting new prohibitions for the future. The penalties were fines, confiscation, banishment, and the lash.⁵ As the enforcement of the regulations proved difficult, the Council authorized an attorney to arrest drunken Indians and compel them to name the Frenchman who sold to them It even said that any citizen might perform this duty, and that, when called

¹ C G , II, f 50. ² C S , vol 1, p 64. ³ Ibid , p 77
⁴ Journal, p 323 ; C S , vol 1, p 174 ⁵ C G , II, f 92

upon, everybody must aid in effecting an arrest The penalty of refusal would be ten livres, payable to the person requesting help.[1]

At Three Rivers the situation was rather peculiar. Governor Argenson had permitted four men to open a liquor store there upon condition that they contributed 1400 livres to the construction of the parish church. In response to a petition from the churchwardens the Sovereign Council now prayed governor and bishop to require payment of the sums due.[2] This was one way of fighting the Devil with his own weapons, but it does not seem to have proved effective. The following year the inhabitants of Three Rivers drew up an "act of assembly" desiring the absolute suppression of the trade because of the abuses committed under cover of the permission to sell the Indians beer and *bouillon*. The Sovereign Council gave them satisfaction and also forbade people to lodge Indian traders in their homes, because under pretence of hospitality some were base enough to hide their guests' baggage for several days in order to exploit them the more thoroughly.[3] But Three Rivers remained full of dissension. The officers of justice were not in accord, several habitants and factious valets were leagued together for mischief; and the minority refused to submit to the majority or to the Council in the matter of the liquor trade.[4]

About this time a new factor entered into the situation, for Colbert began to participate in the discussion. In his instructions to the viceroy, Tracy, he called attention to the fact that Laval and the Jesuits had forbidden the sale of strong drink to the Indians because it deprived them of their reason and caused them to fall into mortal sin. Continuing, Colbert made the following quite erroneous assertion: "This prohibition is so exactly observed that no

[1] C.S., vol. i, p. 181. [2] Ibid., p. 185.
[3] Ibid., p. 340. [4] Ibid., p. 353.

Frenchman dare give a glass of brandy to an Algonquin or Huron." This, he argued, was doubtless right in principle, " but it is very ruinous to commerce, because the Indians, being passionately fond of these drinks, instead of coming to carry on their traffic in furs with us, go to the Dutch, who give them brandy. This is disadvantageous even to religion, for, having that with which to gratify their senses, they then allow themselves to be catechized by the Dutch ministers, who instruct them in heresy. The said bishop and the Jesuits—without reflecting upon the fact that prudence and even Christian charity require us to close our eyes to one evil in order to avoid a greater evil, or to reap a benefit more important than the evil—hold fast to their first opinions." [1]

Clearly Colbert had accepted the prophecies of the traders as accomplished facts. We have no reason to believe that at this time any Hurons or Algonquins had gone to New Holland for their fur trade. Dutch and English brandy was freely distributed throughout the Iroquois cantons and among the Abenakis, allies of the French. But if Protestant ministers had catechized some of these tribes, it was due to their propinquity as well as to the attractive power of alcoholic liquors. We remark in this connection that Colbert supplemented his economic argument with a religious consideration, just as Laval's friends in the Council had buttressed their religious argument with predictions of the ruin of the fur trade. Nevertheless, in spite of his apparent concern for orthodoxy, for twenty long years the great minister was to throw his influence almost entirely against the Church in this controversy.

Returning to our record of events in Quebec, we find that in the spring of 1665 several Indians and one squaw were imprisoned for inebriety. The squaw, it appears, was a good Christian, and Father Chaumonot interceded with

[1] *C.G.*, II, f. 103

councillors and jailer so persistently that the latter seems to have connived at her escape.[1] Chaumonot's intervention reminds one of the incident between Lalemant and Avaugour, but it was not fraught with the same disastrous consequences. Mésy was now on his death-bed Moreover, in spite of the vehemence of his quarrels with the bishop's party, he had never chosen the brandy question as a field of open combat. Yet he had secretly made some grave charges against the clergy in letters to Louis XIV

According to Superior Le Mercier he had accused bishop and Jesuits of enriching themselves secretly and adroitly by giving the Indians liquor in exchange for their furs.[2] This double accusation obliges us to inquire, not only whether the Jesuits bought furs with liquor, but also whether they traded in furs at all.

The Jesuits and the Fur Trade

In our chapter on Acadia we dealt with the partnership in the fur trade between Biencourt and the Jesuits which caused such a clamour among the enemies of the order

This incident was not soon forgotten, and we read that in 1629 Jacques Michel, the Huguenot pilot, echoed what was probably a widespread prejudice, in accusing the Jesuits of coming to Canada " to convert beavers rather than savages."[3]

Soon after the restoration of Canada to France, the provincial drew the attention of Superior Le Jeune to the rule of the seventh General Congregation of the Society of Jesus, which absolutely forbade all kinds of commerce and business under any pretext whatsoever. Their adversaries had been accusing the Canadian missionaries of trafficking and secretly sending furs to France In 1636 Father Le Jeune

---

[1] C.S , vol 1, p 337 [2] A N , M 242
[3] Champlain, 1632, vol ii, pp. 253, 261

explained that peltry was the most economical means of exchange. It was the coin of the country by use of which you saved twenty-five per cent Even the day-labourers preferred to be paid in beaver-skins. The Company of New France allowed every one to employ this money upon condition that all the skins should finally reach its warehouse and cross in the ships. The missionaries to the Hurons paid for their bark houses and their supplies partly with elk-skins The Jesuits received these furs as presents from Indians whom they had aided in distress. If they refused to accept them they would soon be destitute. If the provincial should so command, the Jesuits of Canada would abandon even this harmless use of furs, but in that event the slanderers of the Society ought to make good the deficit of one-fourth or one-third which would result " What then ? " demands Le Jeune sarcastically. " Shall men, who have given up greater worldly blessings than they could hope for (here) in the imaginations of these slanderers, finally decide to exchange France for Canada, to go there for the sake of two or three beaver-skins, and to trade them off unknown to their superiors ? " In conclusion he asked, if the Jesuits were so avaricious, why the Company of New France did not complain.[1]

As the calumnies continued, on December 1, 1643, the directors and associates of the Company declared " that the said Jesuit fathers are not associated in the said Company of New France, directly or indirectly, and have no part in the traffic of merchandise which is carried on by it " [2]

Two years later, under the impulsion of Jesuit counsels, the dowager-queen insisted that the Great Company should abandon control of the fur trade to the Community of Habitants. This local company was to contribute 5000 livres annually to Jesuit missions and transport gratis thirty tons of supplies. The rapacity of its leading members ruined

[1] Thwaites, vol ix, pp 171-81   [2] Ibid , vol. xxv, p 77.

the Community, and in 1654 it refused the religious orders free freight.¹ Meanwhile, in November 1645 it was rumoured that all trade between French and Indians at Quebec and Three Rivers was to be forbidden. Father Vimont inquired of the general manager of the Community whether the Jesuits would now be worse off than under the Company of New France. The answer was No, that they should go on in the ordinary way, but that they must do it quietly. They were to notify Father Buteux of Three Rivers.² From this entry it is clear that the Jesuits were engaged to some extent in barter with the Indians, though we do not hear of their hoarding beaver-skins as did M. Le Prieur, chaplain of the Ursulines In 1647 the Community confiscated more than two hundred and sixty pounds of beaver belonging to this priest, who had boasted that he had some, and that he did not intend to give it to the warehouse of the Habitants except for a good price Apparently such conduct was considered scandalous, for M. Le Prieur returned to France, doubtless at the behest of the Jesuit superior.³ Soon after the exposure of the chaplain's transgression, the Jesuits held secret deliberations as to whether, as confessors of the habitants, they could tolerate the beaver trade carried on illicitly at Sillery. They concluded that if the prices at the Community's warehouse in Quebec were reasonable, one could not in conscience divert the peltry elsewhere; that if they were not reasonable, one could " in conscience dissimulate, the habitants having the right to trade from nature and from the king"; and, finally, that in no case were the Jesuits themselves obliged to trade.⁴ As we have said, the directors of the Community were rapacious. At this time they levied a toll of fifty per cent on all the furs brought to their magazine, and it was only upon the protest of a syndic that the Council reduced the tax

¹ *Journal*, p 3; *C.G.*, I, ff. 239, 286; II, ff. 22, 35, 59.
² *Journal*, p. 13.   ³ *Ibid*, pp 90, 95.   ⁴ *Ibid.*, pp. 91, 92.

THE DEFEAT OF THREE REBELS

to one-fourth in 1653.[1] Evidently the Jesuits were willing to protect the humbler settlers against exploitations, and to feign ignorance when they smuggled their furs on board home-bound ships in order to escape the excessive tax at the warehouse of Quebec In the same year Montmagny and Ailleboust testified that whatever the Jesuits had done in the fur trade had been " for the welfare of the community and for a good object."[2] Two years later Father Ragueneau assured the general, that in spite of the increase in their numbers the Canadian Jesuits would not need any more pecuniary aid,[3] a fact which suggests that they were paying part of their expenses by judicious barter

After the destruction of the Huron nation by the Iroquois the Jesuits cared for the refugees on the island of Orleans. In 1651 they had spent 5000 livres already, and were expecting a new colony of Hurons "In order to provide for the expense," wrote Superior Ragueneau, "we shall use the peltry brought for them last year from their own country, which is worth 20,000 livres."[4] Perhaps the men who had brought the peltry so far to be used by the Jesuits in caring for the shattered fragments of the Huron people were the lay brothers, the *donnés* of the mission, who were permitted to engage in commerce.[5]

However, rumour would have it that the Jesuits of Canada were carrying on the fur trade in the ordinary commercial sense, and General Nickel felt obliged to order an investigation. In October 1656 he wrote Provincial Cellot and Father Le Jeune that the aforesaid accusation was false and groundless.[6] But even from their own accounts the Jesuits were in an ambiguous position. On the one hand, they must have hatchets, kettles, etc., with which to make presents to the Indians. On the other, they

[1] *C.G.*, 1, f. 286.
[2] Parkman, *Old Régime*, ch. xxi
[3] Carayon, March 1, 1649.
[4] Thwaites, vol. xxxvi, p. 250.
[5] Faillon, vol. ii, p. 94.
[6] *Rel inéd.*, vol ii, p 344

must buy these utensils " from the merchants with beaver-skins, which are the money they demand in payment for their merchandise." Accordingly, said the superior, if the missionaries received or gathered a few skins to help to defray the " immense expenses " of distant missions, surely those whose duty it was to make this expenditure themselves ought not to be the first to condemn the zeal of the Jesuits and " to make them blacker than their robes." [1] The calumniators here would appear to be members of the Community of Habitants, which was utterly neglecting its duties to the colony.

In 1657 Father Chaumonot assured the Iroquois that the missionaries were not going among them for the fur trade. Any beaver-skins which might fall into Jesuit hands would be used in the service of the Iroquois.[2]

Nevertheless, the old accusations were revived continually. In 1658 Father du Quen reassured the general that the Canadian missionaries used furs merely as current coin. However, when the general expressed the wish that all possibility of a just quarrel be taken away from the adversaries of the Society of Jesus, the provincial of Paris replied that he would warn his missionaries to abstain from every appearance of beaver trade.[3] This warning was none too effective, as an entry in their private *Journal* shows. Two Jesuits and seven other Frenchmen journeyed to the Ottawa region. Father Albanel and six others of the party ultimately returned to Montreal with thirty-five canoes and one hundred and fifty Indians. The Jesuits' merchandise had been faithfully bartered for beaver-skins, but the cost of the voyage exceeded the value of the beaver by 800 livres.[4] From this entry it is clear that the Jesuits aimed at making their missionary enterprises pay for themselves. Father Albanel seems to have been entrusted

[1] *Rel.*, 1657, p. 16.
[2] Rochemonteix, vol. ii, pp. 176, 177.
[3] *Ibid.*, p. 17.
[4] *Journal*, pp. 287, 320.

for a time with the maternal welfare of the mission of the Madeleine In August 1665 Father Frémin was made superior of that mission, where, says the *Journal*, " the temporal is in good condition " It further remarks that the new superior was to be freed from " tout soin d'aucune traite " in order that he might devote himself to the instruction of the Indians.[1] The care of the trade evidently devolved upon Albanel.

However, the Jesuits were not quite as frank in their public statements as in their private entries In the preceding year, in the Sovereign Council, their attorney had made a declaration on their behalf to the effect that the Jesuits had never made " any profession of selling nor had ever sold anything," but that they gave merchandise to individuals only for the purpose of obtaining their " necessities " Moreover, at present, they had nothing left except for alms and the necessities of their convent. If some work had to be done, they would have to pay for it with wine, *eau-de-vie*, local produce, cash, or drafts on the merchants [2] In brief, the Jesuits of Canada had not made a business of fur trading, but they had traded in furs as circumstances required [3]

However, M de Mésy now accused them of enriching themselves by buying furs from the Indians with the liquors the habitants were forbidden to sell He also

---

[1] *Journal*, p 333 [2] *C S*, vol 1, p 300.
[3] In the Far East they were sometimes less reserved, and the Bishop of Heliopolis brought charges against them. In this connection a noted Jesuit wrote to Father Bagot of the Maison Professe at Paris " If great wealth is injuring our corporation, assuredly it is not so everywhere ; I believe that poverty is doing quite as much harm in several places For a regular himself to appear on a vessel as a merchant is doubtless bad and gives rise to many slanders .. But Mgr of Heliopolis will be much more surprised if he goes as far as Macao and learns that the Jesuits traffic and have a vessel for that. The cause of this is their poverty, and they have permission from the Pope by special bulls in order not to be compelled to abandon everything for lack of sustenance " (*Fds Fr*, 15,796, f 309, Aug 27, 1663)

affirmed that the two houses of Laval and the Jesuits, together with three or four others of the cabal, handled more merchandise than all the rest of Canada. For the former statement we have no corroborative evidence whatever. The latter is a gross exaggeration, for such a state of affairs could not have escaped the sharp eye of Talon, who was soon to pronounce the outward behaviour of the Jesuits of Quebec unexceptionable. Furthermore, in his letter to the viceroy, the dying governor confessed that he may have let himself be too lightly persuaded by the report which men made him of the conduct of the clergy in temporal affairs.[1] This report was undoubtedly made by the traders and merchants whose interests suffered from the Jesuits' war upon their commerce with the Indians in *eau-de-vie*

But M de Mésy had made a third statement, viz. that this mercenary conduct of the clergy caused much murmuring, but that the people feared to complain because of "their servile subjection beneath the clerical yoke"—because of the "captivity" in which they were "enchained by their directors of conscience." In the preceding chapter we have shown how the character and circumstances of the Canadian Jesuits combined to give them an immense authority in all domains Colbert had remarked it already. According to him the Jesuits had caused Laval to be appointed a mere bishop *in partibus*, subject to recall, in order that they might have the real spiritual jurisdiction throughout the whole of Canada Again, at their recommendation His Majesty named M. de Mésy governor-general "So that the Jesuits are in a sense the directors, as all those who hold authority in spiritual or in temporal affairs act on their advice." Now, according to Bishop Laval, the Jesuits showed no favour to those who were "too much attached to temporal goods," and Colbert warned the new

[1] Dom. Arch

viceroy against the spiritual tyranny which might threaten the economic prosperity of the colony.

As it is to be feared that they may wish to constrain the minds of the inhabitants a little too much to exercises of piety and distract them by this means from the culture of the land, from their commerce and from the exercises of war, which are necessary as much for their own defence as for the augmentation of these colonies—it is good that the Sieur de Tracy observe carefully all that takes place in this regard, in order to apply the proper remedies and retrench that which the zeal and the piety of these good fathers might oblige the said inhabitants to do over and above the duty of a good Christian, who ought to apply himself to his work, as much for his own subsistence and that of his family as for the universal welfare of his country [1]

It was quite natural that the men with whose commerce or industry Jesuit piety seemed to interfere should retaliate by insinuating that the missionaries were animated by mercenary motives. To these innuendoes M. de Mésy gave too much heed.

Within a month or so after Colbert's instructions were penned, Mésy had ceased to be the docile auxiliary of clerical forces. A little later he too was making accusations against the Company of Jesus; but in place of the calm and moderate language of the great statesman, the fiery major talked in metaphors of servile subjection, clerical yoke, captivity, and chains. His military temperament was in revolt against a theocracy whose control was soothing or exasperating according as one's mentality was predominantly religious or predominantly secular. The theocracy had remained unchallenged from 1632 to 1658. The first three governors who sought to break it were themselves broken. With the coming of such an imposing trio of royal officers as Tracy, Courcelle, and Talon, New France entered upon a new era.

[1] A E., *Am*, v, f. 59, *Doc inéd*, vol xii, p 259

CHAPTER V

THE TRIUMVIRATE

1665-1672

VICEROY DE TRACY

FOR two years Canada was ruled by a sort of triumvirate. Nominally the viceroy was the dominant member; actually the intendant was the most effective.

The Marquis de Tracy had been sent by His Majesty on a voyage of inspection to all the French colonies of the New World As far as New France was concerned, the king hoped that the viceroy's "address in effectively uniting people's minds" would enable him to "apply specific remedies to the disorders which had reigned there up to the present."[1]

Certainly no one could be better fitted for this task than Tracy Though Colbert had warned him of the necessity of opposing Jesuit tyranny, the viceroy's aim was pacification and not contention. According to Father Ragueneau the marquis was received "like an angel, and performed an angel's functions"; his visit was necessary, for the disturbances had become insupportable.[2]

Certainly his character was admirably adapted to his Canadian environment To Mother Marie he appeared "a man chosen of God for the solid establishment of these regions and of the liberty of the Church " So conspicuous was his piety that he had been seen to "remain in the

---

[1] *C G*, II, f. 103v.   [2] *Mélanges*, 106, f. 617.

church six whole hours " at a time. The perfect unity prevailing among the clergy delighted him.[1]

When the marquis was making ready to carry a war of extermination into the Iroquois country, his avowed object was "to establish the name of Christ" there and the domination of France.[2] To him and to his troops it was "a holy war" which would open to them the gates of Paradise Five hundred soldiers wore the scapulary of the Holy Virgin,[3] and two Jesuits accompanied the expedition.[4]

Tracy's relations with the Jesuits were almost uniformly happy,[5] both within the colony and beyond its limits. In Indian politics, like his predecessors, he welcomed the aid of the skilful and devoted missionary-diplomats. After much negotiation six Jesuits were sent among the Five Nations as Catholic evangelists and French ambassadors[6] According to M. de Courcelle the viceroy treated the Iroquois envoys very well, thanks to the Jesuits, for Tracy was always disposed to respect everything in which his directors interested themselves.[7] The proximity of the missionaries caused no little anxiety to the English governor, Lovelace, who suspected that their aim was to advance not only the Kingdom of Christ, but also that of His Most Christian Majesty[8] In order that they might attain both ends the more effectively, the viceroy advised the court to accord them a monopoly of the Iroquois mission, together with the missions along the St. Lawrence and among the Ottawas To enhance their usefulness among the Huron and Ottawa Indians, he proposed that the Jesuits be allowed to occupy land along the River of the Prairies

To obviate the possibility of friction between rival orders, Tracy advised that the Sulpicians should do missionary

[1] *Lettres*, pp. 251, 600, 609, 622
[2] *C.G.*, II, f. 191v.
[3] *Lettres*, p 610.
[4] *Journal*, p. 350.
[5] *Ibid.*, pp. 347, 348, 351.
[6] *C.G.*, II, f. 192v; A.E., *Am.*, v, ff 184, 196, 228.
[7] *State Papers*, 1666, p. 392
[8] *Ibid.*, 1669-74, p. 110.

work only in Acadia.¹ Such a proposal would be most unwelcome to the Seminary of Montreal,² but the marquis was intent on pleasing the Jesuits. When he learned of the return to Canada of the Abbé de Queylus, he emphasized the necessity of obliging him to live "in the dependence due to his superior and his bishop," and to "conserve with the Jesuit fathers union, if possible, but at least perfect decorum." ³ The viceroy seems to have continued the traditional quarrel with Montreal, and to have disregarded the seigneurial rights of the Sulpicians in his dismissal of the local governor Maisonneuve.⁴

During Tracy's sojourn in Canada the thorny question of precedence cropped up again. This time the contest for the place of honour was between the lesser representatives of Church and State—between the churchwardens and the military officers. "But I did not make any decision on this point," explained the viceroy, "the interest of the king being to maintain peace." However, Colbert surmised that his inaction was due to his being on the clerical side.⁵

At all events, the marquis thought that in processions within the church the wardens should have precedence, while in processions outside the officers should come first. But His Majesty's ordinance of 1668 aimed at preventing such scandalous disagreements by providing that in all ceremonies, inside or outside of the church, the governor should come first, the officers of justice second, and the churchwardens third. Military officers could claim no rank whatsoever in religious ceremonies.⁶

In August 1667 the Marquis de Tracy sailed for France. His two years of office had been marked by unwonted peace in the internal politics of Canada. His profoundly religious

---

¹ *C.G.*, II, f. 327v.   ² *E.g.* F3, III, f. 353.
³ *C.G.*, II, f. 329.   ⁴ Faillon, vol. III, pp. 95, 110, 111.
⁵ *C.G.*, III, f. 17.   ⁶ *C.G.*, II, ff. 325, 328; *ibid.*, III, f. 3.

nature led him to sympathize with the ecclesiastical influences which he found dominant in colonial life. Yet by the prestige of his rank and his wide experience, by his calm, his poise, his tact, and above all by his influence at court, he commanded the respect and obedience of the restless, anti-clerical minority.

The Gallican Talon echoed the general opinion when he said : " The king has in him an excellent subject." [1] Under cover of Tracy's presence the intendant's administrative genius had begun its great work of economic development, which M. de Courcelle could neither help nor hinder.

Governor de Courcelle

During the viceroy's sojourn in Canada Governor de Courcelle could do no more than loyally second the efforts of his superior. After Tracy's departure, in spite of his popularity and fine personal qualities, Courcelle found his commonplace abilities overshadowed by the rare talent of the intendant,[2] whom he was not so willing to second.

Toward the Jesuits his attitude was usually antagonistic. Distrusting their order from the beginning, he was inclined to throw upon them the odium of his disastrous march against the Iroquois. When his Algonquin guides failed him, he rashly accused Father Albanel of having retarded them purposely. Ultimately he seems to have accepted the Jesuit explanation that the Indians had become intoxicated on the road. At any rate, he hearkened to Tracy's advice " not to fall out with the black-robes," and appeared to be reconciled with them.[3]

However, Courcelle was impetuous and aggressive, and Colbert sometimes felt it necessary to hold him in check.

---

[1] *Mélanges*, 133, f. 185.
[2] *C.G.*, II, ff. 153v; III, ff. 244v, 250; Juchereau, p. 218
[3] *Journal*, pp. 342-4; cf *Fds. Fr.*, 4569, ff. 98, 100

When the governor complained of the excessive authority exercised by the Jesuits " under the name of " the bishop, the minister replied · " It is necessary that you act with much prudence and circumspection in this matter, since it is of such a nature that when the country increases in population, assuredly the royal authority will overcome the ecclesiastical and resume its rightful domain. Meanwhile, without any rupture appearing between you, . . . you can always adroitly prevent the too great enterprises they may undertake On this point you can consult M Talon and act in concert with him." [1]

But the governor could not endure to see the intendant too friendly with the clergy During Talon's absence in France he criticized his substitute, Bouteroue, on this score. Colbert replied that M de Bouteroue was in " very good esteem," and that with time he would have ceased to be so absolutely dependent on the bishop and Jesuits Nevertheless, added the politic minister, as a gentle caution, " he is greatly to be esteemed for having shown them esteem and deference " [2]

Toward the close of his administration Courcelle seems to have profited by such suggestions, for in 1671 Colbert was pleased to learn that he was living " in perfect intelligence " with Laval and the Jesuits [3] In the same year a member of the clergy praised the " good order " maintained in Canada by bishop, governor, and intendant · " The ecclesiastical laws are conserved there by those who maintain also the civil laws " [4] However, Courcelle was condemned to a minor rôle throughout his entire administration, and we shall treat of him further only in so far as he was connected with Talon.

[1] B, I, f. 143v (1669)
[2] *Ibid*, f 142 For personal qualities of Bouteroue, *cf* Juchereau, p 195 ; Chapais, p 327 ; and Talon's appreciation, *C G*, III, f. 91
[3] B, III, f 39v.
[4] *Fds Fr.*, 25,081, f 290.

Intendant Talon

His Economic Policy

With Jean Talon we come to one of the few outstanding characters of New France. His two intendancies, separated by a period of less than two years, may be treated as one. His all-absorbing care was the economic development of the colony, and in this respect his work is absolutely unique in the annals of the French régime.

His policy was that of paternalism, of direct administration, for "an uncivilized country cannot form itself," but must be "aided in its commencements." Talon favoured the intervention of the royal government in every domain: for the regulation and stimulation of commerce and industry; for the encouragement of a large emigration and the settlement of the land; for exploration and discovery; and for the formation and increase of families.[1] Colbert and the king, on the other hand, especially in view of the war with England, would have preferred a natural and spontaneous evolution of the colony chiefly by its own efforts. Besides, France could not depopulate herself to people Canada.[2] However, while the indefatigable intendant remained on the field his views prevailed to a considerable degree, and near the end of his term he foresaw, speaking "not as a courtier but with reason," that "this part of the French monarchy will become something great."[3] In 1668 Mother Marie affirmed that since the coming of Talon the country had developed more than in all its previous history.[4]

In spite of his multifarious activities, which often hurt vested interests, Talon's probity seems to have been almost universally recognized. His Majesty and Colbert had

---

[1] C.G., II, f. 143. Talon's general policy. [2] Ibid., f. 199.
[3] Ibid., III, ff. 167, 171. [4] Lettres, p. 634.

absolute confidence in his disinterestedness.[1] His faithful secretary, Patoulet, testified that Talon had been a "good subject" of the king and a "faithful servant" of Colbert. To Canada he was "a father who cherished it," and to his secretary "a good master." Patoulet had never seen in him "anything but great zeal and entire freedom from every sort of interest."[2]

Nevertheless, even Talon did not escape all calumny A merchant of La Rochelle, a creditor of the defunct Community of Habitants, complained of his having storehouses in Canada. The intendant remarked to Colbert that if he had had none several other enterprises would have come to grief.[3] The merchant also tried to besmirch his reputation as an honest administrator, and in fact caused him so much annoyance that Talon begged Colbert either to "reform the bad conduct" of this Rochelais, or to appoint a new intendant. He added: "I have taken upon me fatigues and pains which are not conceivable Long ago I renounced the pleasant things of life. . . I sacrifice everything to work."[4] And in view of his sacrifices Talon was in no mood to allow himself to be harassed by petty enemies

The only other assailant of importance was the great merchant La Chesnaye, whose private interests had suffered from the competition of the king's merchandise, with which Talon's agents provided the colonists at low prices "There was no merchant who could do business in his presence," declared La Chesnaye. "M. Talon, desiring to unite the government with the intendancy, spent a great deal in acquiring friends" The first clause contains an element of truth, for in 1672 the intendant begged the king to recall him or else "leave him alone" in Canada[5] But as to his great expenditures, the mass of evidence proves them to

[1] E g C G , II, ff 206v, 295. [2] C G., III, ff 61v, 66v
[3] Ibid., f. 85v   [4] Ibid , f 114   [5] Ibid., f. 279

have been directed toward the development of " this portion of the French monarchy." That they won him friends was incidental. Talon's initiative and boldness exposed him to the attacks of malevolent critics, but his honesty, both of purpose and of conduct, was well-nigh absolute. He could say without boastfulness "I remain satisfied with myself." [1]

His Relations with the Governor

Unhappily, he was not so well satisfied with the governor. Though he recognized the good qualities of M de Courcelle, Talon himself had not "sufficient talent and genius " to discharge his duties satisfactorily " without succour such as he received from M. de Tracy." [2] Yet he pledged himself to act so wisely toward both the governor and the bishop that the peace of the colony would never be disturbed by him.[3] When he was returning to Quebec after a furlough in France, royal letters demanded for him "an entire credence" from Courcelle and Laval.[4] As he was to represent the royal authority in a distant land " where the prince does not warm his subjects by his presence," he was accorded very wide powers.[5]

Courcelle was naturally rather jealous Moreover, he felt chagrined because the wise and prudent Talon disapproved of his impolitic " manner of acting with the ecclesiastics and the people " and refused to " follow his movements " [6] In return the governor treated the intendant " like a little subaltern," raised obstacles in his path, and allowed him to " consume his health in vigils and toils "[7] However, Talon was resolved to advance the welfare of New France with or without the collaboration of his superior

---

[1] *C G*, III, f. 157   [2] *C.G*, II, f 214v, 227v   [3] *Ibid*, f 303
[4] B, II, ff 34, 37v   [5] *C G*, III, f 50v   [6] *Ibid*, f 89v
[7] A E, *Am*, v, ff 301, 308.

in rank. His views and methods were those of a far-sighted, high-minded, able, and tactful administrator and autocrat.

In the domain of justice he showed this same tendency to paternalism. Observing that the habitants were diverted from the cultivation of the soil by their innumerable lawsuits, and remarking that the Sovereign Council "liked to have affairs," the intendant, says Frontenac, "found no better means of abridging trials than by granting audiences in his chamber." His decisions, "although verbal, were carefully executed."[1]

In view of Talon's exceptional personality, we cannot but regret the royal government's failure to act upon his own suggestion that he be left in Canada with undivided authority.

Talon and the Church

Talon's attitude toward the Canadian Church and toward religion in general has been variously interpreted. To the writer he appears a good Catholic whose mind was nevertheless secular rather than religious. His loyalty to the State was more ardent than his devotion to the Church, but he was anxious to avoid a conflict between these two attachments. In his memorial of 1673 he summed up the policy of Louis XIV as the simultaneous extension of the Kingdom of God and the Kingdom of France. The king's intentions had been fulfilled by his subjects who had carried into unknown countries, "along with the terror of his arms, the cross which they had planted for his religion and the escutcheon of France which they had erected for his state; the name of Christian which they had given with baptism, and the French name which these peoples had received, which they feared and revered."[2] The foregoing lines, while sincere enough, are a conventional exercise in rhetoric, and do not hide the fact that the intendant's Catholicism was

[1] *C.G.*, IV, f. 25; A E., *Am.*, v, f. 306v. [2] *C.G.*, IV, f. 32.

secondary to his patriotism Of like nature was his message to the king after the conversion of some Huguenots · " Thus your Majesty already is reaping abundant glory for God, and, for yourself, renown throughout the whole extent of Christendom " [1]

Talon and the Jesuits—First Impressions

In his instructions of 1664 [2] the minister informed his appointee that " the Jesuits, whose piety and zeal had contributed much toward drawing people to Canada, had assumed an authority which passed beyond the bounds of their veritable profession, which regarded only the conscience." To strengthen their position they had chosen for bishop M. de Laval as being " in their entire dependence." As to the governors, they had always secured either their nomination or their recall. It was absolutely necessary, insisted Colbert, " to hold in a just balance " the temporal authority, which resided in the person of the king and his representatives, and the spiritual authority, which resided in the person of the said bishop and the Jesuits, " in such a manner nevertheless that the latter be inferior to the former." Accordingly, Talon's first duty would be to acquaint himself with the state in which these two authorities now were, as well as with that in which they ought naturally to be With this end in view, he must see the Jesuits in Paris who knew the colony, and, besides, Bourdon and Villeray, who were said to be entirely devoted to their interest. From these two councillors he was to draw what they might know, but without discovering to them his own intentions.

Whatever the result of these interviews, the new intendant wrote from Quebec · " If in the past the Jesuits balanced the temporal authority by the spiritual, they have certainly reformed their conduct ; and provided they keep it as it

[1] C.G., II, f 155.   [2] A.E., Am., v, f. 138.

appears to me to-day, we shall not have to take precautions against it in the future. I will watch it, however, and prevent . . . it from being prejudicial to the interests of His Majesty. In that I believe I shall not have any trouble." Far from opposing the clergy, Talon meant to co-operate with them, for in the same letter he promised, in accordance with the injunctions of Colbert, to encourage " not only the children, but even the heads of families, in divine worship, in the veneration they owe to the ministers of our religion, and in the respectful love they are obliged to conserve for the sacred person of His Majesty." [1] The king's reply expressed satisfaction at Talon's assurance that the only aim of the bishop and the Jesuits was " the advancement of Christianity, the maintenance of the inhabitants in purity of faith and morals, and the upbringing of the children in the fear of God " and the love of work [2]

But about this time a small cloud arose on the political horizon of Quebec. Talon had promised the Jesuits every assistance in the furtherance of their interests, but in their *Journal* we find for December 26 this entry " We present a request to the intendant on the subject of our lands of Notre Dame de Bon Secours. Frustra." [3]

The Three Burgs

A month later, Superior Le Mercier petitioned Talon not to fulfil his design of establishing divers burgs upon the Jesuit seigneury of Notre Dame des Anges. His petition contained the following points :

1. The execution of this design would be so prejudicial to them that it would remove their only means of subsisting in their college and of meeting the immense cost of so many missions . . . after they had pos-

---

[1] *C G*, II, f 143 (Oct. 4, 1665) ; f. 151v.
[2] *Ibid*, f 206
[3] *Journal*, pp. 337, 340

sessed the said land for about forty years, cultivated it in part at great expense, and justly hoped they might continue to develop it in peace.

2. The Jesuits had already established on the said seigneury about one hundred habitations, which were being settled daily. They were going to form others according to the lines already traced, and they were ready to second the intentions of Talon

3. In this way, while enjoying their right, they could work for the end which the intendant proposed to himself, viz the peopling of the country. The Jesuits had "caused it to be cultivated and peopled in so many places that no one would be found who had served and profited the whole country more than they in the last forty years."

4. Let Talon carry on work elsewhere, and let the Jesuits continue on their lands So would the king and the country be better served If, however, he did not yield to their reasons, let him at least give them an acknowledgment that he was acting without their consent, for their justification before their superiors and the Church

But Talon preferred to conduct the debate upon entirely different grounds. For him the supreme consideration was the service of the king and the welfare of the colony. If the vested rights of individuals proved inimical to the well-being of the State, the former must yield So the intendant replied indirectly by proposing a "problem" in which, claiming that his own projects were more conformable to the intentions of the king and the general interests of Canada than were the proposals of the Jesuits, he asked whether he could change his design in the interest of "a community making only one member in the state."

The Jesuits proved as wary as the intendant. Were they to acquiesce in the thesis implied in his problem, they would be endorsing a theory hostile to the Church. Were they to combat it, their credit with Louis XIV would be injured. Moreover, perceiving that Talon's purpose was as settled as it was disinterested, and that all argument would be futile, the Jesuits replied in a respectful tone that, being directly involved in the case in question, they did not deem it proper to answer the problem. Their response, following the advice of M de Tracy, took the form of a new petition.[1] The viceroy evidently sympathized with the Jesuit claims, although he did not wish to interfere openly in matters pertaining to the intendant's jurisdiction.

In the autumn Talon informed the minister that he had "borrowed" from the Jesuits and from certain individuals the ground which he had caused to be occupied by his three new villages in the neighbourhood of Quebec. Having accomplished this result, he favoured leaving them the seigneury and the dues accruing from it, unless His Majesty would rather begin there a royal domain.[2] From this proposition, so advantageous to the Jesuits, we see that in "borrowing" the land for new villages, Talon was impelled by a desire to build up the colony, and not in the slightest degree by any animus against the Society. He evidently felt that no gift of the Duc de Ventadour or of the Great Company could accord "one member of the state" the right to retard the growth of the whole body. The Jesuits were not doing all that needed to be done. In the king's name the intendant decided to ignore their technical right, and, in spite of their protest, to erect new burgs on part of their seigneury. But, to prove his goodwill, when he had thus greatly enhanced the value of their domain, he suggested that they be allowed to reap the benefit. In the case of others, who had made no effort at all to cultivate

[1] A.N., M 247.   [2] C.G., II, f 219 (Nov. 13, 1666).

their concessions, Talon was not so gentle. He proposed simply to redistribute their lands.[1]

However, Colbert thought Talon's proposal over-generous. He replied that it would have been better to form a small domain of these three villages, the revenue of which would be applied to the fort, than to erect them as " a seigneury to the profit of the said Jesuit fathers "[2] This answer caused sharp disappointment in the monastery of Quebec, for in October of the same year, 1667, Talon wrote : " I do not know on what terms I am with the Jesuits since I made them lose their hope that the seigneury of the lands I employed to form these villages would turn to their profit But . . . people assure me that they feel bitter over it Nevertheless, they have the prudence not to show it "

Meantime, in another matter Talon was able to show the Jesuits a kindness. With Courcelle's assent he authorized them to cultivate their concession of the Madeleine opposite Montreal and to form an establishment there for themselves. He advised Colbert to approve this step unless the extent of the concession appeared too great.[3] Thus, by the firmness and tact of the intendant and the unwonted submission of the Jesuits, the threatening storm was averted[4]

Intendant and Bishop

It seems to have been with the bishop and his Seminary that Talon was first aware of strained relations As early as November 1666 he had expressed himself thus : " I well know that I am not here to the liking of everybody, and it is that which, joined to my indisposition, makes me ask leave of absence If I were willing to leave the Church

---

[1] A E , *Am* , v, f 301v   [2] *C G* , ii, f 291v   [3] *Ibid* , f. 308v
[4] Colbert thought that in return for such a large concession the Jesuits should be bound to bring over annually from France fifty young men and twenty young women (*C G* , iii, f 16)

upon the same footing of authority as I found it, I should have less pain and more approbation."[1]

In March 1667 the intendant was moved to protest against what he deemed tyranny on the part of Laval and his priests. We have already mentioned the Congregation of the Holy Family, whose aim was the betterment of family life. On March 14, in the Council, Talon moved the appointment of commissioners to report on the suppression of this society by the prelate, who was dissatisfied with the conduct of some of its members during the Carnival. For, in 1665, Laval had formally authorized this Congregation, had placed it under the spiritual direction of the priests of the Seminary; and had made a rule that its members were to let their piety appear with especial clearness during the Carnival. Though the intendant was evidently intruding here upon the religious domain, the other councillors seem to have sympathized with him in his opposition to an extreme measure of episcopal severity, for even Villeray allowed himself to be placed on the committee of inquiry. He and Tilly reported that nothing worthy of condemnation had occurred in the incriminated gatherings during the Carnival. They probably felt that social liberty was involved quite as deeply as religion, and that an unjust censure of the Congregation would cast a stigma upon the character of some of the most influential women in Quebec.

Perhaps by this indirect protest the intendant had accomplished his purpose; perhaps, on the other hand, the discreet and devout Tracy emphasized the fact that the matter was beyond the reach of the Council's jurisdiction. Be this as it may, Talon's request was struck out with his own consent.[2]

But the Council did not defend all citizens who came into collision with the Church. When an uninfluential habitant,

[1] *C.G.*, II, f. 228. [2] Chapais, pp. 167-75

named Gaboury, was found guilty of eating meat during Lent "without asking permission of the Church," he was condemned to pay, in expiation, one cow plus a year's profit on the said cow ; to be attached to the public post for three hours ; to kneel, with clasped hands and bare head, in front of the chapel of the Isle of Orleans, and ask forgiveness of God, the king, and justice ; also to a fine of twenty livres " applicable to the works of piety of the said parish " ; and finally to pay the costs.[1]

We should hardly expect Talon to approve of such harsh punishment of an offence against the rules of the Church, but he seems to have acquiesced in the sentence. The case was judged by the secular court, and there was at least no question of ecclesiastical usurpation of authority. When the clergy, secular or regular, were to the intendant's mind clearly within their rights, he never failed to give them his support. Recognizing the loyalty, zeal, and spirituality of Laval,[2] and seeing how needy were the thirteen members of his Seminary, he asked for "a foundation for the support of the dignity both of the clergy and of the Bishop of Petræa."[3]

Tithes

With a view to providing for the regular subsistence of the Seminary and the bishopric, Talon had aided Tracy and Courcelle in establishing a tithing system. Their instructions had informed them that the Canadian tithe, at first a thirteenth, had been reduced to a twentieth, whereas most parts of France paid an eleventh They were to examine the question as to whether the existing rate was " really

---

[1] C S., vol. i, p 642 On appeal this sentence was mitigated somewhat

[2] E g A E , Am , v, f 224

[3] C G , III, ff 37, 51 Already, in response to an earlier request from Talon, the king had granted Laval a gratification of 6000 livres (C G , II, f 297v).

too onerous" for the country. If so, His Majesty would have to contribute to the support of the said Seminary.[1]

In 1667 the triumvirs received a request from the bishop that the tithes be at last established and collected, since the inhabitants of Canada were now enjoying the fruits of the earth peaceably and abundantly. Moreover, the condition of his clergy would not suffer that the gathering of the tithes be deferred any longer. In opposition to this request of the bishop a petition from the habitants was presented to the king's representatives. Both in writing and by the mouth of their syndics the people demanded more favourable conditions than those contained in the royal edict.

In consideration of all this, the king's officers, unwilling " to let flow by a time notable enough to carry with it a sort of prescription in favour of the people against the Church," ordered that the tithes be fixed at one twenty-sixth for at least the next twenty years. In the future the state of the country might permit of a heavier imposition, even as heavy as that paid by the " faithful Christians . . . of the viscounty of Paris." The tithes were to be levied upon the produce of the soil and delivered at the principal residence of the curé, or at the mill he might choose.[2] Thus the bone of contention between ecclesiastics and laity was removed for the moment, and the civil authorities, with the agreement of the bishop, placed the maintenance of the secular clergy upon a basis which promised to become adequate.[3]

But the intendant's readiness to aid in the material support of religion does not imply that he was pleased with the situation in general. Three days after the granting of the aforesaid ordinance, a letter to Colbert in Talon's own handwriting said that the minister would receive his first

[1] A E, *Am.*, v, f. 145.   [2] *C G*, v, f. 113-17 (Aug. 23, 1667).
[3] *Cf* C G., II, f. 300v.

impressions of the situation from the returning viceroy,—impressions which might result in regulations prejudicial to the king's service Accordingly, the intendant humbly supplicated Colbert to suspend judgment upon what Tracy might advance touching the Church

For its authority, "far from being diminished, has acquired new force, and has rendered itself so redoubtable" as to retard the augmentation of the colony through "the fear the Church has created of its government, which is too sovereign and extends beyond its proper limits." Nevertheless, he continued, his attitude toward its bishop would be conducive to the tranquillity of Canada. "I am, thank God, born with the spirit of peace, which I will breathe everywhere and which I will try to make reign" among all classes.[1] In October of the same year Talon reassured Colbert that "the illustrious and rare example which the king gives by his piety" would encourage him so to treat the "interests of God" that the minister would receive no "just complaint" "I say '*just*,' because I know that people may well make baseless complaints, especially when they want to confound the magisterial jurisdiction with the ecclesiastical,—a thing that I know you will not suffer"[2]

In conclusion, Talon complained that the bishop had caused some difficulty over the publication of ordinances from the parish pulpits as provided for in the Custom of Paris[3] In response to this appeal Louis wrote rather dryly to Mgr de Laval, desiring him to conform to the usage of France by ordering every curé in Canada to publish from the pulpit at the parish mass all the acts of justice rendered by the officers of the Sovereign Council or by the ordinary judges.[4] Though obliged to submit for the time being, the bishop was to raise this difficulty more than once in succeeding years

[1] *C G.*, II, f 302 (Aug 26, 1667)
[2] *Ibid*, f 315v (Oct 27, 1667)
[3] *Ibid*, f 325
[4] A E, *Am*, V, f 238

Talon and the Jesuits

Meanwhile Talon's relations with the Jesuits had been growing more strained Jérome Lalemant complained to his general that both governor and intendant were unjust toward the missionaries of Canada "Quod scilicet nos minime consentientes habeant in nonnullis in quibus de Dei honore et animarum salute agitur"[1] The allusion is probably to the brandy trade Talon had heard that the missionaries indulged in the fur trade, but he would not vouch for the truth of this report At any rate, to all outward appearance their lives were very regular,—a good model for laymen But, as the colonists were not all of equal strength or of like virtue, or of the same disposition to good, some fell easily into disgrace with these religious for not conforming to their manner of living or following all their sentiments or abandoning themselves to their conduct They extended their authority to temporal affairs, even infringing upon external police which concerns only the magistrate. There was ground for suspecting that their practice (which did not conform with that of the ecclesiastics of France) had for object the sharing of the temporal authority, which, until the arrival of the troops, resided chiefly in their persons This evil, which went so far as to trouble and constrain the conscience and thus disgust the colonists the most attached to the country, might be remedied by counterbalancing with address and moderation ecclesiastical authority by the royal, also by sending back to France one or two of the ecclesiastics who least recognized this temporal authority, and who by their conduct most troubled the repose of the colony; and, finally, by sending to Canada four new ecclesiastics. These newcomers must have full authority to administer the sacraments without being disquieted Otherwise, if they did not

---

[1] Rochemonteix, vol iii, p. 87

conform to the practice of those who were already there, the bishop would forbid them to continue, and thus they would become useless. What he had said about this constraint of conscience could be corroborated by the chaplain of the Carignan regiments, as well as by M de Bretonvilliers, Superior of St Sulpice.[1]

The great confidence which Talon enjoyed at court is exemplified by his receipt of a royal order empowering him to send back to France " all who should act against the service." [2]

A decade later La Salle affirmed that Talon and Courcelle had been " much hated by the Jesuits " and that Father Bardy had preached against them Talon had spoken so frankly that the court gave him to understand that it would rather know less.[3] If the intendant received such a hint at all, it must have been in the interval between his two intendancies

During this interval M de Bouteroue was in Canada His instructions complained of the excessive number of priests, monks, and nuns in that colony, and Colbert warned him of the " fear of excommunication and the too great severity of life " which the clergy made to reign at Quebec. Nevertheless, Bouteroue " ought never to blame the conduct either of the Bishop of Petræa or of the Jesuits in public " If necessary, he was to warn them in private and send memorials to the court, which would confer with their superiors.[4]

The Return of the Récollets

After his furlough in France, and in anticipation of his return to Canada, new instructions were drawn up for Talon in May 1669 [5] If the clergy overstepped the proper limits

[1] C G , II, f. 356. [2] C G , III, f 9 (1668). [3] Margry, vol I, p. 345.
[4] B, I, ff. 88, 90 , C G , III, f. 14v. [5] C G , III, f 39

of their authority, he was to oppose them " by methods gentle and amiable, and carefully inform His Majesty." In one of his memoirs he had requested " four good monks who do not constrain or fetter the conscience." [1] The required monks were now chosen from the Récollets, " it being necessary for the welfare of my service," said the king's letter to their provincial, " and for the salvation of my subjects . to send there certain Récollets of your province." [2]

On the same day Colbert asked the bishop not only to give the Récollets the power of administering the sacraments, but also to procure their re-establishment upon their lands in Canada,[3] while Louis XIV commanded Laval to assist the new missionaries, adding that their return might be " of very great utility for the spiritual consolation of my subjects and for the relief of your ecclesiastics " [4]

A marginal note in Talon's instructions said " The establishment of the Récollet fathers suffered no opposition. It was accomplished with the consent and the joy of clergy and laymen " And in November 1670 the intendant reported that the Canadian clergy were acquitting themselves of their duties very well. The Récollets, " though heretofore undesired by the bishop and Jesuits," were rendering good service. Their provincial's judicious and prudent conduct had won the esteem of all, but they needed the king's help By enabling them to augment their number, His Majesty would forestall any demand the bishop might make for reinforcements. The more Récollets there were, the better would they counterbalance the excessive authority of the others. " Truly, Mgr., it is hard to express the joy of the people at the arrival of these fathers " Colbert's name was everywhere blessed. The provincial would tell him of the constraint under which the Canadians had been

[1] *C G*, III, f 52. [2] B, I, f 132v.
[3] *Ibid*, f 145   [4] *Ibid*, II, ff 38, 39 (April 4, 1670).

hitherto, and "with what delicacy it was necessary for me to deal with the Church in order to conserve the authority of the king and the repose of consciences and to avoid giving the bishop cause to murmur against me."[1]

Colbert was glad to learn of the faithfulness of the clergy, and he added the politic remark. "I did not doubt that the bishop and all the Jesuits would give a favourable reception to the Récollet fathers, since (as they are working upon the same principle and with a view to carrying the light . . . of the Gospel into the regions farthest removed from New France) this will be a succour to animate their zeal all the more."[2]

Although the Récollets were thus cordially received, they were unable to reoccupy their former lands and convent The lands had been taken by settlers, and the convent had fallen into ruin.[3] The newcomers had to seek a home elsewhere.

About this time Father Jérome Lalemant wrote his general a letter which depicted the situation at Quebec from the viewpoint of the Jesuits. Among the religious bodies there was perfect peace. Between the Jesuits and the secular powers the peace was only apparent, since the instructions of royal representatives required them to diminish the supposedly excessive authority of the priests. This was thought to be one reason why they had brought back the Récollets. "Quidquid sit, Patres illos suscepimus et omni officiorum genere prosecuti sumus et prosequemur, nec inde nos depressos habemus, sed adjutos."[4]

Harmony Restored

So we see that Colbert's secret instructions for the "balancing" of their influence had not remained a secret to the

[1] C.G., III, f. 85v.   [2] B, III, f. 30.   [3] *Lettres*, p 647.
[4] Rochemonteix, vol. iii, p. 90 (1), Sept. 19, 1670.

Jesuits. They were none the less resolved to make the best of the situation and to avoid any open conflict.

Talon soon found it necessary to repress their activity in a matter affecting the prerogatives of His Majesty. Dissatisfied with his position as simple Apostolic Vicar, Laval had long sought a definite appointment as titular Bishop of Quebec, and the Jesuits, whose caution at first had made them prefer a bishop *in partibus*, were giving him their hearty support. Ardent Gallican that he was, Talon intervened: " Knowing that the Jesuits were giving him to understand that their Company was working at Rome to have him accorded his title, I let him know that he ought to expect it from His Majesty, who alone could secure it for him ; also that he was to hold all his establishments from His Majesty, because he depended upon him alone." The bishop took this advice kindly and afterwards showed much gratitude.[1]

The Jesuits do not appear to have manifested any ill-humour over the incident, and, with the exception of the fire-water question, no acute difference of opinion seems to have arisen henceforth between the intendant and the clergy. In 1671 Talon was satisfied with the concord which still appeared to reign among the ecclesiastics, Récollets included. His own best efforts tended in that direction, for " peace is the support of bodies which are commencing to take form." Yet he perceived that in this regard his conduct was not agreeable to some people who would that he were " always at loggerheads with the Church." The allusion is probably to Courcelle, who, as we have seen, was sometimes chagrined because the intendant would not " follow all his movements." But, concluded Talon, as long as the clergy had good intentions, he would support them with all the authority the king had entrusted to him , but if they changed their practice, he would change likewise.[2]

[1] *C G*, III, f. 87 (Nov. 10, 1670).   [2] A.E., *Am*, v, f. 299v.

Explorations

In our study of Canada's greatest intendant there remain but three topics to discuss exploration, Indian politics, and the fire-water traffic. The first may be treated in a few words. Throughout his sojourn in New France, Talon eagerly accepted the collaboration of Jesuits and Sulpicians in the work of discovery. The former told him of a rich copper rock in Lake Huron, they themselves had a copper anvil weighing 100 lb. When Talon sent Sieur Péré to find the mine itself, this gentleman stayed at the Jesuit mission and wrote only " very obscurely " of the object of his quest. The intendant was quick to suspect Jesuit intrigue. However, the following spring these missionaries assisted Talon's envoy, St Lusson, in assembling at Sault Ste Marie the deputies of seventeen tribes to acknowledge the sovereignty of the French king. In the summer of 1671 Talon entrusted Father Albanel and Sieur St Simon with a mission to Hudson Bay.[1]

The Sulpicians also did their share: Dollier set out with La Salle to reconnoitre a sea communicating with Japan and China. Dollier and Galinée explored much of what is now old Ontario and furnished the intendant with maps of their discoveries ; while Fénelon supplied him with information concerning the Iroquois country.[2]

The Civilization of the Indians

The second topic is Talon's Indian policy

For Indian politics proper the intendant was much less responsible than the governor. But this did not prevent his strengthening the position of the missionaries when opportunity offered. For instance, on one occasion he took

---

[1] *C G*, II, f 311 ; III, ff 63, 106v, 161v, 162v, 163v, A E, *Am*, V, f 277.
[2] *C G*, III, ff 64, 71, 87, 107.

Father Pierron by the hand, and addressing the Iroquois said "Here is my uncle. I desire that you treat him as you would treat me, and still better."[1]

But though the intendant had little responsibility for the policy of New France toward the Indian nations outside of Canada, yet, with regard to the Indians within the colony, it was to him that the court looked for the realization of its views. In April 1666 Colbert wrote that, apart altogether from the possibilities of immigration, there was nothing which would contribute more to the augmentation of the colony than "to try to civilize the Algonquins, the Hurons, and the other savages who have embraced Christianity, and dispose them to come and settle in community with the French, live with them, and bring up their children in our manners and customs."[2]

A great deal of time, energy, and money might have been saved had Colbert acquainted himself with the history of the question upon which his views were so pronounced. Let us review briefly the efforts that had already been made to civilize the Indians. To do so we must return to the Récollet period. Very soon after their arrival these missionaries formed the design of reducing the errant tribes to a sedentary life, but the same merchants who opposed French colonization also opposed Indian civilization. A Catholic trader threatened to drive the neophytes out of the proposed settlements "à coups de bâton," for fear they would quit the chase. Nevertheless, the Récollet friar Sagard asserted that early failures had proven that the only remaining hope for the evangelization of the Indians lay in making them live together in communities, otherwise the wandering missionaries would become as wild as the red men themselves. Besides, families of "virtuous Catholics" must be mixed with these Indians to show them the practice of what the priests taught. However, by 1626 the Récollets

[1] *Moreau*, 842, f. 75.   [2] *C.G.*, II, f. 205.

THE TRIUMVIRATE

had been able to induce only three or four native families to settle near their monastery, clear a little land, and sow some corn. In their eagerness to initiate the Indian children in French laws and manners the missionaries formed small classes in reading and writing, but these embryo schools came to naught for lack of funds

Champlain heartily approved the Récollets' endeavours not only upon religious but also upon political grounds, since the presence of Indian hostages near Quebec would increase French control over the tribes [1]

After the return of the French to Canada in 1632 the Jesuits seriously undertook the education of Indian children. Withdrawing them from the influence of their relatives, they placed them in a French environment in the society of French children. Then, seeing that the latter were in danger of being perverted by the contact, they removed their Indian pupils to Notre Dame des Anges. It was labour wasted [2]

After five years of sterile effort the Jesuits abandoned their seminary for Indian boys, and concentrated their strength upon the sedentary missions for Indian families at Sillery and at Three Rivers. Experience had brought them to the same conclusion as their predecessors with regard to the necessity of reducing the nomad tribes to a settled life like that of French colonists.[3]

To all the Christian sedentary Indians the Company of New France accorded the same commercial privileges as to Frenchmen, the king granted them the civil rights of French subjects;[4] and the missionaries strove to teach them the principles and practice of agriculture.[5] But, unlike the

---

[1] Le Clercq, vol. i, pp 96, 99, 134, 223, 243, 287; Sagard, pp 168-71, *Rel*, 1626, p. 2; Champlain, 1632, vol. ii, p. 34

[2] *Rel*, 1634, p 12; 1635, pp 19, 20; 1636, p 35, 75; 1637, p. 56, 1638, p 23

[3] *Ibid*, 1634, p 10, 1635, p. 21, 1638, p. 17, 1640, pp 37, 45, 1641, pp. 31, 56, 1643, p 28

[4] C.G., 1, f. 253   [5] *Lettres*, p 322.

Récollets, the Jesuits made no mention of mingling French families among their neophytes, and this isolation of Indian converts was to remain a cardinal point of their policy. In 1644 Mother Marie explained the policy of separation by saying that the Jesuits feared lest their neophytes imitate the immorality of some of the French. Besides, she added, the natives were not yet ready for even the honest liberties of French life.[1] Of the Indians at Sillery, Father Le Jeune made " friends and subjects of France while bringing them to the true faith and while respecting in large measure their manners, their usages, and their language." In 1651, when the Company of New France formally granted the seigneury of Sillery to the Indians, it placed everything absolutely under the control of their Jesuit pastors [2]

It was to this situation that M. de Mésy alluded when he charged that the Jesuits would not " suffer the Indians to be governed under the laws of His Majesty."[3] His accusation that the " religion of the Indians is quite imaginary " was merely an unfriendly way of repeating what all the missionaries confessed, viz. that material motives were the mainspring of Indian conduct, and that when left to themselves these children of the forest soon forgot their lessons in Christianity. It was for precisely this reason that Récollets and Jesuits had developed the sedentary mission, where their own influence would be paramount and permanent. Moreover, these barbarous peoples were as yet " exempt from all the great vices of France,"[4] and the fathers well knew that this exemption would be of short duration if they were to gallicize their converts so completely as to expose them to the influence of the worst elements in Quebec; for the Indians, like other undeveloped races, assimilated the vices more readily than the virtues of European society. Add to this the Jesuits' instinctive

[1] *Lettres*, p. 387.
[2] Rochemonteix, vol 1, pp. 279, 466.
[3] M 242.
[4] *Fds Fr.*, 25,081, f. 289

determination to keep in their own hands the work they had begun and to increase the power of their order by rendering themselves indispensable to the civil authority as the main channel of communication with the natives

But Colbert and Louis XIV, unacquainted with the history of these varied attempts at civilizing the Indians, saw no obstacle in the way of complete "francization," and they exhorted Talon to take up this work with energy In November 1666 the intendant replied that he had already sought to apply to the natives the rules of French life and the punishments which followed their infraction, together with privileges such as the use of liquors, which hitherto had been forbidden them. But he had encountered an obstacle which he would try to remove the following winter. Certainly the Indians ought long ago to have been taught French, so as not to oblige subjects of the king to learn their language in order to be able to communicate with them.[1]

In the spring of the following year Colbert again blamed the missionaries for making very little effort to detach the natives from their savage customs. He encouraged Talon to draw the Christianized Indians into the neighbourhood of the French habitations and, if possible, to mingle them with the colonists "in order that, having but one law and one master, they may form only one people and one blood."[2] Thereupon Talon gently reproached the Jesuits with having neglected to cultivate the manners of the natives as they ought. The good fathers, desirous of the approbation of the civil authorities, promised him that they "would labour to change these barbarians in all their parts, commencing with the language."[3]

But the royal government was resolved to marshal all the available forces for this campaign of civilization, and so Louis wrote to Laval that he had been surprised, since

[1] C.G., II, f. 222.   [2] Ibid., f. 297.   [3] Ibid., f. 317v.

assuming responsibility for the colony, that so few Indians had been led to dwell among the French and to adopt their methods of living. Nevertheless, there was no better means of assuring the salvation of these tribes, and the bishop should incite the missionaries to work for the union of Indians and French into " one same people." This surely would facilitate the conversion of the former However, if the adult Indians proved intractable, every effort must be put forth to give the children a French Catholic education.[1]

It is surely amusing to hear Louis XIV, in his gilded palace of Versailles, giving instructions to the Bishop of Quebec and his Jesuit veterans as to how best to assure the salvation of their savages But in reality the king's motives were chiefly political the aggrandizement of the Monarchy and the extension of the Empire without any drain upon the population and resources of Old France

In a letter of 1668 Mother Marie discusses the king's desire that the Ursulines bring up a number of Indian girls after the French fashion :

If His Majesty wills it, we are ready to do so, by the obedience we owe him. Nevertheless, it is a very difficult thing, not to say impossible, to gallicize or civilize them. We have more experience in the matter than any one else, and we have remarked that out of one hundred who have passed through our hands we have civilized scarcely one. We find them docile and intelligent, but when we are thinking of it least, they climb over our enclosure and go off to roam the woods with their parents, where they find more pleasure than in all the comforts of our French houses. The Indian humour is made thus, they cannot be constrained; if they are, they become melancholy, and melancholy makes them ill Besides, the savages have an extraordinary love for their children, and when they know they are sad they pass over every consideration in order to have them back, and we have to give them up [2]

---

[1] A.E., Am., v, f. 238.   [2] Lettres, p 627

THE TRIUMVIRATE

Thus we see that the experiences of Récollets, Jesuits, and Ursulines had been identical, and no one would accuse either monks or nuns of lack of zeal Yet the king's will must be obeyed.

In his instructions to Bouteroue, Colbert set forth his view of the matter more fully than elsewhere :

It has appeared up to the present that the maxim of the Jesuits has not been to call the natives of the country into community of life with the French, either by the gift of common lands and habitations or by the education of their children and by marriages Their reason has been that they have thought to conserve more purely the principles and the sanctity of our religion by keeping the converted Indians in their ordinary form of life, than by calling them in among the French. As it is only too easy to know how far this maxim is removed from all good conduct, whether as regards religion or as regards the state, it is necessary to act gently to make them change it, and to employ all the temporal authority in enticing the said Indians among the French This can be effected by marriages, and by the education of their children [1]

The king followed this up by exhorting Mgr. de Laval to continue the work of education he had already begun. The amalgamation of the two races could be accomplished only through the assiduity of bishop, Jesuits, and Sulpicians , and this was the most important fruit and the most solid that they could produce there [2]

In compliance with the wishes of the civil authorities the Jesuits made another effort, but with no more encouraging results than previously. When Talon returned to Quebec he found the number of their Indian pupils " much diminished." However, he thought that " their ardour for this charity " was reawakening, and would be further kindled by two or three lines of approbation from Colbert.[3] Meantime, their two principal sedentary missions were making progress. At Sillery three priests and two friars were at

[1] B, I, f. 88v.   [2] *Ibid.*, f 134   [3] *C G*, III, f 88

work, at the Madeleine three priests and three or four friars.[1]

However, in their new effort to gallicize the red man the civil authorities found more enthusiastic collaborators in the Seminary of St. Sulpice at Montreal. The priests sent out by M de Bretonvilliers had already rendered valuable service as curés, without being a charge upon the royal treasury,[2] and Talon now turned to them for aid in the civilization of the natives He told their superior that, to communicate with the Indians, Frenchmen were reduced to learning their language, thus "wounding the dignity" of the French nation The superior offered to open a school for the instruction and complete francization of the Indians, big and little, "provided that we be not traversed or disquieted in these exercises of charity by those who claim to be sole directors of the said Indians."[3] Talon advised that the king accord them the desired protection, so that, "emulation arising between them and the Jesuits, they will vie with each other in the perfection of their task."[4] Accordingly Colbert wrote the Abbé de Queylus, who had returned to Canada, that His Majesty "leaned almost entirely" upon him for the augmentation of the colony of Montreal,[5] and expected him to educate the Indian children until they were "capable of being admitted to the common life" of the French.[6]

The abbé set to work zealously. Indian boys were brought up in his seminary; Indian girls in the congregation of Mlle Bourgeois.[7]

He then proposed to build a hospital for aged and invalid Indians, whose presence would make it easier to detach the children from their relatives in the woods This project and his work in general won him the unqualified approval

---

[1] C.G., III, f 37 [2] Ibid, II, f 227. [3] F 3, III, f. 353 (Oct. 7, 1667).
[4] C G, II, f 317v. [5] B, I, f 146
[6] B, III, f. 35 [7] C G, III, f 87v

of the intendant, who described him as very zealous for the welfare of the colony and extremely generous, inasmuch as he was going to employ all his fortune in the upbuilding of Montreal. In fact, he might need Colbert's protection to withdraw his revenues from France.[1]

Talon and the Sulpicians

There is no doubt that Talon, like Courcelle, felt immeasurably more sympathy for the Sulpicians than for the Jesuits or the Seminary of Quebec. In his memoir of 1667 he had said: "As these ecclesiastics are not a charge to king or country, because of the property they transport to Canada, and as, besides, they do not cause the colonists the spiritual disquiet which they suffer from the conduct of the others, I think it would be well to invite M. de Bretonvilliers to send some of them out here each year."[2] He repeated this suggestion some two years later, continued his eulogies of the Abbé de Queylus, begged of Colbert an audience of "half a quarter-hour" for Abbé Fénelon,[3] and co-operated with the Sulpicians of Paris in choosing young women "well qualified" for life in New France.[4]

In brief, the harmony between Talon and the ecclesiastics of Montreal seems never to have been interrupted, except in the case of Father Rémy, whose knowledge of jurisprudence and activity in settling disputes led to some misunderstanding between him and the intendant.[5]

With the clergy of Quebec, as we have seen, Talon's relations were not so uniformly happy, but, in spite of an

---

[1] *C G.*, III, f. 88; A E, *Am*, v, ff. 300v, 307.   [2] *C G.*, II, f. 357.
[3] It was no easy matter to get an audience with Colbert. We have already mentioned Ragueneau's experience. Lauson de Charny, in spite of his personal rank, failed in several attempts to speak to the minister on "something which regards the welfare of New France." Charny was really a delegate of Laval and his Seminary (*Mélanges*, 142 bis, f. 565).
[4] *C G.*, III, ff. 52, 70, 87; IV, f. 30.   [5] Faillon, vol. III, p. 419.

absence of perfect mutual confidence, his second intendancy drew to its close without any open break between him and the Jesuits or the priests of the Seminary. A fundamental cause of the aforesaid lack of confidence was the extreme divergence of views between the two authorities with regard to the traffic with the natives in *eau-de-vie*.

The Brandy Trade

While Talon was firm in the repression of crime and disorder, he did not see eye to eye with the ecclesiastics in regard to the use of liquor by the natives. He accepted Colbert's theory that the Indians could be completely gallicized if they were only treated as Frenchmen; and this involved the right to indulge in liquor.[1] Nor were his views affected by the disaster which befell Courcelle when intoxication stopped his Algonquins on their way to guide him to the land of the Mohawks.[2] However, he soon realized that brandy was wasting the substance of the French colonists themselves, and he bent his energies to overcoming this waste. His idea was not to repress the traffic, but to oust it from the colony by introducing a competitor. Colbert approved his proposal to manufacture beer, because it was "very healthful and could be sold cheaply," whereas wines and brandy were too dear for many of the habitants. Besides, all the elements in the composition of beer were to be found in Canada.[3] To aid the enterprise, which was endorsed by the most "notable" citizens, the king made Talon a present of two copper boilers. The intendant hoped to economize for the people more than 100,000 livres now spent annually in wine and *eau-de-vie*. In addition to this, the new industry would "incite the habitant to the ... cultivation of the soil, because he would be

[1] *C.G.*, II, f. 222.   [2] *Journal*, p. 341.
[3] *C.G.*, II, f. 296 (April 1667).

assured of the consumption of his surplus grain."[1] Viceroy de Tracy believed that the brewing of beer would promote temperance and help the tillers of the soil, but he also advised the restriction of the importation of liquors whether for whites or for Indians.[2] Early in the following year, 1668, Colbert wrote that a final resolution in the matter of the trade with the Indians ought to be taken in Canada after a mature examination of its advantages and disadvantages. Meantime, let the people accustom themselves to the use of beer Thus money would be kept in Canada, and "the vice of drunkenness and the others which accompany it would cause no more scandal," or at least they would be of less frequent occurrence, for the "vapours" of beer rarely cause the loss of reason.[3] The establishment of a brewery appealed even to the Jesuits as a highly desirable undertaking, and in the *Relation* of 1668 Superior Le Mercier adopted Talon's arguments.

Any plan which would tend even indirectly to diminish the quantity of brandy imported into Canada must needs appear to Le Mercier worthy of commendation, for from some of the missions the reports of Indian excesses grew worse and worse The Jesuits among the Mohawks found that Satan was profiting by the sale of brandy which the "Europeans of those parts had begun . . during the last few years" Sometimes the whole village seemed mad, their licence was unbounded ; they threw firebrands at the heads of the Jesuits, burned their papers, forced their chapel, and threatened their lives. Often for three or four days the missionaries got neither food nor sleep, but they resolved not to quit their posts until death One could "make an angel of a barbarian" if intoxicating drinks were kept from him, whereas brandy "changed Christians into apostates." Almost the only bright spot in the picture was Tadoussac, where the Company of the Occident won

[1] *C.G.*, II, f. 316v (Oct. 1667) [2] *Ibid*, f. 328 [3] *Ibid*, III, f. 16v.

the praise of bishop and Jesuits by conducting a profitable trade without the aid of alcohol. Experience had proven, said Le Mercier, that "the great means of enriching both Frenchman and Indian in their mutual trade is to exterminate all commerce in drink," which "provokes very justly the wrath of God, and can bring down only His malediction."[1] We find the same argument suggested in the private *Journal* of the Jesuits.[2] It naturally calls to mind M. de Mésy's grave accusation against the missionaries, and we wonder whether any of them ever did traffic in brandy. About this time Father Pierron began his apostolic labours among the Iroquois, and it behooved him to lay in his winter supplies. It is worth while to note the extent of his interest in *eau-de-vie*. He sent two letters to two persons in Orange requesting them both to give the bearer ninety pounds of bacon, three or four jugs of good brandy, and a jug of wine. Colonel Nicolls saw these letters and invited Pierron to meet him at Schenectady, adding: "I shall be glad to see you and to serve you in what you seem to desire toward your winter provision."[3] It must be patent to every one that the Jesuit wanted these few jugs of liquor for medicinal purposes in the frosts and storms of the American wilderness. Four jugs of *eau-de-vie* would hardly suffice to build up a clandestine commerce in furs.

Leaving the missionaries, and returning to Quebec, we find that the Sovereign Council has not been idle. Inebriety was, of course, considered an extenuating circumstance in the punishment of crime. For example, two persons "in wine," having killed a soldier, escaped with flogging and branding, while the lesser crimes of theft, incendiarism, forgery, and rape were punishable with death.[4] In 1667 the attorney-general drew the attention of the Council to

[1] *Rel.*, 1668, pp. 3, 12, 22, 30.   [2] E.g. *Journal*, p. 354.
[3] *State Papers*, pp. 496, 497, 508, 513.
[4] *Journal*, pp. 316, 337, 354, 357.

the murders and rapes committed by intoxicated Indians, and demanded better enforcement of the ordinances in remote corners of the colony. A close friend of the clergy, he even proposed the galleys for life as punishment for a second infraction of the prohibitory laws. Indians should suffer the same penalties as Frenchmen. However, the Council refused to take extreme measures, but ordered that drunken Indians be fined and fastened in the stocks for three hours. This decree was to be interpreted to them by the Jesuits and executed by the local judges.[1]

At times the Sovereign Council enforced its own decisions with vigour, though without enduring effect, as when, for instance, it condemned several men, in default of payment of fines, to a month in prison. During the last fortnight they were to be exposed on the wooden horse one hour each day in the public view, bearing placards which were to read : " For having traded in brandy with the Indians." [2]

Two weeks later the councillors had to send one of their number to Three Rivers to investigate the " liquor troubles, which were extreme " ; [3] and in February 1668 they remarked that in Three Rivers, Montreal, and the smaller settlements the Indians had been for some months " perpetually drunk " and in the " worst disorder." More serious still, the habitants had begun to follow them into the woods, " so that there was hardly a band of Indians that had not some Frenchmen with it " When drunk the natives did not hunt well, and their creditors in the colony lost by them. The new ordinance stipulated that only one jug of brandy each week for personal use would be allowed Frenchmen who went off hunting [4]

The Council followed this up with a more radical measure such as M. de Tracy had advised. After the construction of a brewery no one was to import brandy or wines without

---

[1] C G , II, f 332.
[2] C S , vol. I, p 406 (June 1667).
[3] Journal, p 354
[4] C.S., vol. I, p. 474

special permission from the king, and the total annual importation was not to exceed 800 casks of wine and 400 of brandy.[1] However, this decree was doomed to remain a dead letter.

While councillors, missionaries, and intendant were facing the problem, each in his own way, Bishop Laval remained the centre of resistance to the traffic. Early in 1668 we find him warning the confessors against undue leniency toward penitents who plead for exemption from the rules on account of special circumstances.[2] If there was leniency for poverty-stricken penitents, there certainly was none for the impenitent. Witness the remark of the Jesuit *Journal* on the Sieur Bondy, who was drowned while inebriate: "He was buried like a dog near our mill."[3]

In February 1668 Colbert drew up instructions for M. de Bouteroue, who was to relieve Talon of the intendancy.

The commerce in wine and brandies with the natives . . . has been a subject of perpetual contestation between the Bishop of Petræa and the Jesuits, and the principal inhabitants and those who traffic in that country. The bishop and the Jesuits have claimed that these drinks intoxicate the Indians, that they cannot partake of them with moderation; that inebriety makes them lazy in hunting, and gives them every sort of bad habit, both as regards religion and as regards the State. The principal inhabitants and the traders, on the contrary, claim that the desire to have liquors, which are bartered dear, obliged the natives to hunt with more diligence.[4]

Colbert's classification of the contending parties was not quite accurate. Many of the principal citizens were of one mind with the clergy in this matter. Villeray, Bourdon, Gorribon, and several others might be named. As we have seen, the Sovereign Council, with apparent unanimity, supported a policy of repression, although it counted among its

---

[1] *C S.*, vol 1, p 477. [2] *Mandements*, p. 72.
[3] *Journal*, p. 355. [4] B, 1, f. 89.

members Mésy's friends, those " good servants of the king," Tilly and Damours. Nevertheless, Colbert's division is correct in the main.

We now come to a crisis in the history of our subject. It is November 10, 1668, the day of the departure of Talon. The Council is assembled. Latour says that Talon had received a letter from Colbert permitting the liquor trade [1] We have found no trace of such a letter, nor is it mentioned in the minutes of the Council. We are not even sure that the meeting was called at the request of Talon ; it is possible that Intendant Bouteroue wished to have this grave matter settled before the departure of his experienced predecessor In any case, the Council was presided over by Governor Courcelle Bouteroue, Laval, Talon, and all the councillors were present Their object was to fix upon the most suitable remedies for the " disorders arising from the quantity of *eau-de-vie* " which was furnished to the Indians " in contempt of the ordinances." Surprising as it may seem, they found " none more proper than that of admitting the liberty of the Indians to use (these liquors) after the example of the French, in order to introduce them thus into the society and commerce of the most honest people, rather than to see them exposed to live in the woods, where libertines, vagabonds, and idlers, abandoning their cabins . . . go to find them and take away the better part of the product of their hunt, thus depriving them of the means of satisfying their creditors." Moreover, " His Majesty wished the natives to live with his own subjects in a spirit of gentleness and union in order to foment the promised alliance between them and cement it better and better by their continual commerce and frequentation." After due deliberation the Council decided to permit all Frenchmen to sell all kinds of drinks to the Indians It enjoined the said Indians " to use them soberly." If they became drunken, they were

[1] Latour, p. 85.

to be attached by the collar to the stocks or pillory for two hours and to be fined two beaver-skins. Under similar penalties Frenchmen were forbidden to get drunk along with the Indians.¹

It will be noted that neither Laval nor his friends protested against this abrupt reversal of the Council's policy. Were they tired of the failure of repression and willing to test the merits of Talon's theory? Or, did they acquiesce in appearance only, resolved to undo his work when he was gone? Undoubtedly the bishop was in the latter case, for after a brief pause he recommenced the attack. If the sentiments of the ecclesiastical party are reflected in the letters of Mother Marie, they do not seem to have harboured any bitterness against Talon at the time. Writing of the great work he had accomplished, the Ursuline superior concluded: " If God inspires him to root out the commerce in drink, that will complete the immortalizing of his memory in this new Church." ² However, nine years later, a confidential letter to Laval showed that the clergy had come to regard the former intendant as the main cause of their woes,³ and in 1693 La Chesnaye's impression was that M. Talon " peut-être pour chagriner, ou chagrin d'ailleurs, prit le parti de faire permettre la traite des boissons." ⁴

At all events, in the spring of 1669 Mgr. de Laval revived his " reserved case." ⁵ At Easter " the bishop, his mitre on his head, his crosier in his hand, environed by his clergy, ascended a pulpit in the middle of the choir. After a pathetic discourse, in which he took for his text these words of God to Moses, ' Descende, peccavit populus tuus,' he fulminated the excommunication. He set in motion the monks and the clergy, and he was seconded with zeal; they thundered in the pulpit; they were inflexible in the con-

---

¹ *C.G.*, III, f. 19; *C.S.*, vol. i, p. 534; F 3, III, f. 357.
² *Lettres*, p. 645   ³ *Rapport*, 1183, p. xcvii.
⁴ *C.G.*, XII, f. 380   ⁵ *Mandements*, p. 77.

fessional "[1] Hence we see that, whatever their attitude toward the experiment of November 10, 1668, the clergy were resolved to use all their influence and all their authority for the absolute suppression of the evil. In October 1669, in describing the ills which beset the colony, Mother Marie asserted:

The most harm is caused by the traffic in wine and brandy. (The priests) declaim against those who give to the savages; they excommunicate them. The bishop and the preachers publish from the pulpit that it is a mortal sin. Notwithstanding all that, several have formed themselves a conscience which permits it. And, in this voluntary error, they go into the woods and carry drinks to the natives in order to have their furs for nothing when they are drunk. This year the disorder went so far that we were on the eve of beholding all the savage nations in combustion among themselves, or uniting to swoop down upon the French.

Moreover, Frenchmen were beginning to commit numerous crimes against the Indians, and the clerical party could "attribute the cause only to this pernicious traffic."[2]

While the Church was aiming at suppression, the civil authority was engaged in regulation. The new intendant issued an ordinance restricting the liberty of the taverns of Montreal, which plied their trade regardless of the ruin of families. "They respect neither the Sabbath nor hours of divine service; they foment disorder and debauchery"[3] When he was taking the census, M. de Bouteroue heard complaints about soldiers and habitants who forestalled the fur market by carrying brandy fifty leagues into the woods. Upon his report the Sovereign Council decreed that all habitants going off hunting must obtain leave from the commandant or a judge of their district, and have him inspect their outfit. Each man was allowed one jug of brandy for each week of absence. Violation of the regu-

[1] Latour, p. 82.   [2] *Lettres*, p. 642.   [3] *Doc.* 1651 à 1672, vol. i.

lations would involve confiscation of their goods, in addition to fines and corporal punishment for first and second offences respectively. The same decree enjoined the Indians to prevent their squaws from getting drunk, under penalty of being punished along with them.[1]

In France also restrictive measures were being adopted. In a memorial to the court Talon admitted that it had not been deemed expedient to distribute to the soldiers in Canada the brandies and wines intended for them, because, in part, of the " vexatious consequences of intemperance." [2] He then requested the king's Council to confirm the decision of the Council of Quebec in favour of the establishment of breweries and the diminution of the excessive quantity of liquors exported from the mother country to the colony.[3] Talon's petition was granted, and Colbert instructed his relative, M. de Terron, at La Rochelle, to see to it that the merchants, who had " full liberty to carry on commerce " with Canada, exported only the smallest possible quantity of liquors, " so that we can prevent by this means the intemperance and the idleness which are almost inseparable from each other and so harmful to the welfare and growth of this colony." [4]

In the autumn of 1669 the brewery at Quebec was completed,[5] and on November 10, 1670, Talon, who had entered upon his second intendancy, sent off to the Antilles some of the brandy stored in Canada. His aim was to encourage the cultivation of barley through the brewing of beer, which would be used more in proportion as other drinks were less available.[6] A year later Talon's brewery was capable of furnishing 2000 casks of beer for the Antilles and 2000 more for domestic consumption. This, it was hoped, would create an annual demand for over 3000 bushels of grain,

---

[1] *C.G.*, III, f. 59 (June 1669).
[2] *Ibid.*, f. 34.
[3] *Ibid.*, f. 53.
[4] *B*, I, f. 124 (April 1669).
[5] *C.G.*, III, f. 66v.
[6] *Ibid.*, f. 106.

to the great advantage of the tillers of the soil.¹ An ecclesiastical writer suggested a royal storehouse of *eau-de-vie*, for use only in necessity, until vines should be planted at Montreal. He thought there was no longer any need of attracting the Indians by the sale of brandy " as of yore." ²

Here we note a curious incident. Years before, the Community of Habitants had contracted colossal debts in France, which were to be progressively wiped out by a general import tax of ten per cent Now, on October 20, 1670, the Sovereign Council ordained that henceforth this tax should be levied only upon tobacco and liquors.³ At the same time it was advocating a decrease in the importation of liquors. Thus the good councillors were able to promote temperance, encourage home industry, and defraud their tiresome creditors all at one swoop.

And now we turn to the mission fields, whence came in 1669 the familiar tales of woe Among the Mohawks the gravity of the situation had provoked the assemblage of a public council. Upon the advice of Father Pierron, their chiefs had presented to Governor Lovelace, of Manhattan, a petition drawn up by the Jesuits. The rather unsatisfactory reply of the Englishman was that he had taken, and would continue to take, all possible care that the Indians should not receive liquor in excessive quantities.

Another missionary told of how his Iroquois joyed in drunkenness. They would shout " I am going to lose my head , I shall drink the water which banishes reason ! "

The Oneida mission was disturbed by the return of the Indians with sixty barrels of brandy from New Holland. The Jesuit there could not even conduct prayers in the chapel, " as each person thinks only of fleeing and hiding himself to avoid the violence of these madmen." ⁴

From the Senecas the news was less gloomy. The women

---

¹ *C.G.*, III, f. 167. ² *Fds. Fr.*, 23,081, f. 279.
³ *C.G.*, III, f. 145. ⁴ *Rel.*, 1669, pp. 6, 16, 45.

and the old men did not abandon themselves to inebriety, and there was hope that " their example and the zeal of the missionaries would moderate the dissoluteness of the warlike youth, who breathe out only blood and brandy." [1] That was in 1670. But the following year intemperance extended even to the women. Bands of Indian traders brought the liquor eighty leagues overland from New Holland, and the debauch lasted twelve or fifteen days after the arrival of each band.[2]

In 1672 we hear again from the Mohawks. To that tribe peace was proving more deadly than war, for they were now free to carouse on Dutch rum, and a malignant fever had desolated their land.[3]

The most hopeful tidings came from the Ottawa mission, which was still flourishing. " It is fortunate for these peoples," wrote Mother Marie, " and for the establishment of the Faith, that they are at a distance from the French, and consequently from bad examples and intoxicating drinks." [4]

At the Madeleine, too, the outlook was bright. The sobriety of these Christian Indians had become proverbial. At the entrance to their village they placed two memorial trees, to which were attached the figures of Intemperance and Impudicity, both subjugated by the Faith.[5] Joined to a Jesuit memorial of a later date, we find a copy of regulations adopted in Boston in 1672. These laws show that New England was also obliged to attack a problem which in New France was yearly assuming greater dimensions. The sale of brandy to the natives was absolutely prohibited upon pain of a fine of forty shillings for every pint sold, and one-third of this fine was to go to the informer. If doctors prescribed alcohol as medicine, their prescriptions were to be submitted to a magistrate for approval. With

---

[1] *Rel.*, 1670, p. 73. [2] *Rel.*, 1671, p 22.
[3] *Rel. inéd.*, vol. i, p. 4. [4] *Lettres*, p 672.
[5] *Rel.*, 1671, p. 13 ; Rochemonteix, vol. iii, p. 65.

a view to suppressing the "execrable sin" of the brandy trade, the court of Boston granted authority to any citizen to seize liquor in possession of an Indian, or to arrest him and have him imprisoned until he should explain how he obtained his liquor If too obstinate, the prisoners would be forced to labour on the public works.[1] By the inclusion of this extract in their memorial the Jesuits sought to strengthen their case in Canada

Thus far, in discussing ecclesiastical opposition to the brandy traffic, we have quoted almost exclusively from the Jesuits and the secular clergy of Quebec It is worth while, then, to note the attitude of the Sulpicians as expressed by their superior, Dollier de Casson. In his famous voyage of discovery in 1669 he had remarked the ravages of Dutch brandy among the Iroquois These Indians considered a drunk man totally irresponsible If he killed any one, they refrained from mourning over his victim for fear of causing the murderer pain by reminding him of his crime[2] Toward 1672 Dollier wrote as follows :

This liquor is such a diabolical bait that it catches all the savages who are near the French . Let certain casuists say what they will, I do not believe the hardiest would wish to die immediately after giving a savage enough to intoxicate him . . seeing that it is written, 'Woe unto him by whom the offence cometh' To that you will say, if the trade in liquors conducted thus is not permitted to good people, they must make up their minds to die of hunger, of cold, and of poverty, letting everything go to people devoid of conscience, who trade in liquors without discretion. I reply that that is true, and that they must continue to suffer right to the tomb, without allowing their love of ease or of the necessities of life to make them ever consent to sin for their own interest or that of their family, which they ought quite naturally to sacrifice to God no matter what compassion . . . they have for them.[3]

This pious argument of a celibate priest, we may suppose,

[1] *C G*, XII, f 129   [2] *Supp. Fr.*, 2490, f. 3.   [3] *Montréal*, p 114

would not appear convincing to the average habitant charged with a numerous family.

In the autumn of 1672 Talon returned to France. In his memorial upon Canada he pointed out how fur might be used as an article of export to the West Indies. By this means His Majesty could ruin Dutch commerce with the Isles to the profit of his own colonies. Talon also believed that Canada could very profitably exchange French wines and brandies for masts and dried fish from Boston [1]

The administration of Talon was the most successful of all the administrations of intendants or governors of the seventeenth century. Strong in the confidence and support of the king and his minister, he had achieved a double triumph, economic and political. In the economic sphere he had given a wonderful impulse to the development of Canada; in the political field he had "balanced" so effectively the power of the Church that its authority became indeed "inferior" to the civil power, as Colbert had wished. Yet so tactful had been his manner, that even the Jesuits seem to have submitted without rancour. And when governor and intendant sailed away, the Jesuits, following the rule of publishing only what is charitable and edifying, expressed "some chagrin" at their departure. "Eternally we shall remember the former for having so well brought back the Iroquois to their duty, and eternally we shall wish for the return of the second to put the finishing touch to the projects he has commenced so advantageously for the welfare of this country." [2]

In her history of those Sisters of Charity whom Talon had so constantly befriended,[3] Mother Juchereau summed up their views of him in these words: "One may well say in comparing him to those who followed him: 'Non est inventus similis illi.'" [4]

[1] *C G*, iv, ff 37, 42.
[2] *Rel.*, 1672, p 1.
[3] *E g C G*, ii, ff. 319v, 358; iii, f. 37.
[4] Juchereau, p 217.

CHAPTER VI

THE FIRST ADMINISTRATION OF FRONTENAC

1672-1682

INTRODUCTION

ON its political side the work of Talon was continued by his successor, but his economic programme was unhappily forgotten During the administration of Count Frontenac the power of the Church was still further reduced, for not only was the new governor, like Talon, a strong Gallican, but, unlike the great intendant, he loved to dominate in form as well as in fact.

Talon had suggested a one-man government for New France, and none was so well fitted for the task as he. Unfortunately, the king seems to have shrunk from the experiment then, only to try it later with a different type of administrator. For three years this martial figure ruled unhampered by a colleague. His troubles with the Sovereign Council and the clergy convinced Louis XIV that the experiment was proving a failure. Accordingly, in 1675 he sought to remedy matters by sending out a new intendant, Jacques Duchesneau. The remedy accentuated the disease, for Duchesneau, far from pacifying the hostile parties, embittered the strife by entering the clerical camp From 1675 to 1682 the political history of the colony is mainly a record of struggle between Frontenac and his supporters on the one hand, and the clergy, backed by their adherents, on the other.

FRONTENAC AND THE JESUITS

Before Frontenac sailed for Canada he received royal orders which instructed him to continue toward the Church the policy of Talon, i.e. to hold the Jesuits in check and to offset any aggressive tendency on their part by protecting the Récollets and the Sulpicians.[1]

Enamoured of pomp and mindful of the traditions of the old nobility, Frontenac sought to organize the political and social life of the young colony by calling an assembly of the estates "As far as I am concerned personally, I have every reason in the world to praise the civility and the decorum of the Jesuit fathers," reported the governor, for of their own accord they had offered him their new church decorated for the occasion.[2] Nevertheless, Frontenac showed his inbred suspicion of their order by adding on the same page that the Jesuits were the secret instigators of a small difficulty he had had with the grand vicar of the absent bishop. Another thing which displeased him was that the grand vicar and the priests of the Seminary were entirely dependent upon these monks, and thus the latter were "indirectly the masters in what concerns the spiritual, which . . . is a great machine for moving everything else." There was need of more Récollets, men of sufficient talent " to counterbalance a little that of the others."[3]

Meanwhile, the count himself seized the first opportunity of making the missionaries feel his influence Whereas hunters and traders were obliged to get passports when leaving the settlements, the missionaries had been accustomed to come and go at will. Frontenac now gave the Jesuit superior to understand that "they ought to be the first to set an example of submission and obedience." The Jesuits submitted without demur,[4] although in 1675 the

[1] B, IV, f 42v.   [2] C.G., III, f. 248
[3] Ibid., f. 247v.   [4] Ibid, f 246v

king ordered his representative to leave all the ecclesiastics liberty to come and go all over Canada without passports.¹ Nevertheless, the following year His Majesty placed a restriction upon this liberty by observing, that though not compelled to ask for passports, the missionaries ought to do so, and that when they went beyond the limits of his government, Frontenac ought to know their destination.²

Another point of attack soon presented itself to the watchful guardian of secular interests. In the second year of his administration he urged that holders of vacant lands within the city of Quebec be compelled either to build within a certain time or to sell at a fixed price. Many people were demanding building sites, but not an inch of ground remained free. Most of the land belonged to the religious communities, who, thought Frontenac, were either indifferent or hostile to the growth of the town.³

From this point he proceeded to the more general subject of Jesuit domination. First he advised an increase in the salaries of the councillors. Assuredly the money would be as well employed that way as in the "vain pretext" of Jesuit missions, the fruit of which did not appear very considerable. He was trying to combat the monopolistic spirit of these missionaries by securing to the Récollet friars their share of the work.⁴ Inside as well as outside the colony the Society of Jesus aimed at supremacy. Laval and the principal members of his Seminary belonged to the congregation of Father Bagot, and differed from the Jesuits only by their bands. Instead of counterbalancing the usurped authority of these monks, the episcopal authority served to augment it every day.

All the priests were so anxious to know the domestic

¹ B, vi², f. 12v.   ² B, vii, f. 17.
³ A.E., Am., v, f 316. In 1666 the Jesuit Beschefer had written: "La ville haute n'est considérable que par les églises et par les maisons religieuses" (Moreau, 842, f. 341).
⁴ E.g. ibid., ff. 318v, 345v.

affairs of their people that they had "salaried inspectors" in town and country. In the confessional, too, their curiosity led to the abuse of their spiritual authority, for they wanted to know " the names, the accomplices, and a thousand other circumstances which are not of the essence of confession." Then, either directly or through their emissaries, they would inform the husband of the conduct of his wife, or the mother of that of her daughter, so that something which never happened at all, or which was at any rate secret, became public in no time. Frontenac, foreseeing " a sort of inquisition a thousand times worse than that of Italy or Spain," reminded the ecclesiastics that " this practice was a little contrary to that of France and to the maxims of the Gospel which taught us . . . the manner in which Jesus Christ wished us to correct our neighbour." Finding all his remonstrances unheeded, the governor warned the priests that the first informer who caused domestic scandal by making charges he could not prove would be treated as a calumniator and severely punished. Soon afterwards, upon the advice of a missionary, a woman informed one of the habitants that his wife was unfaithful to him. Outraged by such treason after sixteen years of conjugal happiness, the habitant was tempted to slay the alleged adulteress, who appealed to Frontenac. When questioned, the tale-bearer avowed that she had acted upon " mere suspicion and by a principle of conscience, fearing lest God should be offended " by what might ensue. The governor threatened her with imprisonment, obliged her to retract before a notary, and then reconciled the husband and wife. This example had a salutary effect upon the scandalmongers, but such incidents proved to Frontenac the wisdom of opposing even the smallest of the daily attempts against the king's authority.

The preceding winter, in a well-advertised sermon, a Jesuit preacher had advanced certain " seditious propositions."

Among them was his denial of the king's right to intervene in the controversy over the brandy trade. His Ultramontane doctrines were couched in insulting terms which "assuredly might make a bad impression on the people." His superiors made humble apologies to Frontenac, who told them that if such a thing ever occurred again, he "would put the preacher where he would learn how to talk."

However, this lesson did not change the clergy's "intention of persuading the people that their authority ought to be respected before all others, even in secular things." Accordingly, knowing how many they held in tutelage, Frontenac let nothing pass unchallenged, but gently and with a show of friendship he assured the ecclesiastics that he would be deeply pained if he had to complain of them to Colbert. "I hope, Monseigneur," he added, "that you will keep this secret." Secrecy, of course, was good policy from the governor's standpoint, but it was hardly fair to the objects of his criticisms, who were thus prevented from defending themselves. Meanwhile, in spite of this sense of rivalry, the count assured Colbert that he got along very well with the churchmen (especially with the "wise and prudent" Jesuit superior), and that he granted them every possible favour.[1]

Nevertheless, his distrust of the Society of Jesus was profound. After the famous Perrot affair, in which he had excited so many antagonisms, Frontenac wrote home. "The Jesuits alone have not appeared in this, although, perhaps, they have as large a share in it as the others. But they are cleverer and cover their play better."[2] Still thinking chiefly of them, he reminded the minister of what had been done and said against preceding governors, "of what the ecclesiastics have been and are capable of doing

[1] A E., *Am.*, v, ff. 319-22 (Nov. 13, 1673)
[2] *C.G*, f. 70 (Nov. 12, 1674)

in this country, of their credit, their confessorships, and their other subterranean means "[1]

This obsession caused the governor so far to forget his duty as to intercept the letters of the clergy and to refuse them liberty of correspondence—offences for which he was reprimanded by His Majesty.[2] It may be pleaded as an extenuating circumstance that Frontenac suspected his enemies of rifling his own mails. On one occasion he wrote the provincial of the Récollets as follows: "As there are people here very curious to know what one person communicates to another, if you are writing to me and the Father Commissioner, send your letters to my wife, who will put them in her packet."[3]

Frontenac's attitude toward the Jesuits was determined in part by the influence of his ally, La Salle. With all his heroic qualities, the great explorer was afflicted with one fundamental weakness—brooding suspicion. The old Norman sea-captain, Beaujeu, found him "an impenetrable man," "of an incredible distrustfulness." At Rochefort he had suspected the treasurer of the port of having received "money from his enemies to cause the failure of his enterprise." One of his acquaintances complained of his *humeur saturnienne*. From Villermont he withdrew his friendship "without cause and upon petty conclusions and frivolous, ill-founded suspicions." He doubted the sincerity of even Frontenac's friendship: "I know that those who protect me in appearance, do it not through friendship but because they are in a way honour bound to do so." And further on: "It is not surprising that I do not open up to any one, distrusting everybody and having reasons for it that I could not write."[4]

[1] *C G*, f 71 (Nov 12, 1674)
[2] B, vi², f 12v ; *Rapport*, 1885, p cv
[3] *Mélanges*, 171, f. 54
[4] *Fds Fr*, 22,799, ff 103, 148, 164, 179, Clair, 1016, f. 177. All printed in Margry, vol II, pp 234, 425-61

To such a nature, after his unhappy experience in their order,[1] the Jesuits of Canada were necessarily a source of haunting suspicion

They were his evil manitous, and in all his troubles his gloomy imagination could see the treacherous hand and hear the stealthy step of the black-robe   Accordingly, while he evidently meant to be honest, his reported indictments of the Canadian missionaries are replete with violence and exaggeration , and a comparison of the most important of them [2] with Frontenac's famous arraignment of the Canadian clergy [3] proves a remarkable community of ideas and sentiments between these two men. They both accuse the Jesuit missionaries of having deliberately fomented war between the Iroquois and the French in order to embarrass Frontenac and ruin the work of La Salle.

The explorer's establishments, actual or projected, on Lake Ontario and westward, interfered with the free communication (and commerce) which the Jesuits in the Cantons wished to enjoy with the Ottawa region and with Mexico, and La Salle was convinced that the Society was planning " to make of these quarters a new Paraguay " According to both memoirs, it was by disregarding the urgent letters of the missionaries and by visiting Fort Frontenac with a small company that the governor maintained the peace.   Unhappily, we are not in possession of the proofs by which the count's indictment seems to have been accompanied, but the truth of his main charge seems more than doubtful   That the Jesuits were resolutely hostile to La Salle and his friends is certain , but we have no reason to believe that they ever sacrificed the interests of New France or planned wholesale slaughter in order to rid themselves of an enemy.

Besides, whenever trouble was brewing between French and Iroquois, the missionaries were in danger of their lives

---

[1] Rochemonteix, vol iii, pp 40-8   [2] Margry, vol 1, pp 345-402.
[3] *Clair*, 1016, f. 43, and Margry

La Salle himself remarked this in 1673,[1] and the Jesuit *Relations* mention it repeatedly.[2] Voluntarily to stir up trouble would have been for the missionaries suicidal. Moreover, we have direct evidence to disprove such a charge. In 1673 both La Salle and Frontenac remarked the effervescence of warlike feelings among the Iroquois.[3] Father de Lamberville accused the Dutch of inciting the Cantons to rid themselves of the black-robes,[4] and in 1674 the governor proudly asserted that his journey to Lake Ontario had procured " the surety of all the missionaries who are among the Iroquois."[5] However, peace with the Five Nations was always of uncertain duration, and in 1676 Superior Dablon reported: "The war with which the Iroquois threaten the French exposes the fathers . . . to an imminent danger of being massacred, and, besides, it retards the progress of the Gospel. These barbarians, since they have finally exterminated the Andastes . . . have become so insolent that they talk only of splitting the heads of the missionaries in order to start the war."[6] This manuscript *Relation* was meant for circulation only among a select circle of readers in France, whom the superior could have no likely object in deceiving, and the facts as given in the foregoing extract would seem to discredit the suspicion of La Salle and Frontenac that the " authors of the rumours of war " were the Jesuits. If they urged the governor to take vigorous measures against the Iroquois, it was probably because, on this as on other occasions, they felt that war was coming inevitably and that the French ought to assume the offensive before their enemies were thoroughly prepared. In spite of all Frontenac's genius for managing the Iroquois, the threatening storm eventually broke just as the colony lost its valiant protector.

[1] *G G*, IV, f. 9.
[2] *E g. Rel. inéd.*, vol. ii, pp. 99, 196.
[3] *C G.*, IV, ff. 9, 12.
[4] *Ibid.*, f 48.
[5] *Ibid.*, F 68v.
[6] *Rel. inéd.*, vol. ii, p 99.

THE FIRST ADMINISTRATION OF FRONTENAC 143

In 1677 Jean de Lamberville reported to his superior at Quebec that the missionaries were being struck and threatened with death by the Iroquois, who wanted to begin a war[1] The honesty of this message cannot be doubted In 1679 the Jesuits advised Frontenac that General Andros was intriguing to rouse the federation against the French, and the count seemed to find corroborative evidence from other sources[2] In 1681 he announced to Seignelay that the Iroquois were alienating themselves from the French, but that he was not in a position to follow the ex-superior's suggestion that he commence hostilities against the Senecas That counsel, he added, " is only the sequel to those they have given me for several years, to which I have not thought it my duty to defer."[3] Here, Frontenac refers to the military weakness of the colony as his chief reason for not listening to Jesuit advice, and he no longer suspects the missionaries of " intrigue " or " design." Finally, shortly before Count Frontenac's departure from Canada, Father de Lamberville warned him that the Iroquois had no fear of the French, and that they were promising themselves, after having destroyed their allies, to fall "all together upon Canada in order to overwhelm it in a single campaign." The experience of La Barre and Denonville was soon to justify the Jesuit warnings

But even apart from the Iroquois war, Frontenac showed a tendency to distrust of Jesuit motives. In 1673 Father Bruyas informed him of Dutch designs upon Acadia. The governor sought more complete information, but did not place confidence in Bruyas' response. " The trouble is," he explained to Colbert, " that they send us whatever word they like and whatever they believe may favour their interests, there being no one who can explain the truth " He hoped that through Le Moyne, the expert *truchement*, he would be able to clear up everything and discover the

[1] *Rel. inéd.*, vol. ii, p. 196. [2] *C G.*, v, f. 5v [3] *Ibid.*, F 272v.

true disposition of the Dutch and the Indians.¹ In fact, he did not know what he would do if he lost Le Moyne, the only good interpreter in the colony, for he would then have to "pass through the hands of the Jesuit fathers, who would make us believe what they wished." ²

The next year, 1674, he asked Colbert for funds for the maintenance of two interpreters, "in order not to pass through the hands of the Jesuit fathers when we have to treat with the savages." ³ His request does not seem to have been granted, for he repeated it seven years later—this time without any mention of the Jesuits.⁴

But, in spite of his suspicions, throughout his administration Frontenac was indebted to the missionaries for valuable aid. In 1673, when Groseilliers was working for the English interest at Hudson Bay, the governor delegated Father Albanel to counteract his influence over the Indians and to win him back to the service of France.⁵ Three years later we find the Hudson's Bay Company complaining of the priest's effective intrigues against their interests : "He hath endeavored under the pretence of propagating the Christian Fayth to divert ye Indians from trading with your Petıconers." He was now in Paris together with Groseilliers and his companion Radisson. "From all which, your Petıconers have great reason to suspect some farther ill designe agt. theyre Colony and Trade in Hudsons Bay." ⁶ In response to this petition the English government made representations to "the Most Christian King" requesting him to "hinder the Jesuit and the 2 persons aforesaid from undertaking anything that may be prejudicial to the Trade or Interest of the aforesaid company." ⁷

---

[1] A E , Am., v, ff 338, 346.
[2] Ibid , F 336v. La Salle, whose suspicions were more fantastic than Frontenac's, declares that Le Moyne was devoted to the Jesuits (Margry, vol 1, p. 345, et seq.)   [3] C G , iv, f 87   [4] Ibid., v, f. 274v
[5] A E , Am., v, f. 345v   [6] B.M , C.O. 389, vol iii, p. 42
[7] Ibid , 134, vol 1, p 21 (Jan 26, 1676).

THE FIRST ADMINISTRATION OF FRONTENAC 145

It was from Father Nouvel, of Sault Ste Marie, that Frontenac learned of the activities of Groseilliers and the English at Hudson Bay Nouvel had warned him of the crisis threatening French commerce from north and south. The missionaries at the Sault were urging their Indians to continue their commerce with the colony and " to remain in close union with both God and the French, assuring them that in this union they have nothing to fear." [1]

At the same time the Jesuits in the cantons contributed to the success of the great council at Cataraqui to which Frontenac summoned the Iroquois ambassadors in the summer of 1673 The missionaries, says Father Millet, made the deputies desire an establishment there " as a means of facilitating their trade . . . with the French." Alarmed at the founding of Fort Frontenac, the intendant of Manhattan had invited Father Bruyas to meet him at Orange and explain its meaning The Jesuit replied by letter that it was " the beauty of the spot " which had determined Frontenac's action " rather than the design of turning aside the Iroquois from trading at Orange " [2] This collaboration was rewarded by the governor's hearty endorsement of the missionaries in his harangue to the assembled envoys.[3]

In the face of all these instances of Jesuit devotion to French interests—a devotion which by this time had become traditional—we cannot lay great stress upon Frontenac's memoir of 1677 when it accuses the Jesuits of playing into the hands of the English Certain missionaries might easily attend special English councils, " make several journeys to Orange and Manhattan," and appear to accept Andros' protection, without disloyalty to His Most Christian Majesty. The English themselves were convinced that the Jesuits were formidable adversaries Moreover, after his

[1] C G., IV, f. 5 (May 29, 1673).
[2] F 3, II, f 30; cf also C G , IV, f. 8   [3] C.G., IV, ff. 10, 14v.

K

slashing attack of 1677, composed when he was especially under La Salle's influence, Frontenac never again impugned Jesuits' loyalty to the Eldest Daughter of the Church. In the spring of 1682, when war-clouds were gathering dark over the feeble colony, it was above all to the Jesuits of Quebec that the governor turned for counsel.[1] To those of the Ottawa mission he entrusted orders which were to be communicated to the Indian allies upon the commencement of hostilities.[2] And from Father de Lamberville he received assistance. In his last letter, referring to Count Frontenac's distrust of his order, this apostle to the Onondagas said: "In any case, Monseigneur, permit me to tell you that assuredly some one has slandered us to you . . ."; and, continuing, he insisted that he and his confrères had "never thought of anything but seconding with their very feeble ability all the good intentions" that Frontenac had had for Canada. "But the past is past," he concluded tactfully, "and I do not believe that you have ever placed much reliance upon all the representations that people have made you without sufficient grounds."[3] Had the governor really turned a deaf ear to the impugners of Jesuit patriotism he would presumably have received still greater services from these missionary-diplomats.

In the work of exploration the Jesuits did their share during this administration, and here again they received unfair treatment from Frontenac. For instance, in 1674, when discussing the discoveries of Jolliet, he says not a word of Father Marquette.[4] And again, in his indictment of 1677, he accuses the Jesuits of vaunting Jolliet ahead of time, although he had been preceded by La Salle, who would testify that Jolliet's narrative was false in many particulars. This double injustice, like several others in the same memoir, may be attributed to the influence of La Salle,

[1] C.G., VI, f. 22v.
[2] Ibid., f. 12.
[3] Ibid., ff. 15, 21, 47 (Sept. 20, 1682).
[4] Ibid., IV, f. 81v.

THE FIRST ADMINISTRATION OF FRONTENAC

for five years earlier Frontenac himself had shown a due appreciation of the discoverer of the Mississippi [1]

Another subject of contention between Frontenac and the Jesuits was that of commerce Repeatedly and violently the governor accused the monks of trading for profit. As we treat this question further on, we shall not discuss it here. We turn now to the study of another religious body

THE RÉCOLLETS AND THEIR PROTECTOR

We have already seen that the Récollets came to Canada under the auspices of two ardent Gallicans, Talon and Colbert Under Frontenac they were to continue their rôle as servants of the State in its conflicts with the Church. In 1673 Colbert repeated his motive in sending them: they were to counterbalance the "too great authority which the Jesuits had given themselves in that country." [2] Two years later the king himself wrote: "I am sending to Canada five Récollets to strengthen the community of these religions which is already established there, my object being by this means to give a little more liberty to (people's) consciences." [3] Frontenac welcomed the newcomers as useful auxiliaries, and claimed that their disinterestedness made them better fitted for the work than were the others.[4] In 1674 he wanted more of them, "picked men," "the best" of the order, for they would encounter strong opposition. "Strange stratagems are played here, and unless one is wary, one is often caught" Frontenac's friendship for these Minor Brothers of St. Francis is illustrated by the fact that he made a dormitory above his own apartment in the Récollet convent for the reinforcements they were expecting. He thought Colbert might well inform the bishop that the Récollets had been sent to New France not to lead a "con-

[1] C.G., III, f 243v.
[2] B, v, f 27v.
[3] B, vi², f 15
[4] A.E , Am , v, f 319

templative life only, but to help work in the Lord's vineyard." There would soon be employment for fourteen or fifteen of them at Quebec, Fort Frontenac, Three Rivers, and the Ile Percée. The fine sermons of their superior, Eustache Maupassant, had aroused envy, and were the reason why he would not be allowed to preach that year; "for which," concluded Frontenac, " I am in despair, as no one can preach better than he preaches "[1] In a dispatch to Colbert he expressed his admiration with almost equal fervour . " The superior . . . is a great preacher who has thrown into the shade and caused some chagrin to those of this country who assuredly are not so clever."[2]

On his side, Eustache Maupassant showed a lively sense of gratitude for the " very great kindness " and the " very strong protection " the Récollets were receiving from the governor However, these favours aroused jealousies. " We have perceived," wrote the superior to Colbert, " that those who have the guidance of the Church are doing what they can underhand to decry our ministries and to render us useless in the country " The Récollets feared that their opponents wished to establish " maxims which were unheard of in the Church and in the world." " If I had wished to enter the cabals which are formed against the respect due to Monsieur the Governor, I should have found much favour with the people who have great power in the country But I am too good a servant of the king to depart ever so little from the obedience I owe to him who represents for us his person."[3]

However, his loyalty to his protector did not save Father Maupassant from the consequences of his own faults. Latour, an unfriendly critic, says that his community deposed the Guardian because of his improper life.[4] In any case, when he returned to France, Bishop Laval reported

[1] *Mélanges*, 171, f. 54 (Nov. 10, 1674).   [2] *C.G.*, IV, f. 79
[3] *Mélanges*, 171, f. 57 (Oct 12, 1674).   [4] Latour, p. 205.

unfavourably on him to Colbert. This incensed the provincial and all the Récollets, who had him preach in the Convent of Paris to restore his reputation. M. Dudouyt assured them that Laval had written advantageously of the others, but that Maupassant had by his "bad conduct caused the scandal"[1]

In his memoir of 1677 Frontenac eulogized the Canadian Récollets in general. They had brought solace to many, were wished for everywhere, even at Montreal, but were persecuted and calumniated by the rest of the clergy People were forbidden to confess to them, and their penitents were driven from the communion table. When the governor alleged as a reason for this persecution that the Récollets "do not take sides," he meant, of course, that they did not side with his adversaries.

Although their presence was desired by many people in different parts of Canada, their firm friend, Colbert, believed that they ought to place their Quebec establishment upon a firm footing, rather than build in several places. However, in 1681, under pressure from many habitants, the Sulpicians granted the Récollets a site for a convent at Montreal.[2]

In the same year the king gave them the site of the former Sénéchaussée in the Upper Town Of this favour Frontenac wrote to His Majesty that it "would be of great service to the bourgeois of the City of Quebec" had not the bishop rendered it useless by allowing the Récollets to build only a home for their infirm members and not a chapel where divine worship could be held publicly, "as the people would wish for their consolation." Furthermore, fearing lest the Récollets should be accorded the Old Warehouse in the Lower Town, Laval had decided to anticipate them by erecting an altar there.[3] As he took this liberty without permission, the Major of Quebec put a sentry there to close the entrance.[4]

[1] *Rapport*, 1885, p cvi.
[2] *C G*, v, f. 388.
[3] *Ibid.*, ff 388-9
[4] *Ibid*, f. 381.

And now we come to the concluding episode in our account of the relations between Frontenac, the Récollets, and Laval. In December 1681 a Récollet preacher touched lightly, says Frontenac, upon the existing "divisions, partialities, and cabals." As we might expect, the governor had listened to these sermons with "great edification," but the bishop reproved and removed the preacher. In the discussions which followed, according to Récollet testimony, Laval's representatives had submitted propositions in doctrine "very extraordinary both for religion and for the State." In order to inform the king and conclude the whole matter, Frontenac requested Superior Valentin to give him a full account of the affair in writing [1]

The Seminary of Quebec
(a) 1672-1675

From 1672 to 1675 Mgr. de Laval was absent from Canada, and it was with his grand vicar, Dudouyt, that M. de Frontenac had to deal

The count lost no time in reprimanding the bishop's representative for ignoring the Sovereign Council in the rehabilitation of a certain marriage, [2] but their first serious disagreement was over the wearisome old question of precedence. The councillors claimed the right to attend church in a body and to precede the churchwardens in processions The grand vicar contested the point "I own I was astonished at this dispute," wrote Frontenac, "which showed me their fondness for maintaining their own authority even in the smallest things, while trying to lower the royal " He thought the ecclesiastics ought to feel honoured to have a Sovereign Council attend service in a body, as would the curates in France were the parlements to do so. At home he had often known the wardens

[1] F 3, VI, f. 18.   [2] C.S., vol. i, p. 770

to plead against the curates, but seldom had he seen the curates uphold the wardens Moreover, he considered the matter settled by the king's ordinance of Tracy's time, but the clergy disputed his interpretation of that. After requesting definite instructions, Frontenac concluded : "Although these sorts of things are mere bagatelles, yet, in countries as far away as this and composed like it, they are of some consequence and give impressions of respect and obedience to the people and to the Indians." [1]

On March 4, 1675, the Council decreed that in all processions and ceremonies the officers of justice should follow the governor and precede the churchwardens.[2] At Lauson the publication of this decree caused a riot, and the Council deputed Sieur Desperras to inquire into the "opposition, violence, and disobedience" of the curate, the wardens, and the habitants. The priest, Thomas Morel, refused to appear before the councillor, and demanded to be tried by Henri de Bernières, his grand vicar. In spite of the attorney-general, Auteuil, the Sovereign Council enjoined M. de Bernières to oblige Morel to appear before the commissioner. The grand vicar's reply was that the criminal code did not require him to do so, since he was a superior of secular and not of regular clergy. Meantime, Frontenac and his friends in the Council had reproached the attorney-general with the "uniformity between his conclusions and the responses of the ecclesiastics," and urged him to show more zeal for the authority of the Council and the service of the king; but all to no purpose. When Morel disobeyed the aforesaid decree he was imprisoned in a chamber of the Château. Thereupon Jean Dudouyt, claiming to be promoter of the ecclesiastical court, petitioned the Council to hand over M Morel for trial by his ecclesiastical judge either alone or in conjunction with a commissioner. However, this sug-

[1] A.E., *Am.*, v, f. 323; or *C.G.*, IV, f. 25v.
[2] *C.S*, vol 1, p 904; *C G*, IV, f 110.

gestion was rejected, as the Council had never recognized any ecclesiastical court, and Bernières and Dudouyt were ordered to produce the "titles of their alleged jurisdiction." Accordingly Dudouyt brought forward copies of the royal edict of 1659 establishing the ecclesiastical jurisdiction of M de Laval. The Council did not pronounce upon the validity of this title, but meanwhile, upon the security of his superiors, it set Morel at liberty.[1]

While this quarrel over secular and ecclesiastical jurisdictions was in progress, Frontenac was challenging the authority of the Seminary in other matters. Moneys belonging to the *fabrique* were being diverted from their original destination without the consent of the wardens. Contrary to the rules of the Church, these moneys were not in the hands of the wardens at all, but in those of ecclesiastics. The latter, on their own authority, had turned a cemetery into a garden for the Seminary, and had exceeded their rights in other directions. The governor therefore enjoined upon the wardens the necessity of guarding more carefully in future the moneys and rights of the *fabrique*.[2]

These incidents portray for us the situation at Quebec during the absence of Laval. Frontenac and the Sovereign Council, of which he was master, were constantly on the alert to block what they considered clerical aggression and to enforce civil rights. With the return to Canada of Monseigneur de Laval, and with the coming of Intendant Duchesneau, the secular forces began to disintegrate.

(b) 1675-1682

Generally speaking, the antagonism between governor and bishop was less open and violent than it had been in certain previous administrations. Yet they were both conscious of

[1] C.S, vol. 1, pp 924, 934, 940, 942, 948, 950, 953, 959.
[2] *Ibid*, p. 908.

the opposition of interests which they represented. The eternal wrangling over precedence continued. In 1676 Louis XIV informed Frontenac that the honours accorded the governor in the cathedral of Quebec were greater than those enjoyed by the governors of the French provinces, and that he had reason to be content. However, he was to signal any infraction of the rights and privileges of the crown and of "the liberties of the Gallican Church in matters spiritual."[1]

For a moment in the controversy even Duchesneau supported the civil claims to the extent of demanding that the Council receive incense and other church honours immediately after the bishop and before all his clergy, but Colbert informed him that no such practice existed anywhere in France.[2] In 1679, weary of this petty strife, His Majesty warned Frontenac that he heard of more troubles in the Church of Quebec than in all the rest of his kingdom: "I desire that you pass over all these difficulties, which are of no consequence." In future Frontenac was to conform to the practice of France as indicated in a recent decree for the province of Picardie and the city of Amiens, and, with regard to points which were undecided, he was to let the bishop do as he pleased. "Since you represent my person in that country, that ought to be sufficient."[3] Likewise, Laval was requested to accord the governor of Canada the same honours as were due the governor of Picardie according to the aforesaid decree.[4] Thus, for the time being, was closed a source of contention which had disturbed Canadian life.[5]

Although Frontenac and Laval never came into collision in any noisy or scandalous manner, their correspondence proves that each felt the other to be an adversary. For instance, in writing of such an apparently neutral matter

[1] B, vii, ff. 15, 16 [2] B, vii², f. 7v. [3] B, viii, f. 7v.
[4] Ibid., f. 18. [5] Cf. C.S., vol. ii, p. 116.

as the manufacture of tar, the count found an opportunity of giving the prelate a passing thrust. " Since M Duchesneau has adjudged to Monsieur the Bishop of Quebec the habitation of a man named Pitoin ... and all the pines which M. Talon had had barked at the expense of Your Majesty, no one has worked (at the manufacture of tar), and at present only this prelate has the material to make any." [1]

That this thrust was rather disloyal is evident from the intendant's report· "People will not apply themselves seriously to the manufacture of tar until the country is more populous It costs twice as much here as in France." [2] So Laval was not playing dog in the manger after all.

At another time, in 1681, the bishop offered to act as mediator in the violent conflict between Frontenac and the son of Duchesneau. We have Laval's own account of the incident. It appears that toward the young chevalier the governor was overbearing and violent, but that toward the prelate his manner was courteous enough The one exception to this courtesy was when he told him that he was not surprised at his knowing less about this affair than about theology and cases of conscience, upon which he would consult him willingly [3]

It was, however, in his memoir of 1677 that Frontenac made his most vehement attack upon the Canadian Church and upon its head Of his criticisms in general Dudouyt wrote to Laval that same year : " M. de Frontenac has written what he is accustomed to say at Quebec against you and your clergy and the intendant His letters were not communicated to me to answer. I believe it was because they were filled with calumnies too great, and that that would have made it necessary to say many things." [4]

One of the greatest of these alleged calumnies was the count's reiterated charge that the clergy were enriching

[1] *C.G*, v, f 14v.
[2] *Ibid*, f 61.
[3] F 3, II, f. 78.
[4] *Rapport*, 1885, p cviii.

themselves in Canada. However, it was only in the memoir of 1677, drawn up under the influence of La Salle, that he made an elaborate attempt to substantiate his statements.

Here he enumerated the revenues of Monseigneur de Laval and found them to reach 40,000 livres a year. But some of his items will not bear scrutiny. For instance, take the first: 6000 livres from the king. This royal gift had not been forthcoming since 1672. The second item was 6000 livres from the two abbeys annexed to the bishopric of Quebec. In a public audience with Colbert, Laval's grand vicar asserted that the annual revenue from this source had not exceeded 2000 livres.[1]

Dudouyt knew whereof he spoke, and he could have no hope of deceiving the minister, even had he so desired. Frontenac's estimate of the tithes was excessive, and probably his remaining calculations erred equally through over-statement. Certain it is that the episcopal revenues were entirely inadequate, and it was with a feeling of despair that Dudouyt wrote: " It is hardly possible to get any money out of M. Colbert. It all goes for the war." Apparently the court would have willingly allowed Laval to abandon the field to the Récollets and Sulpicians.[2]

Returning to the memoir, we find the governor more trustworthy in his description of the " great and superb buildings" erected by the bishop. The Seminary, this four-storey " palace," with walls seven feet thick, was to cost 50,000 écus.[3] However, as far as Laval was concerned, its construction represented vast debts rather than vast revenues.

Referring to the prelate's other establishments, the governor hinted that perhaps the ecclesiastics were supported by " rich and powerful people " and that they had " some great designs we do not know." The episcopal possessions,

---

[1] *Rapport*, pp cix, xcvii.   [2] *Ibid.*, p. cix.
[3] *Bernières*, p. 135; Pothene, vol i, p. 235.

added to those of the religious orders, were so extensive that there remained for laymen only a little more than a third of the country. The revenues derived from this property were supplemented by gains from commerce.

With the support of his clergy, Monseigneur de Laval was resolved to raise the power of the Church as high as possible. In the Council he had declared that he would not govern himself by the usage of France, and that if the other bishops would not do their duty he would do his. Thus it was that he sought to elevate the churchwardens above the local judges and to diminish the honours due the parish seigneurs, which he termed "usurpations committed in France." To Frontenac's remonstrance Laval retorted that he had power even to excommunicate governors. In order to augment the credit of the clergy, Monseigneur attended the Sovereign Council "with an assiduity never seen in any other bishop."[1] With the same object in view he was educating in his two seminaries "the sons of his creatures," whom the clergy wished to inspire with their own policy. From their first entry into the country the ecclesiastics had sought to "make for themselves an absolute empire in Canada," and from their ambition, said Frontenac, sprang nearly all the disorders of New France: they wished "to join to the spiritual power an absolute authority over temporal things"[2]

In Laval's aversion to fixed curacies Frontenac saw an illustration of the prelate's resolve to maintain his priests in absolute dependence upon him. Moreover, in spite of the high cost of living in Canada,[3] the governor held that 500 livres was an ample stipend for a curate, since the

---

[1] In 1676 Laval seems to have been present nineteen times to Frontenac's eighteen. In 1677 Laval's presence is noted ten times and Frontenac's twenty (C.S., vol. ii passim).

[2] Clair, 1016, f 43, or Margry

[3] E g A E., Am ,v, f. 338, where Frontenac complains that the workman held his "foot on the habitant's throat"

THE FIRST ADMINISTRATION OF FRONTENAC 157

curates of France lived on much less When some of the clergy petitioned for 800 livres, Frontenac insisted that the Council should hear the seigneurs and habitants before acquiescing.[1] As in the time of Mésy, the people still opposed the collection of tithes, and pleaded their poverty. Unlike his colleague, Intendant Duchesneau, Frontenac sympathized with them in their resistance to the demands of the Church.

The " imaginary " cathedral chapter was another point of attack for the watchful enemy of episcopal power, for all the revenues of the chapter remained in the hands of the bishop " as in a monastery of *religious*."[2] Although after his onslaught of 1677 Frontenac's criticism of Monseigneur de Laval never became extravagant or violent, yet the opposition between the heads of Church and State was fundamental and permanent, and no loyal collaboration could ever exist between them Especially deep was the gulf which separated them in their attitude toward the traffic in alcoholic liquors with the native tribes, but we shall discuss this phase of their relations toward the close of this chapter. We now pass to a consideration of Frontenac's dealings with the bishop's auxiliaries in another part of Canada, viz. the Sulpicians of Montreal.

THE SULPICIANS OF MONTREAL

While Frontenac came to Canada with strong prepossessions against the Society of Jesus, toward the priests of St. Sulpice he was well disposed. To begin with, the Sulpicians were on good terms with the court of France, and M. de Bretonvilliers was an intimate friend of Colbert. Later on the Abbé d'Urfé became the minister's relative by marriage, and the governor was frequently advised to show special consideration for the ecclesiastics of Montreal [3]

[1] *C.G.*, v, ff 9v, 14v   [2] *Ibid*, f. 14v.   [3] *E g* B, vi², f. 18v.

Furthermore, there had always existed between Montreal and Quebec a latent rivalry in things religious as well as secular, and the Gallican court of Louis XIV showed a natural inclination to utilize it in "counterbalancing" the power of the Jesuits. This rivalry had led the Society of Montreal to oppose Laval's appointment as bishop *in partibus*, and it cropped out from time to time, notably in Dudouyt's letter of 1677. The grand vicar feared that the Sulpicians were always planning for one of their friends to succeed Laval, and that thus they might secure "the principal conduct of the Church"[1] Frontenac knew of this hidden jealousy, and was prepared to take advantage of it to further the royal policy. His first reports commended the Sulpicians for their readiness to gallicize the Indians and for their effort to develop industry[2] The governor's favourable impressions were marred by the famous Perrot incident, the details of which are too well known to require repetition here. In this affair at first only Frontenac and the governor of Montreal were concerned, and the question at issue was the illicit commerce carried on by the latter. When Perrot was thrown into prison at Quebec, and deprived of his office without the consent of the seigneurs of Montreal, the latter naturally felt aggrieved. This was especially so in the case of the Abbé Fénelon, who, while intending to act as mediator in the quarrel, had been made to appear like a betrayer of Perrot. Though the Sulpicians had long chafed under the local tyrant they had set over themselves, Fénelon now began to work vigorously in his behalf against the governor-general. When summoned before the Sovereign Council, then the governor's tool, the abbé behaved rebelliously and defied its authority. He demanded an ecclesiastical trial before Bernières, the grand vicar of the absent bishop, and the clergy of Quebec supported him strongly. Finally, the Council wavered and shrank from its responsi-

---

[1] *Rapport*, p. cix. [2] A E., *Am.*, v, f. 325.

bility. Fénelon was sent home with Perrot to be judged by the king For his interference in a secular quarrel he was forbidden to return to Canada, while Frontenac was gently reproved for not having handed over a priest to his ecclesiastical tribunal.

During this affair not only Fénelon, but also Rémy of Montreal and Francheville and Bernières of Quebec, had refused to appear before the Sovereign Council. In fact, the clerical revolt had been general.[1]

That is the story in brief, but Frontenac's narrative contains some interesting observations "It seems," he wrote to Colbert, "that it is a fatality for all the governors to have similar quarrels, and you did me the honour to say, when I was taking leave of you, that I should be very happy if I were exempt from them"[2]

Speaking of Fénelon's defiant attitude, he remarked that a man had only "to wear a black robe here in order to believe himself independent and by no means obliged to recognize any secular jurisdiction." Fénelon had written him two letters "so full of insults and scorn that one would not write in these terms to the lowest of men."

On the question of jurisdiction Frontenac was positive: "Even if his jurisdiction were as well established as that of the titular bishops of France, the Bishop of Petræa could never withdraw an ecclesiastic from a sovereign court before which his case had been brought" However, this was pushing the prerogative of the State further than even the head of the State would go, for His Majesty replied that the governor ought either to have handed over Fénelon to his bishop or the grand vicar, or to have arrested him and sent him back to France by the first vessel.[3]

The uncompromising attitude of the Sulpicians, even including Dollier de Casson, had surprised and disillusioned

[1] C S., vol 1, pp. 817, 862, 866, 878.
[2] C G., IV, 72
[3] B, VI², f. 10v

Frontenac. " I had thought the Seminary of Montreal in a different frame of mind ...," he confessed, " but I see now that they have let themselves fall into the sentiments of the others, who, being cleverer than they, have perhaps made them do more than they wished " In every untoward event Frontenac was willing to see a sinister intrigue woven by the Jesuits or their allies, and so comes the astounding conclusion : " All this has been, properly speaking, nothing but a plot formed to set M. Perrot and me at variance and to make trouble for both of us." It would seem to the onlooker that Frontenac and Perrot had been sufficiently at variance before any ecclesiastic entered the arena. At all events, after Perrot's return to Montreal he and the governor-general formed an alliance that neither intendant nor Sulpician could break.[1] In extenuation of any faults he might have committed, Frontenac pleaded : " A governor here would be much to be pitied if he were not supported, having no one in whom he can confide, being obliged to distrust everybody." [2]

The storm of which Perrot was the centre had hardly blown over before the *affaire Roland* again placed the Sulpicians in antagonism to the Council. In this event, which we narrate elsewhere, the aggressors were mainly the Sulpician Guyotte and his superior, Lefebvre. The new head of the Seminary of Paris described the former as overconscientious, and the latter as marked by his " imperious air," " haughty manner," and " absolute conduct." [3] The net result of this incident was the repulse of the Sulpicians, who had encroached upon the secular domain, and M. de Tronson laid it down as a rule that " when there is an interdicted man in the church, it is for the curate to cease saying mass, but not to ask the people to put him out." And later on, writing to the curé of Montreal, he observed : " The

---

[1] *C G.*, I, f. 289 and *passim*.   [2] *Ibid.*, IV, ff. 70-8
[3] *Tronson*, vol. ii, pp 137, 144, 145

THE FIRST ADMINISTRATION OF FRONTENAC 161

example quoted to you of the emperors they used to put out of the church appears to me rather extreme for the time in which we live, and still more so for the matter in question" Then speaking of Dollier de Casson, the successor of Lefebvre, he wrote · " He knows the world and the genius of our century well enough to see that it is not procuring the welfare of the Church to carry things thus to extremes"

Toward the civil authorities Tronson was quite as conciliatory as his predecessor Bretonvilliers, and when, in 1677, the curé of Montreal offended the Sovereign Council by giving the churchwardens precedence over the bailiff, in defiance of the ordinance of 1675,[1] Tronson reproved him thus : "It is not the business of a curate to settle questions of rank between the officers of justice and the churchwardens, and to give precedence in church to the ones rather than to the others " [2] Right from the beginning M. de Tronson considered it necessary to hold in check the excessive zeal of his ecclesiastical troops in Montreal He exhorted them to be ready to "suffer a little for the sake of peace," and to put *Monseigneur* when writing to Frontenac "You must not give him cause to complain for so little, and it is not just that a word prevent you from living in peace " He added reasons for believing that the governor was anxious to be on good terms with them.[3] Again, he counselled them against the tale-bearing which Frontenac had condemned in the clergy, and advised them to avoid criminal lawsuits [4]

Meanwhile, however, Frontenac had criticized the Sulpicians almost as harshly as the rest of the priesthood in his memoir of 1677 Among other things he told how they had refused to bury a habitant shot by accident, on the pretext that he had not communed at Easter, an allegation

---
[1] *C S*, vol. ii, p 116
[2] *Tronson*, vol. ii, letters of April 5 and 17, 1678, and May 20, 1679.
[3] *Ibid*, p 175 (July 1, 1678)   [4] *Ibid.*, p 227.

later proven to be false; and how they had deposed the judge of Montreal after eighteen years of faithful service because he did not "defer blindly to their will."

After this indictment of 1677 his indignation seems to have abated. The general work of the Sulpicians commanded his admiration, and their tendency to spiritual tyranny was curbed by their superiors both in Paris and in Montreal. Nevertheless, he continued to protect their oppressor Perrot, whom some of them had once championed so boldly against him, and he doubtless derived a good deal of pleasure from his revenge. In 1682 Tronson wrote of the great number of "oppressed ones who groan."[1] However, in face of the approaching danger of an Iroquois attack, the factions within the colony began to draw together, and we find Frontenac, Perrot, and the Sulpician superior working together for the defence of the Island.[2]

The Civilization of the Indians

A question upon which the Sulpicians and Récollets were practically in accord with the civil power was the best method of civilizing the Indians. As we have seen, this problem was debated in the time of Talon. When Frontenac came to Quebec in 1672 he was disappointed at finding so few traces of civilization among the native inhabitants of Canada. In his harangue to the assembly of the four estates at Quebec he exhorted the clergy to use every means to make the Indians "subjects of Jesus Christ and of the king, both together."[3] Then in conversation with the Jesuits he expressed his astonishment that not one of their Indian converts at N. D. de Foy could speak French. If they were going to become good subjects of the king they must speak his language. "The true way to make them

[1] C G., v, f. 289; Tronson, vol ii, p. 244.
[2] C G., vi, ff. 22v, 33, 38-43.
[3] C G., iii, f. 225.

Christians was to make them become men." However, he had little hope of the Jesuits, and, "to speak frankly," he wrote Colbert, "they think about the conversion of beaver as much as about that of souls; for most of their missions are pure mockeries."[1] There was just a chance that jealousy of the Sulpicians would give them the needed stimulus.[2] In his reply Colbert insisted that all the clergy must labour to "change the spirit of wildness which possesses all the savages into that of humanity and society that men ought to have naturally."[3]

The governor himself soon grew quite enthusiastic over the idea of gallicizing the Indians. He even determined to study the native languages a little, become "a good missionary," and see who would succeed the better, the Jesuits or himself. Resolved to set the monks a good example, he provided for the education of a few Indian children. "For ten louis one can make a Christian of an Indian girl," he declared, "by having her brought up with the Ursulines"; and he urged the continuance of the royal bounty to aid these nuns in the work.

Then, turning to the sedentary missions, he informed Father Chaumonot that the Hurons of Sillery, who were going to build a new village, must construct their cabins regularly and equip them with French chimneys.

The next subject which drew the governor's attention was the missionaries' demand for more land for their neophytes. Suspicious as always of Jesuit designs, he imputed this request to divers motives of self-interest. First of all, he declared that the Jesuits ought thoroughly to gallicize the existing missions rather than extend their efforts into regions where there were "more beaver-skins to gain than souls to convert." After lecturing the missionaries on their duties he pointed to the example of the New Englanders, who, he claimed, taught their Indians the English language

[1] *C G*, III, f. 246v.   [2] *Ibid*, f. 247.   [3] B, v, f. 28.

and certain trades. "But," confessed this ardent apostle of francization, "up to the present I have tormented myself over it uselessly because two reasons keep them back." The first was the Jesuits' desire to master and manipulate their converts. The second was their apprehension that if the natives were completely Frenchified "they would wish to escape from their tutelage and share in most of the lands which the Jesuit fathers enjoy here, and which have been given to the Indians by the Commandeur de Sillery and others." These lands had been placed under the control of the missionaries, who at first granted title-deeds to settlers in the name of the Indian owners. "But now," alleged Frontenac, "they have changed their style, and they grant them in their own name in order to remove the memory of the manner in which they were accorded."[1] We can hardly tell how much weight to attach to this accusation, for the king's reply ignored it altogether.[2] At all events, in 1699 the seigneury of Sillery was legally transferred to the Society of Jesus. The avowed reason for the transfer was that, the soil being exhausted and the forest cleared, the Jesuits had bought other lands for their Indians at their own expense.[3] In the time of M. de la Barre most of the early Canadian clearings were being abandoned after twenty years of cultivation,[4] and we should expect the mission Indians to exhaust their soil much more rapidly.

In 1677 the Jesuits sought from Colbert a title-deed for new lands at the Sault St. Louis. Their plea was that the ground at the Madeleine was too moist for seeding and for the maintenance of the increasing number of Iroquois established there. If the new concession were not granted these Indians might desert the mission.[5] Frontenac was loth

---

[1] A. E., *Am.*, IV, f. 324 (1673).   [2] B, VI, f. 26.
[3] A.N., M 242.   [4] C.G., VI, f. 329.
[5] F 2, f. 5. At the same time the Jesuits demanded the *amortissement* of their other lands, since the bishop had obtained this favour for his seigneuries (*Mélanges*, 174, p. 80). They advanced as a reason that they

to credit the sons of Loyola with a touch of sincerity:
"Their real reason is, I believe, that they will have no
neighbour who may watch them closely."[1] A fairer way of
expressing the fact would be to say that the Jesuits wished
consistently to pursue their policy of isolation. The
governor was also piqued because, although he and Duchesneau had promised this domain to La Salle, the intendant
had subsequently granted it to the Jesuits on his own
authority. In his memoir of 1677 Frontenac's charges
were more direct than before. The Jesuits, he said, exploited their Indians by making them clear the land, which
was then rented to Frenchmen, so that after all their labours
not one Indian owned an inch of ground. The latter part of
this accusation is not as serious as it appears. Their early
experiences had dissuaded the Jesuits from trying to raise
their neophytes to the status of independent farmers and
landowners. However, it is possible that they sometimes
were tempted to make use of their converts to increase the
domains of their order. In any case, when, in spite of
Frontenac, Colbert confirmed the Jesuits in their possession
of the Sault, he inserted a proviso calculated to frustrate
any ulterior motive of self-aggrandizement that might be
cherished by the Society of Jesus: "The said land . . .
shall belong, all cleared, to His Majesty when the Iroquois
abandon it."[2]

Meanwhile, Frontenac had unearthed another hidden
motive impelling the Jesuits to covet the Sault St. Louis.
This time it was a "political reason": the resolve to secure
for the Church "all the avenues of the great river." And
the count enumerated the strategic points from Michili-

were being pressed, according to feudal law, to give an "homme vivant et
mourant" to represent them in their property (cf. *Littré*, vol. ii, p. 2036).

[1] *C.G.*, IV, ff. 63, 83v. Frontenac thought the lands at the Sault might
better be given to good habitants with grown-up sons, who were asking
for them.

[2] *C.G.*, v, f. 183.

mackinac to the Baie St. Paul already held by the Canadian clergy.[1] In this final allegation he was more nearly correct than in the others. The Jesuits were animated by a perfectly natural desire to establish themselves at a point of vantage where they would be constantly in contact with the Indians of the north

Returning to a royal dispatch already cited, we see that the king wished the Jesuits to concentrate their attention upon the sedentary missions in the colony. His hope was, as he told Talon, the fusion of the two races. When Frontenac urged the royal policy upon the missionaries, they "declared plainly that they were here only to try to instruct the savages (or rather to win beavers) and not to be curés for the French." In fact, in 1674, when there were not enough Indians calling at the Cape of the Madeleine, the Jesuits wanted to withdraw their two priests and leave the habitants without spiritual aid[2] Though this attitude excited Frontenac's indignation, it was entirely in harmony with the professed aims of the order and with the Jesuit policy in Canada At Quebec and at Montreal the Jesuits had discharged the duties of curates only when the absence of secular clergy rendered it necessary. However, although the count despaired of the Jesuits, his ideas met a more cordial welcome from the Récollets and the Sulpicians At Fort Frontenac the former aided La Salle in his effort to Europeanize some of the Iroquois.[3]

At half a league from Villemarie the Sulpicians founded their Mission of the Mountain, which Frontenac hoped the Jesuits would be obliged to imitate in their own interest and in spite of themselves.[4] Soon, indeed, he was able to report that, following the example of Montreal, the Indians of the Jesuit missions were raising

[1] Memoir of 1677
[2] C G, IV, f 79v
[3] C.G., IV, f. 97 Memoir of 1677.
[4] C.G, V, f 15.

poultry, pigs, and wheat. And that was just what he had expected.[1]

So Frontenac seems to have left Canada under the impression that, in the matter of civilizing the Indians, his theory—the royal theory—was being justified by success.

THE SOVEREIGN COUNCIL

Thus far we have been discussing the relations between the governor, as head of the State, and the various elements of the Canadian Church. To complete our survey of this decade, 1672-82, we must also give an account of the rôle played by two other important representatives of the civil authority, viz. the Sovereign Council and the intendant.

At the outset of his administration Frontenac had been informed by the king that the sole purpose of the Council was " to prevent the oppression of the poor by the most powerful and wealthy of the inhabitants."[2] However, although in the first three years of his governorship the count was well pleased with the councillors,[3] whom he controlled successfully, yet he followed Talon's example and sought by personal mediation to eradicate the continual chicane to which " these people, who are mostly Normans, are inclined."[4] During this first period the Council remained submissive, and supported the governor loyally in his differences with the ecclesiastics of Quebec and Montreal. But in 1675, when His Majesty took over the colony from the Company of the Occident and reorganized the Sovereign Council by increasing the number of its members and appointing them himself, Frontenac found that the balance of

---

[1] *C.G.*, v, f. 388. In fact, the Mission of the Mountain enticed some neophytes from the Madeleine (*Tronson*, vol. ii, p. 165).

[2] B, IV, f. 40.

[3] He says they make up in diligence and disinterestedness what they may lack in intelligence and experience (A.E., *Am.*, v, f. 318 (1673)).

[4] A E, *Am.*, v, f. 316.

power had shifted to the side of the Church. First among the new councillors was Villeray, "one of the principal props" of the Jesuits.[1] Auteuil, a staunch friend of the Church, was attorney-general, while the second place of honour in the Council was set apart for the bishop or his grand vicar. Moreover, tired of the experiment of a one-man government, the king had sent out a new intendant, who was to occupy the third seat of honour and act as president.[2]

Thereafter the secular forces were hopelessly divided. Frontenac and a few satellites were left to battle for control against the clergy, their new ally, Duchesneau, the most influential merchants, and a majority of the seven councillors.

On behalf of the latter a memorial was drawn up by Auteuil, which recounted the misdeeds of their would-be master. In 1672, without consulting the bishop or his representative, as the law required, Frontenac had appointed whomever he pleased to membership in the Council. In his vanity he exacted the titles of "High and Mighty Lord" and "Monseigneur." When the councillors proposed to consult His Majesty on another point, Frontenac replied "haughtily, threatening them in very rough words, that he would not wait eighteen months for the king's orders, and that he would make the officers of the Council obey him." Then he exiled not only Villeray and Auteuil, allies of the Church, but also Tilly, Mésy's "good servitor of the king." Only the fear inspired by his continual threats and by the forces at his command had prevented more vigorous opposition to the governor's pretensions.[3]

The assertions of this memorial are no more extreme than those contained in the correspondence of the intendant.

[1] A.E., *Am.*, v, f. 342v. [2] *C.G.*, IV, f. 104; *C.S.*, vol. 1, p. 988.
[3] F 78; F 3, II, f. 26.

Intendant Duchesneau

His Relations with Frontenac and the Church

In 1681 Duchesneau wrote: "He often interrupts opinions, threatens by signs and gestures, and all the officers of the Sovereign Council are perpetually in fear . . ." People dare not testify against him for fear of exciting the "indignation of a man choleric, powerful, and vindictive—in short, everybody is in despair."[1] Almost from the beginning of his intendancy Duchesneau assumed an attitude hostile to Frontenac, and the ceaseless duel between these two heads of the colony was perhaps the chief factor in the recall of them both. The governor's domineering, imperious temper infallibly antagonized those whom it could not cow into submission. Duchesneau, though of a quieter nature, was as tenacious of purpose as his rival. Though often petty and prejudiced he was courageous, persistent, and honest. It was probably without hypocrisy that he said: "I have acquired nothing save the satisfaction of having done my duty, which I esteem more than all the goods of the world."[2] Year after year, in spite of rebuffs from Colbert, he repeated his accusations that Frontenac was profiting from the fur trade and protecting law-breakers. Partly to test and partly to repress him, king and minister answered him harshly. Quietly and doggedly, after each reprimand the intendant returned to the charge and finally forced the court to believe him. Nevertheless, there was much truth in the king's observation that Duchesneau never failed to approve or disapprove of individuals " in proportion as they were friends or enemies of the Sieur de Frontenac."[3]

Among these enemies, or, more properly, opponents, were the Jesuits and most of the clergy, for whom Jacques Duchesneau had a sincere reverence. His attachment to them made his break with the governor irreparable. In

[1] *C.G.*, v, f. 289v.   [2] *Ibid.*, f. 69v.   [3] *Ibid*, f. 340 (1681).

1675 Father Frémin wrote with enthusiasm of "this illustrious minister of His Majesty," whose arrival was so fortunate for New France;[1] and the understanding between intendant and priests was complete. As was his custom, Colbert cautioned the intendant to confine the ecclesiastics within the bounds of the authority they enjoyed in the Kingdom.

This general maxim ought to serve you for all the difficulties of this nature which may arise, but to achieve this end it is necessary that you work to make yourself skilled in these matters by reading the authors who have treated of them . . . One sees clearly that, although the bishop is a good man and does his duty very well, he affects none the less a domination which goes far beyond the bounds set for the bishops in the Christian world and particularly in the Kingdom.

The problem was how to reduce that domination, and Colbert thought of the royal edict which assigned Laval a seat in the Sovereign Council.

As I see that Monsieur the Bishop . . . affects an authority a little too independent of the royal authority, and that for this reason perhaps it would be well that he should not sit in the Council, you ought to examine closely all the occasions and all the means one might employ to make him wish not to come there any more But in this you ought to conduct yourself with great reserve and secrecy, and make very sure that no one discover what I am writing you on this point [2]

However, Duchesneau was not well qualified by his training and ideas to act effectively for the Gallican party. According to Frontenac, he and Laval had both belonged to the famous congregation of the Jesuit Father Bagot, and one of their rules was to support each other and to observe great secrecy.[3] In his official correspondence Frontenac invariably represented the intendant as a blind partisan

---

[1] *Rel. inéd.*, vol. ii, p 66.   [2] B, vii¹, ff. 7v, 8v (1677).
[3] Memoir of 1677

of the clergy, and soon Colbert began to complain that, for example in the fire-water controversy, he followed the bishop "too exclusively."[1] In the matter of Church honours the minister remarked on the part of both Duchesneau and Laval the pretension of establishing equality between intendant and governor.[2]

Notwithstanding the rebukes of his masters Duchesneau remained unshaken in his loyalty to his friends. He could find no fault in the ecclesiastics. They were all "very regular and very pious."

Upon the subject of all the ecclesiastics in general, I ought to tell you, Monseigneur, that I consider them all very submissive, and it is my duty—although people have striven to make me pass for a man who is devoted to them—not to conceal the truth from you, but to assure you that by gentleness and reason I have put them in a state of mind not to refuse anything which is just, and that they conform easily to whatever is practised in France.[3]

So much for Duchesneau's general attitude toward the Church. We have now to touch again upon the question of tithes.

Tithes and "Curés Fixes"

Dissatisfaction was rife in the colony. Frequently the habitants claimed to be paying their tithes and getting little service. On the other hand, they sometimes paid their tithe " only according to their fancy, retaining a part of it," so that the Council felt constrained to decree that the tithes should be collected by four men, two representing the curate and two the habitants.[4]

The bishop had long alleged that travelling missionaries could cope with the situation better than settled curés, and now for the first time he had the moral support of an

[1] *C.G*, iv, f. 189 (1678).   [2] B, viii, f. 14.
[3] *C.G.*, v, ff. 49, 50 (1679)   [4] *C.S.*, vol. i, pp. 793, 815, 943.

intendant. But Colbert informed Duchesneau that revocable curates were "directly contrary to the canons of the Councils, and to the laws, ordinances, and usages of the Kingdom." Moreover, he insisted that "people to whom the sacraments are not administered ought not to be obliged to pay tithes." Fixed curacies could be established for much less than the minimum advocated by Laval. Were there not 4000 curates in France receiving less than 200 livres?[1] The following spring, 1679, a royal edict provided for permanent curates who should live on the tithes of their parishes, and derogated the ordinance of 1663 by which the Seminary of Quebec received all tithes and appointed and recalled all curates[2]

Duchesneau's response was full and clear. The stipends of French curates could not be used as an argument. In Canada, so high was the cost of living that board and lodging alone would cost 300 livres. Even then the curate would have no wine most of the year, and he would eat only lard and coarse bread. For his expenses he would need 200 livres more, as the governor himself had agreed, besides a canoe in summer, and a man in winter to carry his chapel and personal effects. The long distances and the rough weather were hard on clothes, which cost twice as much as in France So immense were the parishes that, though tramping or paddling incessantly, the tired curés could say mass in each place only once in a month or six weeks In spite of the size of these parishes the seigneurs and habitants showed no intention of agreeing even to the minimum stipend of 500 livres. They were powerless because of their poverty, and were willing to pay only the one twenty-sixth on grain required by the ordinance of 1667. Hence the impossibility of ministering to them except through missionaries and in proportion to the value of the tithes they might pay voluntarily.

[1] *C.G.*, IV, f 190v.   [2] *C.G.*, v, ff. 88-93 (May 1679).

The only remedy for a desperate situation would be that His Majesty should give 4000 livres a year to aid in the establishment of fixed curacies in the most populous places. Otherwise certain districts would remain abandoned, which would work great ill to the spiritual and even to the material well-being of the colony [1]

In the afore-mentioned edict of May 1679 Louis XIV, citing the example of "the first Christian emperors," made regulations designed to "excite the zeal of the faithful by marks of honour with which the ancient Church was willing to recognize the piety of founders"—designed, that is, to encourage seigneurs of parishes to acquire the patronage of churches

On this subject Duchesneau's comments were as discouraging and as frank as on the preceding. In the whole colony there were only eight parish churches built in stone, and none of the seigneurs was rich enough to build a church "solidly, at his own expense" They were all filled with vanity, and each wanted a curé on his lands Yet they were all in debt and dire poverty.[2] In short, the king's desire could not be realized

The Civilization of the Indians

Another question which engaged the attention of Duchesneau was that of the civilization of the native races Though His Majesty approved of the existing *bourgades* under missionary direction, he thought it would be much better to mingle the Indians among the French in such small numbers that the latter could assimilate the former and fulfil the royal dream of "a single body of people."[3] In reply Duchesneau emphasized the value of the existing missions. The Iroquois at the Sault St. Louis were so many hostages, whose presence had saved the colony from war

[1] *C.G*, v, f 176   [2] *Ibid*, f 293 (1681).   [3] B, VIII, f. 14

174 CHURCH AND STATE IN EARLY CANADA

with the Five Nations. On that all Frenchmen were agreed.[1] In 1680 there were in all about 960 Indians living in the various *bourgades*, and thanks to Sulpician effort the following year saw an increase of fifty-six. At Sillery, Lorette, the Madeleine, and the Mission of the Mountain, the children were being gallicized as far as possible. Certain exceptions had to be made, since Indian food and clothing were better adapted for hunting than the French. However, at the Madeleine, in deference to His Majesty's wishes, the Jesuits had established a school, and some of their pupils could read, write, speak French, and play upon instruments. "It seems also that we must content ourselves at present with inducing them gently to come and build villages in the midst of our settlements." Infinite tact and patience must be employed in the effort to Europeanize the red men, "for these people greatly love their liberty, and are very easily repelled." The intendant himself had spared no pains in trying to domesticate some Indian lads whom he was educating with his own sons, but, he remarked regretfully: "Already three have left me after I had clothed them extremely well . . . the least constraint repels them."

Duchesneau extended his approbation not only to Récollets, Sulpicians, and Jesuits, but also to the Daughters of the Congregation of Montreal, who taught the Indian girls how to sew, and to the Ursulines of Quebec, who did likewise.[2]

The Fur Trade

On the subject of the clergy's connection with the fur trade Duchesneau and Frontenac probably differed as widely as upon other questions.

Since M. de Mésy no one had brought any definite accusations of mercenary conduct against the Canadian priesthood. On a single occasion Talon had alluded to the apostolic

[1] C.G., v, f. 26v.   [2] *Ibid.*, ff. 49, 178v, 291, 316v, 335v.

THE FIRST ADMINISTRATION OF FRONTENAC 175

labours of the Jesuits as a "work worthy of their zeal and piety if it is exempt from the mixture of interest to which they are said to be susceptible through the trade in peltry that people affirm they carry on among the Ottawas and at the Cape of the Madeleine. 'Ce que je ne sais pas de science certaine.' To all outward appearance the life of these ecclesiastics is very regular." [1] In our fourth chapter we have indicated the nature of the trade at the Madeleine of which Talon had heard rumours.

However, Frontenac made no fine distinctions of motive or method. Although he was aware that in Canada furs were "a kind of money," [2] yet with characteristic violence, in his first dispatch to Colbert, he accused the Jesuits of thinking "as much of the conversion of beaver as of that of souls." [3] Two years later he complained of great irregularities among the Jesuits of Sault Ste. Marie, where a certain tribe "apparently had come rather to bring their beaver-skins than to seek baptism." [4]

In view of these and similar charges His Majesty replied: "As to what you say of the facility with which the ecclesiastics, secular and regular, carry on the fur trade by means of the missions, you ought to examine with Sieur Duchesneau the way to prevent it."

The king also emphatically forbade any ecclesiastic to participate in commerce of any kind.[5] He wrote again: "I am surprised that you have admitted that, notwithstanding my previous prohibitions, the ecclesiastics continue to carry on some commerce in peltry with the Indians." If they persisted Frontenac was to warn them, not that he had informed, but that he would inform, His Majesty.[6] At the same time Duchesneau was instructed to take every precaution "to abolish entirely the custom the

---

[1] C G., II, f. 356.
[2] C G., III, f. 245.
[3] Ibid., f. 246v.
[4] C.G., IV, f. 83v.
[5] B, VII, ff. 17v, 18 (1676).
[6] B, VII², f. 20v.

ecclesiastics . . . had adopted, of trading or having their valets trade." [1]

In his memoir of 1677 Frontenac accompanied his accusations with alleged proofs, which unhappily have disappeared. According to this document a Jesuit (Frémin) confessed to an annual profit of 4000 livres in two neighbouring localities (the Madeleine and the Sault) ; Father Chaumonot had promised the Lorette Indians to keep all sorts of merchandise in the Jesuit store ; two missionary canoes had been found laden with tobacco, the most profitable medium of barter ; Father de Lamberville had told La Salle how to send beaver to New Holland ; and the missionaries among the Ottawas had bought goods from French traders. Frontenac offered to present further evidence if Colbert so desired. He next asserted that the bishop and his friends were planning to build habitations at the falls of the Ottawa. "That would be the utter ruin of the colony, which would have only their leavings." Finally, Frontenac attributed great wealth to the bishop, and in so doing multiplied the cost of the Seminary by nearly three. The Jesuits, too, had amassed riches "in a manner surprising for a country very poor in itself."

After this memoir, composed under the influence of La Salle, Frontenac ceased to accuse the Jesuits of trafficking to enrich themselves. However, he repeatedly affirmed that their neophytes of the Madeleine and of the Sault carried on a regular commerce in furs with the English.[2]

The accusations formulated by La Salle himself are extremely direct, and some are substantially just. When he says that at the Madeleine Father Albanel sold bread, wine, wheat, and lard, we recall what the *Journal* itself implied as to Albanel's duties in that mission.[3] In the same sen-

---

[1] B, VII², f. 3v.   [2] *C.G.*, v, f. 12v ; vi, f. 54 (1681).
[3] Jérome Lalemant called Albanel a "virum parum ad modum religiosum" (*Fds. Roche.*, 19, f. 60).

THE FIRST ADMINISTRATION OF FRONTENAC 177

tence La Salle asserts that at Quebec Brother Joseph kept shop and gained 500 per cent. The Jesuit College cost 400,000 livres, paid in part out of their profits. By their two forts at Michilimackinac and Sault Ste. Marie they had made themselves absolute masters of northern trade, and one motive for the construction of Fort Frontenac was the breaking of their monopoly. On the other hand, to conserve this monopoly they had secured from the Council the abolition of the *congés*[1] In the Baie des Puante was " a convent of Jesuits who really hold the key of Beaverland, where their friar-blacksmith and two companions convert more iron into beaver than the fathers convert savages into Christians."[2] During his voyages of discovery La Salle tried to secure testimony from the Récollet Hennepin, but the latter was too shrewd " to inveigh against people whom he wanted to make pass for traders."[3] In most of La Salle's accusations there was palpable exaggeration and gross misrepresentation; but there was other evidence.

In his memoir of 1671 Dumesnil had stated that a clerk whom the bishop and Father Ragueneau hired to trade for them bought furs from the Indians with liquors, and that for a time the clergy had a monopoly of this traffic.[4] Had this charge been well founded the commerce in question could hardly have escaped the keen eyes of Jean Talon.

And yet the reputation of the clergy was being compromised. In that same year an anonymous ecclesiastic urged that they be forbidden all commerce, direct or indirect, even under the pretext of receiving presents from the Indians If they received a present, let them make use of it in the locality, without selling it or sending it to France.[5] Even when the Jesuits were not accused of trading directly, they sometimes appeared as accomplices. For instance, in 1681 the Council made a seizure of the furs and merchandise

---

[1] Margry, vol. 1, p 345 [2] *Ibid.*, vol. 11, p. 257, or *Clair*, 1016, f 182v
[3] Hennepin, p 114 [4] *Old Régime*, ch. xxi [5] *Éds. Ér.*, 25,081, f 280.

belonging to a strolling trader who had carried on illicit commerce at the Sault. The goods were found in the possession of Father Frémin.[1]

However, against all aspersions on their character the Canadian Jesuits defended themselves vigorously. An anonymous charge against the steward of their college had reached the general, and an investigation had been ordered. In 1678 Superior Dablon reported that the incriminated friar had merely imported thread, needles, and other merchandise with which to purchase supplies for the monastery and to pay the peasants who worked for him. " Every one gives him a thousand benedictions for it." In Canada it was necessary to use these articles in exchange, as in the West Indies they used sugar.

Later on, Father Garnier gave the general a detailed account of the use made of peltry in the Canadian mission. Among the new points he mentions is the fact that votive offerings in furs were received by the churches from French hunters. In the Christian missions, when a convert died, his goods were usually given to the church in order that solemn rites might be celebrated. All these gifts were designated " the things of the temple," and the missionary acted as temple guardian. Upon the arrival of the ships from France he used these accumulated offerings to buy advantageously whatever was necessary for the service or adornment of the church. In no degree was he any the richer himself. The slanders came from greedy men who coveted whatever fell into the hands of another.[2]

After weighing the evidence on both sides we come to the conclusion that during this period, as during the preceding, the Jesuits traded in furs only in so far as the welfare of their missions demanded it, and not with a view to enriching the order or to luxurious living. La Hontan, by no means an indulgent critic, remarked : " Several persons

[1] C S , vol. ii, p. 620.   [2] Rochemonteix, vol. iii, p. 138 (1).

THE FIRST ADMINISTRATION OF FRONTENAC 179

have assured me that the Jesuits were carrying on a great commerce in merchandise of Europe and in peltry of Canada, but I find it hard to believe ; or, if it is true, they must have correspondents, clerks, and factors as secret and as clever as themselves—which would be impossible " [1]

But, as we have seen, the Jesuits were accused of trading in brandy as well as in furs, and we now resume our narrative of the fire-water controversy.

THE BRANDY TRADE

Upon his arrival in Canada, M de Frontenac was much impressed with Talon's brewery, which was " an ornament to the city," and which joined " magnificence to convenience " The beer manufactured there was very good, and, he opined, when they could sell it cheaper it would be of great utility to the country [2]

However, in spite of promising beginnings, in the absence of its founder the new industry languished and died. By 1679 the brewery had fallen almost into ruin, but was used, nevertheless, as a powder magazine. Originally it had been a great building 180 feet in length, built partly of stone, partly of wood, and standing outside the town near the Hôtel-Dieu [3]

---

[1] La Hontan, vol ii, p 76   [2] C G , III, f 235v.
[3] There was some talk of fitting it up as a home of local manufactures, and de Meulles valued the building at 6000 livres His Majesty bought from Talon the brewery itself, but not the copper boilers, which were estimated by a commission to weigh 2500 lb Denonville and Champigny advised against taking them, on the ground that the maintenance of a brewery would be too expensive They thought the habitants ought to brew their own beer, and that perhaps La Chesnaye might be persuaded to make use of the boilers That would help to make Canada self-supporting, and would increase the demand for grain The minister's reply was that whoever was going to use the boilers must buy them (C G , v, f 135 , VI, ff. 82, 86v ; VII, f 134 ; IX, f 11v , x, f 140 , B, xv, f. 16v). Later on the brewery was transformed into a palace for the intendant and a meeting-place for the Sovereign Council (Chapais, *Jean Talon*, p 284 (1))

One of Frontenac's first acts was to begin a war upon the *coureurs de bois*, who deserted the colony and, charged with merchandise, wine, and brandy, voyaged toward distant tribes, without a permit from the governor An ordinance of September 27, 1672, rehearsed their misdeeds and condemned the habitants who secretly played into their hands. Hereafter, the penalty for going off on the fur trade without a *congé* was to be a flogging by the hangman for the first offence, and the galleys for the second.[1] This was followed up by a royal decree which warned the settlers against " making vagabonds of themselves in the woods." Upon pain of death they were forbidden to roam more than twenty-four leagues from their domicile without leave from the governor [2]

At the same time Frontenac observed that the taverns were sometimes centres of debauchery and scandal Hereafter only persons of recognized probity would be allowed to keep them, and they must put up a public sign. Moreover, they were forbidden to serve liquor during the hours of divine service [3] Four years later, under the presidency of Intendant Duchesneau, the Sovereign Council made these regulations more stringent. Tavern-keepers were forbidden to loan or give credit to young men of quality, to soldiers, valets, or others, or to take securities from them, or to serve drinks after 8 P.M [4]

In 1675 the king took over the domain of the Company of the Occident, and the import tax of ten per cent. on wines, brandy, and tobacco formed an important part of the royal revenues [5] In 1681, at the request of the religious com-

---

[1] Chapais, p. 222. A letter from Bellefontaine, a corporal, to the lieutenant of Frontenac's guards, indicates that the governor sold one *congé* to Sieur Dupas for twenty-five pistoles Dupas was indiscreet enough to publish the fact everywhere , but it would have been known anyway, for M Perrot had learned of it (*C.G.*, IV, f 93)

[2] *Ibid* , f 11v   [3] F 3, II, f 112
[4] *C G* , IV, f. 133   [5] *Ibid* , f 114

munities of Canada, His Majesty accorded them perpetual exemption from these entry duties on liquors imported for their own use up to thirty-nine casks of wine and ten casks of brandy annually. This amounted to a gratification of 2000 livres altogether During the time of their lease the farmers of the Company of the Occident had accorded the religious communities the equivalent of this amount, and it was only during the preceding four or five years that they had been required to pay like the other inhabitants Their petition cited a decree of the king's Council of 1675, which forbade cities, when levying imposts for their communal debts, to include ecclesiastics in the levy [1] Hence we infer that part of the import tax still went to pay the debts of the Community of Habitants, which La Chesnaye assures us were never entirely paid

Although the Jesuits, along with the other religious bodies, benefited by the importation of liquors, they by no means encouraged the trade even indirectly When they ceded parts of their seigneuries to habitants, they exacted an agreement that no traffic in strong drink should take place upon these lands or with the Indians of neighbouring missions [2] Notwithstanding such precautions, by 1673 the Algonquin missions had been ruined by alcohol, and intemperance was the single foe of the Hurons near Quebec The Madeleine alone escaped, and dissolute Indians could find there " neither women nor drinks " [3]

We have seen that Frontenac was ready to repress drunkenness among Frenchmen. However, his attitude toward the brandy trade with the Indians was always a heart-break to the ecclesiastics, and in this decade the quarrel between Church and State reached its climax.

It was in the spring of 1673 that Frontenac made his famous voyage to Lake Ontario. In passing Montreal

[1] *C G*, v, f 373. [2] *E g C S*, vol. 1, p 1005.
[3] *Rel. inéd*, vol 1, pp 166, 184

some of his Indians got drunk in the house of a certain Roland, and were committing disorders. This obliged Frontenac to punish the offending parties. Nevertheless, two or three days later, when the Hurons had made amends for their misdemeanour, the governor regaled them and all the squadrons with brandy and tobacco. At Cataraqui he presented the Iroquois delegates with wine, brandy, and food. But he warned them that, in order to obviate all possibility of rupture of their friendship with the French, they must prevent their young men from drinking to excess ; nothing was so unworthy of a reasonable man ; the French held drunkards in great contempt; and if the Iroquois would adopt the same attitude toward their youths they would correct them infallibly.[1]

In a dispatch to Colbert, Frontenac had occasion to refer again to his experience on this trip. He urged that the whole question be settled while Bishop Laval was in Paris, so that the clergy should no longer refuse absolution to those who sold brandy to the Indians. Quite recently they had even refused to absolve a woman before child-birth. Their attitude troubled people's consciences extremely. Frontenac declared that until he had word from the court he could not do otherwise than execute Talon's last ordinance. The priests could not persuade him, in spite of all their allegations respecting Indian intemperance, that, when one gave a native brandy with no design of either intoxicating or cheating him, there was any more harm in it than when the men of Bordeaux sold their wines to the Dutch and English, for these peoples were at least as much given to inebriety as the Indians. The clergy could not impose upon him with their stories of Indian excesses and disorders, for in his journey to Lake Ontario he had obtained first-hand knowledge of the facts. There he had seen all the Iroquois nations together—something, he added proudly, perhaps

[1] *C.G.*, IV, ff. 12-15v.

THE FIRST ADMINISTRATION OF FRONTENAC 183

no missionary had ever witnessed. " I had not remarked that they had done anything extraordinary or scandalous, although some of their youths had drunk heavily for four days of brandy obtained from the English . . . because none of the French with me had dared to give them any in view of my commands to the contrary." [1]

In this confidential communication we see that Frontenac had already taken sides in the dispute. What he stated in regard to the good behaviour of the Iroquois was doubtless true, but, as we have observed, he had given them a special warning. As to the misconduct of his Hurons at Montreal, he said not a word.

A few months later the governor issued an ordinance, the preamble of which admitted on the part of the Indians a passion for alcohol, which his dispatch to Colbert had seemed to deny. They stopped at nothing in their desire for stimulants. They traded off their capotes, blankets, guns, powder, and lead, and were reduced to such a condition of nudity as to be unable to go hunting, and so to pay their debts toward the " good habitants " who had advanced them food and clothing. Frontenac forbade all Frenchmen to trade with the Indians for the coverings they were actually wearing or for their guns and ammunition. The Indians themselves, who were so intemperate, would be imprisoned and fined one moose-skin. However, they might trade the old clothing which they no longer needed.[2] Continuing, the governor prohibited the Indians from setting up taverns on the shores of the St. Lawrence ; they must carry their brandy directly to their villages, upon pain of being pillaged.[3]

In his afore-mentioned letter to Colbert the governor complained bitterly of a seditious sermon delivered by a Jesuit the previous winter. The preacher had dwelt at

[1] A E., *Am.*, v, f. 322v.
[2] Beaver-skins increased in value when worn for a time.
[3] Faillon, vol. iii, p 491.

length upon the "reserved case," which the bishop had reviewed, in spite of the fact that Frontenac had just taken exceptionally stringent measures against whoever should carry liquor to the Indians in the woods. The Jesuit had declared it vain to allege the king's permission to trade, for that exceeded his authority; there were certain things in which the temporal powers were not allowed to alter what was done by the spiritual powers. "He exaggerated that in terms quite offensive to the royal authority—terms which assuredly might give the people a bad impression." Several times Frontenac was tempted to leave the church with his guards and interrupt the sermon, but he contented himself with going afterwards to find the grand vicar, Dudouyt, and the superior of the Jesuits. To them he expressed his surprise and submitted his demand for justice. Did they not read in Scripture that kings had indeed been sovereign pontiffs, but not that sovereign pontiffs had ever been kings? His superiors blamed the preacher, and, according to their custom, attributed his fault to an excess of zeal.[1] From this incident we see how the liquor question could provoke a conflict of theories which sounds like an echo from the age of Hildebrand. In his reply to Frontenac's complaints Colbert accepted his view that the liquor traffic constituted a question of police, and so concerned the ordinary judges and the Sovereign Council. "But," he added, as if to caution the impetuous count, "it is difficult to enter into the secret of the confessions."[2]

In December 1676 we find the Sovereign Council judging the famous Roland case. Roland was the inhabitant of La Chine who sold liquor to Frontenac's Indians on the voyage to Lake Ontario. He now comes before the Council with a petition which states that he has faithfully observed the regulations governing the sale of brandy to the Indians, but that though he confessed at Easter to his curé, the

[1] A E, *Am*, v, f. 321.   [2] B, vi, f. 25v

THE FIRST ADMINISTRATION OF FRONTENAC 185

Sulpician Guyotte, the latter refused him absolution. Soon after Bishop Laval granted permission to absolve him, but the Sulpicians refused, alleging that he gave liquor to the Indians in excessive quantities. Thereupon Roland confessed to the Jesuit Frémin of the Madeleine, who wrote in his favour to Guyotte. Nevertheless, the latter declared publicly that Roland had not received the sacrament at Easter, that he was excluded from the prayers of the Church and from attendance upon divine service. Upon Roland's complaint Intendant Duchesneau interfered in his behalf. Later on, though he had been unable to visit Father Frémin, as Guyotte had requested him to do, Roland entered the church on Sunday. A week later he went again. The curé ordered him to leave. Roland refused to leave a place which was "for all Christians." Then the priest called upon those present to eject him by force. A churchwarden and "several others of the faithful" threw themselves upon him, and "dragged him out of the church by the hair like an excommunicated person, dealing him several blows."[1]

In January 1677 the Council received a second petition from Roland. In this he asserted that the bishop had begged him not to pursue the matter further, for one ought to act like a Christian; moreover, his trip to Quebec would be paid for by those who had ill-treated him. When he returned to Montreal he learned that Guyotte and a churchwarden had made the people sign a report against him at the church door. Moreover, in his sermon the curé had begged those who had expelled "these wretches" not to repent of it, for it was only a "little cloud" which would be dissipated by a thunderbolt. Besides this, the ecclesiastics of Montreal forbade Roland to ignore his own curé in favour of a Jesuit confessor. Thereupon, seeing that they did not respect the promises of the bishop, Roland decided to appeal again to the Council.[2]

[1] *C S*, vol. ii, p. 97 [2] *Ibid*, p. 103

On February 3 Bishop Laval denounced Roland's petition as contrary to truth and insulting to him. Interrogated before the Council, Roland drew back a little, and admitted that the bishop had not promised that he should be reimbursed. Some one, however, had given him this assurance. Hence the confusion in his memory. In any case, the Récollet Custode had been present.[1]

When Father Custode was called he supplicated the court not to oblige him to testify, because, first, being religious, he was dead civilly and incapable of giving testimony; second, having learned nothing of this affair outside of the bishop's cabinet, he ought to keep the secret in all points; third, the sacred canons forbade a priest to give any evidence against his bishop; besides, it was not just that the words of a simple monk should prevail over the sentiments of the bishop.[2] Evidently the cautious Récollet was afraid of being brought into contradiction with Laval and incurring his displeasure.

By this time the unhappy Roland, finding himself without support, would have gladly withdrawn because he was involved with " too strong adversaries," and because he lacked the means to carry through a lawsuit. But the Council, always anxious for cases, would oblige him by advancing the necessary funds.[3]

Fortunately for the plaintiff, M. Lefebvre, superior of the Seminary of Montreal and deputy of the ecclesiastical court of Quebec, intervened in the contest. Roland refused to be tried by his adversaries, the Sulpicians, who were " powerfully incensed " against him, and sought " each day to cause him trouble upon trouble."[4] Accordingly he appealed to the Sovereign Council against Lefebvre's abuse of authority. The Council, jealous for its own prerogatives, supported him heartily. It declared that the superior had

[1] *C.S.*, vol. ii, p. 105. [2] *Ibid*, p 107.
[3] *Ibid.*, p 108. [4] *Ibid.*, p. 118 (March 30, 1677).

proceeded " ill and abusively," and forbade him and his ecclesiastics to take further cognizance of this case.¹ It went further: it fined one of the habitants who, at his curé's behest, took the signatures of the people right in the church; and it forbade Guyotte and all other ecclesiastics to read in the churches or at the church doors any documents except those which regarded purely ecclesiastical affairs, or which might be ordered by the courts.²

This is one of the many instances in which, either directly or indirectly, the liquor question brought into collision the two authorities, secular and spiritual. In the present case, Roland's victory was a mere incident in the Council's assertion of its rights against Sulpician encroachments.

The next scene is at Versailles. In 1675 the professors of theology at the Sorbonne had renewed their approval of Laval's attitude toward the brandy question,³ and in 1678 the prelate sent his representative to the court of France. M Dudouyt met with a harsh reception. Speaking in " a very loud and severe tone," Colbert told him that the bishop and his clergy were meddling with what did not concern them, and that because they were far from the Sun they wished to encroach upon the royal authority. In a second interview Dudouyt blamed Talon for his act of November 10, 1668, urged that the Indians be prevented from transporting liquor to their villages, asserted that the French would not lose five hundred beaver-skins annually from Dutch competition, and assured Colbert that if the bishops of France were in Canada they would do as Laval was doing. Dudouyt's impression of Colbert was that " when one makes him understand the truth and justice, he renders it." ⁴

If Colbert was austere in his manner toward the bishop's representative, he was severe in his treatment of the intendant. In April 1677 he reprimanded him for forbidding

[1] *C.S*, vol ii, p. 122. [2] *Ibid*, p. 132 (June 21, 1677).
[3] *Mandements*, p. 91. [4] *Rapport*, 1885, p. xcvii.

people to keep tavern without his consent. "That is in no wise your affair. . . . It ought to be free to every one to choose the trade he pleases."¹ Three days later he reproved him for taking sides with Laval before informing himself exactly of the number of murders, fires, and other outrages caused by the sale of alcohol to the Indians. If the bishop's allegations were well founded, the piety of the king would rigorously suppress this traffic. However, the testimony of Talon, Bouteroue, and others proved the contrary. In order to prevent the abuse by a few individuals of a thing good in itself, Laval wanted to abolish the use of an article which attracted commerce and drew the Indians amongst orthodox Christians instead of abandoning them to the heretics. Although Duchesneau could hardly hinder the bishop from maintaining his reserved case, he ought to join with the governor in preventing its evil results.²

A fortnight later Colbert wrote Frontenac in a similar strain, though in a friendly tone. The clergy drew general conclusions from particular examples. Nevertheless, the governor and intendant were to examine all the memorials and all the facts together and let His Majesty know the truth. If the awful disturbances described in Laval's consultation in the Sorbonne were general among the Indians, the king intended his representatives in Canada to suppress the traffic. But if the Indians were only a little more subject to drunkenness than the Germans and Bretons, then His Majesty wished Frontenac and Duchesneau, without making any direct pronouncement against the episcopal authority, to prevent it from taking any action outside the Church upon a matter which concerned the police and the judges.³

Meantime, in the course of a general indictment against the clergy of Canada, Frontenac scored with special emphasis their conduct in connection with the liquor traffic.

[1] B, VII, f. 3v.   [2] Ibid., f. 6.   [3] Ibid., f. 23v.

Carefully avoiding a direct personal attack upon Laval, he told Colbert that "*they*" were clinging obstinately to the reserved case through interested motives. Though the Sovereign Council by its decree of November 10, 1668, permitted the sale of brandy to the Indians, the clergy interdicted Roland for that alone, amidst "circumstances violent and odious to the last degree." Even a Récollet father was refused absolution himself because he would not promise to withhold it from the governor of Three Rivers, who, though engaged in the brandy trade, had never intoxicated any Indian. The ecclesiastics refused to absolve not only the traders but also their valets, who were obliged to obey their masters by drawing the liquors. They refused absolution to a trader named Lapaille, and after his sudden death they would not bury him in holy ground. They added insult to ignominy, "car un religieux de Sillery fit sur ce pauvre Lapaille un emblème d'un ange qui vanne du grain et d'un autre qui en brûle la paille." That shows just how far their passion and their obstinacy could go, and how necessary it was to attend to the matter. But Laval himself refused to relax even a little. Not content with interdicting the sale of brandy, they wanted to prevent the sale of wine, and they had secured from Duchesneau—who never refused them anything—an ordinance prohibiting cabarets in all the country villages.[1]

These charges, couched in the violent and often inaccurate language habitual with Frontenac, reveal truly enough the intensely partisan spirit which prevailed on both sides. Yet, in spite of Colbert's sympathy with the party of commerce, by an ordinance of May 12, 1678, the royal government forbade the transportation of wine and brandy to the Indian villages, as well as the sale of it, in quantity sufficient to intoxicate, in the French habitations.[2] This proclamation came partly in response to Duchesneau's accusation

[1] *Clair.*, 1016, f. 46; or Margry. [2] *C.G.*, IV, f. 185.

that, under cover of hunting permits, Frontenac was eluding the decree aimed at the *coureurs de bois*. His Majesty now desired the provost to be "continually on horseback to seize and arrest" those who contravened this ordinance At the same time Colbert indicated that he did not give full credence to the intendant's charge.[1] Three days later he told him bluntly, à propos of this controversy, that an intendant's duty was to examine facts, not formulate opinions "But that an intendant, without examining these facts, should be of an opinion which has no usage in the whole Christian world,—that can come only from a too great self-abandonment to the sentiments of the bishop or from a too great contrariety to those of the governor" This spirit, evident in all the intendant's letters, prevented Colbert from believing his accusations against the governor in the matter of commerce.[2]

And now a decisive step was taken A memorial stating both sides of the controversy was drawn up by the king's command. It was to be studied carefully by governor and intendant,[3] as well as by "twenty of the most ancient and principal inhabitants of the country,"[4] of the "number of those who apply themselves to commerce." Their written opinions would be considered by His Majesty.

As most of the arguments contained in this memorial are mere repetitions, we shall cite only a few distinctive phrases. One of these says that when the Indians have secured enough brandy for fifteen or twenty men, the majority prefer to deprive themselves of their share in order to give three or four of their number the pleasure of intoxicating themselves An argument from the other side of the question says that "never have the bishops meddled with what concerns commerce in all legitimate commodities." Another is that as this traffic is not reputed a sin elsewhere,

---

[1] *C G*, IV, f 190 [2] *Ibid*, f 189.
[3] B, VII, f 24v.   [4] F 3, V, f 75.

there is danger that Canadians "accustom themselves to neglect or despise the regulations, orders, or injunctions of the Church" when it makes a reserved case of the brandy trade.[1]

On October 10, 1678, a historic assembly was held in the Château St Louis Each of the habitants summoned had previously received a copy of the memorial, and now gave his opinion in writing These men were all interested in commerce even when not professional merchants They nearly all favoured the continuance of the liquor trade with the natives, and their reasons necessarily overlapped and repeated themselves. According to Berthier and Sorel, the Iroquois obtained brandy in such abundance from the Dutch that in the preceding summer they had transported forty barrels to Cataraqui; the French there would give them none, since the bishop had raised a scruple in their minds All this was very prejudicial to commerce, and could be checked only by the competition of French brandy, which was far better than that of New Holland Religion would not suffer thereby, for in the sedentary missions of the Madeleine, Montreal, and Lorette there was little drunkenness, though their Indians could have liquor when they would. Here Berthier and Sorel give a false impression, for, as we have seen, the temperance of these neophytes was due to the influence of the missionaries, the vigilance of the Christian chiefs, and the absence of cabarets; to get brandy the Indians had to go elsewhere Continuing, Berthier and Sorel affirmed that they were unaware of any Indian crime caused by drunkenness in the previous six years. If the sale of brandy were suppressed, several hundred Indians between Sillery and Montreal would rejoin their own people near Orange Thus the French would be deprived of their furs and of their labour in the cultivation of their lands We may observe that the last phrase is of

[1] *C.G.*, IV, f 197.

such a nature as to mislead His Majesty, for except in the sedentary missions the Indians made no serious contribution to the culture of the soil

Next comes the Sieur Dubué, who agreed with the first two, and who feared that the English and Dutch would either oblige the Indians " to fall into heresy" or leave them to their superstitions.

Repentigny and Bécancourt would have prevented the *coureurs de bois* and vagabonds from carrying liquor to Indian hunting grounds, but the habitants must not be deprived of the only commerce which yielded some profit ; the other merchandise was very dear. As to the murders, incests, and adulteries attributed to alcohol, they were due rather to Indian barbarity. Laval's reserved case had done no good, but had caused perhaps the damnation of certain habitants

Sieur Crevier declared that the Ottawas, who did not use liquor, and who were taught by the Jesuits, nevertheless committed daily all sorts of crimes.

The Sieur de Belestre maintained that during the two years that the brandy trade had been repressed the Indians (meaning probably some of the Iroquois) had withdrawn to their own country in order with greater facility to carry their furs to the English This caused great prejudice to the habitants who depended upon the fur trade alone for the subsistence of their families " It is very difficult to attain salvation as long as the reserved case subsists, inasmuch as one cannot help giving drink to the savages "

Another member of the assembly thought that, if deprived of liquor, the disgruntled Indians would make war on the colony.

Charron foresaw the possibility of " all the libertines and *volontaires* " ranging themselves on the side of the foreigners and robbing the colonists of their commerce

Romain believed in completely gallicizing the Indians.

THE FIRST ADMINISTRATION OF FRONTENAC 193

Let them live as Frenchmen among Frenchmen, taught by missionaries and the good examples of their neighbours. Then liquors would harm them no more than the Indians of the Madeleine. There were "plenty of impoverished people in the country without the bishop's reserved case making more of them."

La Prade remarked the quarrels and the mutual accusations between neighbours caused by fear of the penalties contained in the new ordinances.

Verchères said the habitants could not bear to have their profit diverted to distant nations, and so they did not hesitate to pass over every consideration to attain their ends. The alleged avidity of the Indians for brandy was quite natural, since, receiving it only in secret, they felt that they were treated like beasts and distinguished from Frenchmen. As to the disorders, they were few in proportion to the numbers of the Indians, especially where the royal authority was known.

La Salle, himself a sort of superior *coureur de bois*, demanded unreserved liberty for the transportation of liquor to the Indian tribes, as the right to sell it only in the colony would be of small utility to commerce. The Indians came to get French brandy, not to drink on the spot but to take home in large quantities. The tribes who bought liquors counted about twenty thousand souls. They bartered a beaver-skin for a pint of brandy. So if each Indian drank only one pint a year, that would account for a third or a fourth of all the beaver New France received. Conclusion: either the Indians got drunk rarely, or Canada depended upon brandy for most of its fur trade. In any case, intemperance was suffered more in New England than in New France, for some Iroquois deputies told Governor Andros they were withdrawing to Canada to avoid debauch and drunkenness. Moreover, all the twenty thousand Indians aforesaid committed fewer disorders in five or six years than were committed in two or three fairs in a small Breton town. The real danger came from the visits of libertines to the tribes. Now, if complete freedom were granted, the Indians would come to the colony themselves and secure supplies of liquor at cheap rates rather than depend upon the vagabonds with their extortionate prices. La Salle was responsible for the safety of Fort Frontenac, and he anticipated war with the Iroquois on account of the dearness of merchandise, unless complete freedom were accorded the overland trade in brandy, for this drink was his only means of attracting these Indians and removing the distrust people instilled into their minds [1] Finally, La Salle enunciated the view that " it is for laymen alone to decide what is good or bad for commerce, and not for ecclesiastics "

Without a doubt the principal motive determining La Salle's attitude on this question was his anxiety for the success of his plans at Fort Frontenac. Given a good supply of brandy there, he could manage the Indian tribes with comparative ease.

However, the assembly was not unanimous. Five of its members favoured the total or partial suppression of the trade.

Gastineau laid emphasis on the religious side of the question, and reproduced the arguments of the ecclesiastical party. One Indian, said he, spent more on drink in two months than he would spend in two years for the maintenance of his family. Intemperance was continual and was destroying Christianity.

Jolliet, unlike La Salle, was a real settler. He would forbid upon pain of death the carrying of liquor into the forest, but would allow its moderate use at centres of trade and in the houses of the habitants Though a friend of the Jesuits, Jolliet declared that all Indians were not prone to drunkenness.

[1] "La défiance qu'on leur inspire": *on* probably means the Jesuit missionaries.

THE FIRST ADMINISTRATION OF FRONTENAC

Dombourg held that if this traffic were absolutely abolished, the colonists would give themselves up to the cultivation of the land, and the country would flourish. He, too, dwelt upon the religious argument, and added that it was a great sin to take six or seven francs of beaver in exchange for one franc of *eau-de-vie*. He believed that brandy was killing off the natives [1]

In quoting the opinions of most of the members of the assembly, we have chosen only the ideas which were not a simple repetition of familiar facts or arguments. The majority of these commercial men were inclined to minimize the importance of the crimes caused by *eau-de-vie*. It was their interest to do so, and, besides, living for the most part among Frenchmen, they were not as well situated as were the missionaries to observe the effect of a few barrels of brandy in an Indian village. On one thing, however, they were practically all agreed, viz. that liquors cost less and bought more than any other French article of commerce. In other merchandise the English and Dutch had an enormous advantage [2]

In the early days, when the French depended for their furs upon the tribes along the Ottawa and north of the St. Lawrence, English competition was not a real danger; brandy was used not to attract the Indians but to exploit them. Since then the situation had changed: the great fur traders now were the Iroquois who crossed and recrossed French territory. In fact, most of the members of the

---

[1] F 3, v, ff 75-83. This report is signed by Frontenac, Duchesneau, and the members of the Sovereign Council. Latour (*Vie de M de Laval*, p. 85) accuses Frontenac of assembling the habitants in his house without consulting the Council; the habitants "signed whatever he wished." There seems to be no truth in this accusation. Latour also states that the bishop believed this whole manœuvre of such great consequence that he undertook a voyage to France expressly to counteract its effect. People remarked that all who signed this deliberation were visibly punished by a dismal death.

[2] E g C G., VI, f. 60v, VIII, ff. 121v, 157

assembly used *sauvages* as almost synonymous with Iroquois. These Indians were in constant communication with Dutch and English, and, if discontented with the French, could carry their furs the longer distance to their Protestant rivals. The French merchants felt that if they were to continue to enjoy the advantage in the fur trade which their geographical position had seemed to guarantee them, they would have to offset the cheapness of English goods by the superiority of French brandy. They were in no wise entranced by Dombourg's vision of a flourishing agricultural country. For the present the beaver trade was more lucrative and more attractive.

In his interview with Colbert, Dudouyt had admitted a possible loss of only five hundred beaver a year if the clergy's views were adopted. But his arguments applied to the recent past rather than to the immediate present, and if the commercial tide once turned toward the south, it would sweep with it an ever-increasing share of French profits.

Clearly the problem could not be resolved within the bounds of the colony. If brandy were freely imported, it would be sold to the Indians. If its importation were to be restricted to such proportions as would supply the needs of the French colony alone, the restrictive measures would have to be applied in France rather than in Canada. And if New France was not to be handicapped in the race for furs with New England, the government of Louis XIV would have to open negotiations with the English court with a view to joint action. Louis and Colbert entertained no such project, nor shall we hear it mooted before we reach the time of Denonville.

In t'_ autumn of 1678 Laval returned to France to combat the influence of the deliberation at the Château St. Louis. According to Latour [1] the prelate had to face every kind of "difficulty, rebuff, and scorn," for the court was pre-

[1] Latour, p. 86.

THE FIRST ADMINISTRATION OF FRONTENAC 197

judiced by the governor.[1] However that may be, the king received the Bishop of Quebec,[2] and heard his reasons for making a reserved case of "the sin which is committed in the drink traffic with the savages of Canada"[3] His first reason explained the difference between the temperament of the Indians and that of other nations, and related the enormities which accompanied Indian drunkenness Hence the Canadian bishop must take exceptional measures

The second reason was that it is a "principle generally received in theology that a bishop can make a reserved case of a mortal sin which ... is causing the ruin of his Church." The sin committed in the brandy trade in Canada was causing the "desolation and the ruin" of the Canadian Church In similar circumstances other bishops would do as he had done

Thirdly, there were eighty ecclesiastics, regular and secular, in New France, who were continually with the Indians, and who were ordinarily the sole witnesses of the crimes perpetrated. They were the most natural, competent, and enlightened judges in this matter, and Laval had convoked them to frequent deliberations. Always they had judged it absolutely necessary to employ the authority of the Church to remedy so great an evil But for greater assurance, in 1662 Laval had consulted Cornet and Grandin, doctors of the Sorbonne, whose sentiment conformed to that of his clergy. Accordingly, he could no longer hesitate to excommunicate "all those who should give intoxicating drinks to the Indians" Later on he assembled several doctors, including six professors of the Sorbonne, who unanimously endorsed his action.

Another document of the same date, prepared under the direction of Laval, was entitled "Responses to the Reasons

[1] Latour, with his usual inaccuracy, adds, "and by the intendant"
[2] B, XIII, f 2   [3] *Fds Fr*, 13,516, f 95.

which favour this trade." [1] It recalled that the Popes excommunicated those who furnished arms to the infidels, inasmuch as this caused a " notable prejudice to religion." The commerce in brandy did the same. Two years ago Governor Andros, of New York, prohibited the traffic, and he removed his prohibition only when he learned that the French were still trading The Boston ordinances of 1672 called it an " execrable sin." To the argument that the Indians would go and were going to the English for liquors, and were thereby exposed to Protestant influences, the response was that they did not stay there long enough to be " perverted by these heretics, who moreover had not yet begun to instruct them, nor had ever taken pains to administer to them the sacrament of baptism which is necessary to salvation."

Another response maintained that some Iroquois reserved their best beaver to purchase garments from the Dutch. With the inferior they bought French brandy, which they bartered for the furs of Indians from the north who would otherwise bring them down to the colony Hence this part of the Iroquois trade was really robbing Canada. Instead of selling them liquor for transportation, let a French barque supply the upper Iroquois with merchandise at reasonable prices and with brandy in moderation, following the example of the farmers of the king's domain at Tadoussac.

When Louis had heard the Bishop of Quebec, he called upon the Archbishop of Paris and Father La Chaise to examine the question. After a conference with Laval, they made a recommendation to the king which resulted in the royal edict of May 24, 1679.[2] The preamble recalled the laws which forbade leaving the colony to trade or even to hunt except with a hunting permit, good from January 15 to April 15. The new ordinance forbade all Frenchmen to

[1] *Fds. Fr*, 13,516, f. 101 . *Mandements*, p. 149.   [2] B, viii, f 17.

carry brandy to the *bourgades* of Indians remote from the French habitations under penalty of a fine of one hundred livres for the first offence, of three hundred for the second, and of corporal punishment for the third [1]

As we have observed, the royal decision was based upon the report of the king's confessor and an archbishop. Two years earlier M. Dudouyt had found La Chaise well disposed toward the Seminary of Quebec, and we should expect the archbishop to be predisposed toward the ecclesiastical side of the controversy. Nevertheless, these two dignitaries (evidently impressed with the economic and political arguments of the party of commerce, and perhaps convinced that the missionaries had painted the situation in too livid colours) recommended a compromise. To keep the libertines and vagabonds from debauching the Indians, all Frenchmen were forbidden to carry them brandy; but the Indians themselves might obtain it in the colony retail or wholesale. The decision was a cruel disappointment to Laval and his friends. Nevertheless, in November Duchesneau wrote Colbert that the bishop's grand vicar had reduced the reserved case in conformity with the intentions of His Majesty, and that everybody was inclined to live " in great peace on this subject " [2]

The assembly at the Château St. Louis and the consultation of La Chaise and the archbishop mark the climax of the *eau-de-vie* controversy during the first administration of Frontenac. In the remaining three years of his term of office we find only questions of detail and ordinances of secondary importance.

At Montreal, by virtue of an ordinance of Duchesneau, French creditors were authorized to attach furs brought back by their Indian debtors resident in the colony, and deposit them at the office of the bailiwick until a settlement was reached by mutual consent or by the authority of the

[1] *C.G.*, v, f. 119. [2] *Ibid*, f. 54.

bailiff.[1] On the Island the royal edict of May 24, 1679, proved ineffective in the repression of the "grand libertinage" of the *coureurs de bois*, who sought "only their own interests." Some of them (in order to appropriate much beaver, to the detriment of the farms His Majesty wanted established at Quebec, Three Rivers, and Montreal) circulated false rumours among the Indians to the effect that the pestilence was in these places and the merchandise poisoned. This prevented the Ottawas from coming down in 1681, and the colony was in danger of perishing. The attorney-general asked that it be forbidden to spread such rumours, and that the offenders receive corporal punishment as "destroyers of the colony."[2]

In spite of everything most of the *coureurs de bois* continued their long voyages of two or three years, while the others persisted in carrying brandy to meet the Indians coming down for the trade; and having intoxicated them they robbed them.[3]

Intendant Duchesneau was firmly convinced that French prestige and even French commerce demanded that religion should be solidly established among the natives. Unhappily the Council did not punish those who set them bad examples and gave them brandy. Intemperance was the greatest obstacle to religion, and ultimately it ruined commerce, for when it had plunged them hopelessly into debt, its victims shunned the colony and thus cheated the settlers who had lent them goods.[4] Meanwhile, in their last year of office, Frontenac was insinuating that Duchesneau himself had an illicit interest in commerce. Fifty casks of *eau-de-vie*, and a very great quantity of other merchandise, had been imported in October in his name and under his seal.[5]

[1] F 3, v, f. 374.
[2] C.S., vol. ii, p. 658.
[3] C.G., v, f. 297, Duchesneau to Seignelay.
[4] Ibid., f. 307.
[5] Ibid., f. 361.

Before this accusation could be examined, Louis XIV determined to recall both intendant and governor.[1]

Conclusion

All things considered, Duchesneau's testimony as to the work and conduct of the various bodies composing the Church of Canada seems nearer the truth than Frontenac's disparaging accounts. The intendant, as a devout Catholic, as a "clerical" (to borrow a modern term), could see all the good to which the governor was blinded by his prejudices and his animosities His sympathy with the whole clergy qualified him as an excellent apologist for the Canadian Church On the other hand, his reverence for all that was ecclesiastical rendered him uncritical. He saw no fault even in the Récollets, or if he saw it his lips were sealed

Frontenac once complained "M Duchesneau always begins by accusing others of what he does or intends to do"[2] This was a very ingenious thrust, calculated to cast suspicion upon all the intendant's criticisms of the governor The count was not only bold but crafty, and his remark

[1] In New England, too, this same question came up again in acute form On December 1 Captain Wyborne read a report before the Committee for Trade and Plantations According to him, "the chief if not the only cause of the Indians making war upon the English is the tyrannical government of Massachusetts, who made a law that every Indian coming into their towns, . . who was drunk, should pay ten shillings, or be tied to a gun and whipped The Indians are great lovers of all sorts of strong liquors, and would not leave that pleasure notwithstanding the lash" So the Boston magistrates changed the punishment to ten days' labour on a fort commanding the harbour. The ninth day the prisoners were often purposely intoxicated and thus kept another ten days, and so on up to three months Finally, the Indians vowed vengeance, and hence the war (*State Papers*, p 307)

In the following year we have records of a further discussion of the causes of the Indian war against Massachusetts Some again attribute it to an over-strict enforcement of the law against Indian intemperance Others blame "the machinations of vagrant and Jesuitical priests" (*ibid*, p 466)

[2] C G., v, f 278 (1681)

characterized himself rather than his duller rival. We must bear this in mind when he accuses the clergy of enriching themselves through the fur trade and through commerce with the English.

Finally, Louis XIV became convinced that Frontenac was abusing his confidence "The bishop," he said, "and his ecclesiastics, the Jesuit fathers and Sovereign Council, in a word all the *corps* and all the individuals, are complaining."[1] This general turmoil was intensified by the ceaseless struggle between the king's two chief representatives, and in 1682 His Majesty recalled them both.

On the whole, during the decade 1672-82, Frontenac's commanding personality had dominated the political stage, and the Church's power had been diminished though not broken.

[1] *C G*, v, f. 198.

CHAPTER VII

LA BARRE AND DE MEULLES

1682-1685

GOVERNOR AND INTENDANT

NEARLY twenty years before the Chevalier de la Barre came to Canada, Colbert described him as "rather violent and not very susceptible to counsel."[1] In the interval advancing years tempered his violence, and reduced it almost to pusillanimity, but, according to M. Tronson of St. Sulpice, he had the "reputation of a man moderate and disinterested, who loves order and peace."[2] Though physically infirm, and, from a military standpoint, incompetent, yet in civil affairs La Barre remained intellectually vigorous. While, in his correspondence on the Iroquois wars, temerity alternated with timidity, bombast with irresolution, nevertheless in his attitude toward the Church he showed moderation, if not independence.

La Barre and his intendant, de Meulles, soon found a way to "pacify most of the schisms" engendered by the strife between Frontenac and Duchesneau. They both sympathized with the count. The bishop, they said, had contributed a great deal to their divisions, and Duchesneau had fallen into many snares which had been set for him. The party spirit reigned everywhere, and everything was done by cabals.[3]

---

[1] *C.G.*, II, f. 104. [2] *Tronson*, vol. ii, p. 246.
[3] *C.G.*, VI, ff. 59, 62, 64, 66v.

De Meulles at once settled numerous lawsuits which the local judges had "maliciously eternalized." "They say that the more doctors there are in a town, the more sick there are. It is the same with judges."[1] By such intervention the intendant made himself enemies.

De Meulles was active, not only in the pacification, but also in the economic development of the colony, and in this sphere the mantle of Talon seemed to have fallen upon his shoulders.[2]

Though their term of office was not marred by the scandalous quarrels of the preceding administration, yet La Barre and de Meulles did not always see eye to eye. The latter felt that it was impossible for a governor to be in the Council without being jealous of the intendant who presided over it. The most virtuous governors would never be prepossessed in favour of the intendants,[3] while M. de la Barre was resolved "to do alone absolutely all that he desired in the country."[4] On the other hand, the Marquis de Seignelay, who had succeeded his father, Colbert, wrote de Meulles: "I must warn you that you want to establish for yourself a power which has never been known of any intendant."[5] The main purpose of the minister's warning was to impress on the intendant's mind a due sense of subordination, for immediately afterward he entrusted him with a new responsibility.[6] The following year His Majesty's application was more just: "I am satisfied with the deference you have had for the Sieur de la Barre, and with the care with which you have avoided controversies which might have sprung from his encroachments upon your functions."[7]

On the whole, the behaviour of governor and intendant toward each other was dignified and worthy of their station.

[1] C.G., vi, f. 91   [2] Ibid, ff. 168, 183   [3] Ibid, f. 177v; vii, f. 152.
[4] C.G., vi, f. 179   [5] B, xi, f. 20v.
[6] Ibid, f. 21   [7] Ibid, f. 19v (March 10, 1685).

Laval and the Civil Power

Their relations with the bishop and his clergy next demands our attention. La Barre's first dispatch seemed to prove him a man after Colbert's own heart: "What will cause us most trouble . . . will be the spirit of Monsieur the Bishop, who by every sort of means is bent on maintaining an authority in things political and civil such as he has in things spiritual, and who makes use of the one . . . to arrive at the other. We shall have for his person and for his character the highest respect (I speak for both of us), but we will go our own way . ." Laval was the cause of much of the trouble in the preceding administration. "That will make us both distrustful" of him [1]

La Barre was also indignant at Laval's treatment of the Hospitalières. Though they were already in debt and dire poverty, the bishop was urging them to build, and to bring over more nuns from France Worse still, he made them pay 800 livres a year for masses said by his seminarists, which the Récollets offered them for 300 livres. Finally, he had forbidden them to receive any patients, and they had complained to the governor La Barre was surprised that Laval should arrogate to himself the quality of sole director of a hospital largely dependent upon the liberalities of the king The intendant ought to be at its head. In any case, the nuns must be helped or their Hôtel-Dieu would fall.[2]

Thus far, then, La Barre's feelings toward the Bishop of Quebec were none too cordial, but during the ensuing year they changed noticeably One of the first questions to come up for settlement was that of the *cures fixes*. The court had informed the new governor, that while the king favoured

---

[1] *C G*, vi, f 59v

[2] *Ibid*, ff 60, 65, 82, 140v As for Talon's general hospital, neither La Barre nor de Meulles approved of the project The former said there were many poor in the country but few mendicants, and there was no need for "an establishment for titular beggars"

settled curacies, Laval had always preferred his curates to be "revocable in order to conserve over them a greater authority."¹ La Barre now reported that the prelate showed signs of yielding the point.² By the autumn of 1683 he had come to the conclusion that the bishop was "very well intentioned" toward the colony, and ought to be given credence.³ So much had the governor come under Laval's influence that he had agreed to a minimum stipend (*portion congrue*) of 500 livres for the permanent curacies —a sum which the minister considered excessive, since 300 livres was a high salary for the curés of France. The court wished the Canadian Church to become self-supporting, and the royal bounty of 6000 livres was to be reduced progressively.⁴

While the governor was swinging away from his first attitude of latent hostility toward the prelate, the intendant's sentiments were veering in the opposite direction. Soon after his arrival, reporting on the *cures fixes*, he declared Laval "extremely reasonable." Owing to the meagre yield of the tithes, he admitted a general system of settled curacies was impossible without a royal supplement, and so at present only a few could be established. However, in some cases, the habitants, passionately desiring a settled curé who would remain in their parish and instruct their children, were willing to assume collective responsibility for the *portion congrue*.⁵ The following year de Meulles visited all the settlements of Canada under the guidance of Laval's grand vicar,⁶ and he seems to have changed his mind as to the reasonableness of the bishop's attitude. French priests, he declared, would content themselves with the tithes of several of the villages he had seen. However, Laval's ecclesiastics, instead of living cheaply by themselves, were lodged by their parishioners, and clothed and controlled

¹ B, viii, f 3v ² C G, vi, f 66 ³ Ibid, f 140v.
⁴ Ibid., f 244 (April 10, 1684) ⁵ Ibid, f 83 ⁶ Ibid, f 181.

from the Seminary. This was an expensive system. Moreover, whenever de Meulles spoke to the prelate and his grand vicar about the *cures fixes*, they enumerated the necessities of the curates " as a young man of quality might do to a very rich father." The intendant went so far as to suggest that the king might send out some " good and virtuous ecclesiastics " from France, who would content themselves with the tithes of the better curacies. Some good monks could serve as missionaries in the poorer districts The Récollet, Father Sixte, for several years curé of Three Rivers, subsisted easily on less than 300 livres If monks, " accustomed to live soberly in their monasteries," were brought out as curates, " one cannot imagine the good the inhabitants of Canada would derive from it, at least three-quarters of them hear mass less than four times a year The result is that often they die without the sacrament, and are no more instructed in our religion than savages who never hear tell of it, a fact which has excited in me an extraordinary compassion."[1]

In the summer of 1684 His Majesty wrote the prelate a letter inspired by de Meulles' suggestion,[2] while in the following autumn the intendant reiterated his views. Every day the people were asking him for monks to serve the poorer *cures*, but the maxims and the policy of the bishop were opposed thereto " If he were of good faith on the subject of the curacies, all his ecclesiastics would be content with whatever you wished, most of them being of low birth, brought up in his Seminary through charity." However, concluded de Meulles, without more energetic action on the part of the court, they would never see the " execution of this noble design " in the time of Laval.[3] In this dispute over the country livings, while Laval's repugnance to the whole scheme of settled curacies may have been an underlying cause of his placing the minimum stipend rather high,

[1] *C G.*, vi, ff. 184-6.   [2] B, xi, ff. 44, 46   [3] *C G*, vi, f 399.

we must remember that Frontenac had agreed to the 500 livres, that de Meulles himself found merchandise twice as costly in the colony as in the mother country, and that La Barre declared labour thrice as dear.[1] Accordingly, when the king bade Laval reduce the *portion congrue* to 400 livres, he was fixing for the Canadian clergy a standard of living which would give their brethren in France little reason to envy them. Although the king's annual gift of 6000 livres was intended exclusively for the maintenance of curates, the intendant now charged that the royal bounty and the other funds which passed through the hands of the Seminary served "principally to pay the great debts that Monsieur the Bishop contracted in building a habitation which is two or three times more magnificent than it ought to be."[2] Though incomplete, it had cost him nearly 50,000 écus, and whatever he might say, the bishop would liquidate his debts as much as possible with the money from the curacies. For though he clothed and supported his priests with the aid of the king's money, he also received all their revenue. It was, therefore, useless to expect his co-operation in the establishment of regular curacies.

De Meulles recounted an incident which suggested the financial pressure to which Monseigneur must have felt himself subjected. For the construction of an intendant's residence Colbert had assigned 9000 livres, and de Meulles thought of buying the site of the cemetery of the Upper Town. In justice, he said, 300 livres would be too good a price for it, but the prelate, wishing to profit by the occasion, demanded over 10,000 livres. "One must not expect any favour from Monsieur the Bishop, and it is a great misfortune to depend upon and have dealings with him."[3]

[1] *C.G.*, VI, ff. 62, 81v. The workmen "frightened" La Barre by asking 6000 livres for what would cost 2000 in France.

[2] In the same year La Hontan speaks of this building "dont la grandeur et l'architecture sont surprenantes" (vol. i, p. 18).

[3] *C.G.*, VI, ff. 409v, 417v.

LA BARRE AND DE MEULLES 209

Within a few days the intendant's secret prayer was answered Mgr de Laval sailed for France,[1] and the following summer saw the arrival at Quebec of his successor, the Abbé de Saint-Vallier.

The Abbé de Saint-Vallier

For some time Laval had foreseen the necessity of entrusting his beloved diocese to a younger man. Early in 1685 M Tronson of St Sulpice wrote as follows:

However His Grace of Quebec may desire to return to Canada this year, it is very doubtful whether he will be able to do so because of his illness He has resolved to take a successor, and he has chosen the Abbé de Saint-Vallier, who was for a long time chaplain to the king The new bishop is zealous and, provided that he do not go too far, he will be in a position to accomplish great good, for he is very well liked at court The king esteems him, and there is nothing to fear for him except the excess which might make him lose his credit there, as has happened to his predecessor As he has a great deal of fire, all those of whom he might ask advice must try to moderate him [2]

Besides this, we learn from Laval's grand vicar, Dudouyt, that the abbé was wealthy and of high birth, that he would consent to being a bishop in Canada only in order to avoid being one in France, and that he was over-ardent.[3]

La Hontan's comments upon the change of bishop doubtless represented the feelings of a considerable class of men in the colony. He hoped Saint-Vallier was less rigid than Laval. "But what appearance is there that this new bishop is conciliatory? If it is true that he has refused other good bishoprics, he must be as scrupulous as the monk Draconce . Well, if such he is, people will hardly put

---
[1] C G, vi, f 365. [2] Tronson, vol ii, p. 274
[3] Rapport, 1887, p xxiii.

up with his rigidity, for they are already very tired of the excommunications of his predecessor."[1]

The Marquis de Seignelay recommended the abbé very highly to de Meulles,[2] and the intendant found him "an honest man," of "extraordinary zeal," anxious to carry out the royal will in the matter of the curacies.[3] But his good opinion of Saint-Vallier did not prevent his continuing to assert civil rights as against clerical privilege. That very autumn he again drew Seignelay's attention to the Upper Town: it was "a little mountain" which would never be inhabited, because the finest part of it (eighteen or twenty arpents overlooking the St. Lawrence) belonged to the bishopric.[4] However, with the new prelate personally M. de Meulles seems to have had no disagreement. We turn now from the episcopal authority to the most important of its supports, the Company of Jesus.

THE JESUITS AND LA BARRE

In spite of Colbert's warning against allowing their authority to extend too far, the governor's attitude toward the Jesuits seems to have been friendly from the beginning.[5] Harassed by the external dangers which menaced the colony, the old general was only too glad of the counsels and aid of men so experienced and adroit in Indian affairs. In his very first dispatch he dwelt upon the significance, from a patriotic standpoint, of the Iroquois mission at the Sault St. Louis. This Christian settlement had almost depopulated the village of the Mohawks, and all the tribes except the Senecas were represented there.

Thus the French were informed of all the war news from the cantons.[6] Moreover, through this mission the

---

[1] La Hontan, vol i, p 134.   [2] B, xi, f. 23
[3] C G., vii, f. 143.   [4] Ibid, f 145 (Sept 28, 1685)
[5] B, viii, f. 2 (1682).   [6] C G., vi, f. 64v

Jesuits had "acquired for the king ... 200 good Iroquois soldiers,"[1] while, from the neighbouring mission of the Madeleine, La Barre was able to choose four Iroquois chiefs to accompany Le Moyne on his embassy to their cantons.[2] To the intrepid missionaries of the Upper Lakes, La Barre also gave his confidence. His instructions to the Commandant Durantaye read as follows: "As the Reverend Father Jesuits are the most *savants* in the way of treating with the savages, and the most zealous for Christianity, he is to have confidence in them, to please them in every way, and to treat them as people for whom I have profound respect and great esteem."[3] From the Jesuits of Ste. Marie the governor received assistance,[4] and in a crisis he appealed to Father Enjalran to exert "his usual zeal and capacity" in keeping the Ottawas loyal. At Quebec, when a general council of war was called, the assembly met in the commodious home of the Jesuits, who told how the English were inciting the Iroquois to commence hostilities against the colony.[5] Another assembly decided to pray the Jesuit missionaries in the cantons to make every effort to cause divisions among the Iroquois.[6] But if the alliance between governor and Jesuits was so complete in face of external danger, it was no less real in domestic politics. Shortly after his arrival at Quebec, La Barre came entirely under the influence of the faction which had long combated Frontenac and La Salle; and he soon echoed their suspicions and their accusations. In a dispatch to the minister he referred to La Salle as "a man who causes violent suspicions that he is plotting something which does not conduce to the good of the service"; there was reason to believe that he had "peculiar designs that he did not wish people to penetrate."[7]

[1] *C.G*, vi, f. 143. [2] *Ibid.*, ff. 135v, 137 [3] Baugy, p. 166.
[4] *C G*, vi, f. 231. [5] *Ibid.*, f. 68. [6] *Ibid.*, f. 308.
[7] C 13, iii, f. 37 (Nov. 14, 1682).

The Chevalier de Baugy was sent to take possession of La Salle's Fort St. Louis, while La Chesnaye and Le Ber seized Fort Frontenac.[1]

In 1688 the Marquis de Denonville reported that this "misunderstanding" between La Salle and La Barre had been "a very great evil for the colony" and had caused the missionaries great pain.[2] However, as we have shown in our treatment of the preceding administration, the clique of merchants was hardly more hostile to the great discoverer than were the Canadian Jesuits; and a letter of Father Enjalran proves a close co-operation between missionaries and governor for the expulsion of La Salle from Fort St. Louis.[3] The explorer had protested in vain to La Barre that his "unique crime" had been his loyalty to Frontenac, and that the Récollet Zenoble would vouch for his good conduct.[4] La Barre's friends were Frontenac's enemies, and, in La Salle's own forts, the grey robes gave way to the black. So his only hope now lay in the court, for which he drew up a memorial containing counter-charges of mercenary motives against La Barre.[5]

The governor's project of attacking the Iroquois was extremely unpopular at first. It appeared a purely commercial enterprise. The people "said boldly that they were going to war solely to conserve the beaver of five or six merchants of the Lower Town of Quebec, who alone carry on all the commerce." Although de Meulles agreed with them he hushed their murmurings, for the success of the campaign.[6] The intendant agreed with the Jesuits of Quebec that, if peace were now made, the country was lost.[7]

---

[1] Baugy, pp. 164, 175, 186, 188.
[2] C.G., x, f. 66
[3] Margry, vol v, p. 3.
[4] C 13, III, f. 43.
[5] Ibid., f. 60; cf. C.G., vi, ff 216, 242.
[6] C G., vi, f. 382v. "Quoique toutes ces raisons soient véritables, il ne laisse pas d'être d'une très grande conséquence de ne pas laisser la liberté au peuple de dire son sentiment" (de Meulles to Seignelay).
[7] Ibid., f. 391.

But while Jesuits and merchants both wanted the war, the former were somewhat scandalized to see La Barre making himself so evidently the tool of the latter. They all had grave misgivings as to the governor's real intention, and when he embarked for the war *tête à tête* with the big merchant, La Chesnaye, that "appeared very extraordinary," said de Meulles, " to Monsieur the Bishop, to all the Jesuits, and to all the honest people in the country." [1]

Their forebodings were realized the expedition was a humiliating failure from the viewpoint of Jesuits and merchants alike La Barre had only one comforter, Jean de Lamberville, who, " whatever Messieurs the merchants might say," [2] hailed him " saviour of the country " because he had wisely avoided a disastrous war. Unlike his confrères of Quebec, the apostle to the Senecas was a consistent advocate of peace. Possibly he recognized the incompetence of the aged governor to carry a punitive expedition to a successful issue. At any rate, we feel that de Meulles misinterpreted his motives when he explained to the minister that Lamberville, foreseeing La Barre's design, was " wise and discreet enough to write him according to his inclinations " [3]

But though in this crisis the Jesuits of Quebec could not applaud the governor, yet generally they exercised a potent influence upon his mind Hence his gradual change of attitude toward their bishop and his lack of cordiality toward their rivals, the Récollets.

THE RÉCOLLETS AND THE BISHOP

In the royal instructions to La Barre we find a marginal note in the hand of Colbert, which runs :

He is likewise to give protection to the Récollets established at Quebec, and to observe that, as the said bishop has

---

[1] *C G*, VI, f 385. [2] *Ibid*, 540v. [3] *Ibid*, f 391.

shown on several occasions great animosity against them, he ought, with prudence and without compromising himself with the bishop, to support them by his authority, these monks being very necessary in this country on account of the spiritual succour they have given . . the inhabitants.[1]

Two years later the Récollets charged that "M de la Barre, far from giving them any protection, has often declared to them that he would take such action that in a few years there would not be a Récollet in Canada." [2] Even if this accusation be an exaggeration of the truth, one cannot fail to be struck by the contrast between the court's orders and La Barre's conduct. It is fairly clear that, under the influence of their opponents, the governor came to regard the Récollets as intruders Moreover, they were friends of La Salle, upon whom La Barre had made war. Hence their ejection from Fort Frontenac to make place for Jesuits.

It was during this administration that the famous quarrel occurred between Laval and the Récollets over their new *hospice* and its belfry. As their monastery was half a league from Quebec, the monks petitioned the king for a place whereon to build an inn to shelter them when " the night and the bad weather " surprised them at their work in the city. His Majesty granted them a site in the Upper Town whereof they might dispose " as of something belonging to them " [3] Laval gave them permission to build there a *hospice*, meaning a sort of " infirmary for their sick," but forbade anything resembling a residence. Later on we find him charging the Récollet superior with having " against every sort of right and of ecclesiastical discipline undertaken an enterprise of this nature," for the monks were placing a bell-tower on their hospital. The bishop ordered them to pull it down; the monks parleyed: " The belfry is inseparable from the *hospices* intended for the solace of the

[1] B, VIII, f. 2 (May 10, 1682). [2] Margry, vol i, pp 18-33
[3] F, II, f. 21 (1681).

infirm and the sick." "We do not intend to establish a regular community in . . . Quebec without the express permission of the king and of His Grace the Bishop." They meant to say mass only in private. These and other assurances were contained in a collective letter signed by the seven Récollets at Quebec. The prelate severely reprimanded their superior for thus rendering his priests "participants in and guilty of a fault," for which he alone should bear the responsibility. He was misconstruing the royal permit and using it as a pretext for setting up a regular convent. Laval forbade him to say even private mass without his permission, or to build a chapel or oratory; and again he ordered the demolition of the belfry.

Then, as the king had instructed him to address himself in spiritual matters to Father La Chaise and the Archbishop of Paris, the prelate complained to them both of the conduct of the Récollets, whose enterprise was "as rash as it was prejudicial to the Church." To Seignelay he declared: "All the communities of this country and the veritable interests of religion and politics are opposed" to a new convent. He accused the Récollets of dissimulation and insubordination. Their new superior had declared that if Laval forbade them under pain of suspension to say mass in their new *hospice*, he would be excommunicated himself by virtue of the privileges of their order.[1]

About the same time La Barre reported that the calm within the colony would be complete were it not for this enterprise of the Récollets. The bishop was entirely in the right. Besides, "the multiplicity of mendicant houses in this country is not advantageous to a people as poor as those of this whole colony."[2] The following year he informed the king that the Récollets were not as complaisant toward their bishop as good religious mendicants ought to be.

[1] F 3, IV, ff. 36, 37, 39, 59v, 73v.
[2] C.G., VI, f. 143v (Nov 4, 1683).

Witness their stubbornness in regard to that "miserable bagatelle" of a belfry, to the demolition of which they preferred the general interdiction of their order in Canada Probably the intendant was encouraging them in that attitude. Though the court had censured their disobedience in regard to the belfry, their new superior, Exupère, appeared willing to yield to neither king nor bishop, while, on the contrary, Laval desired only reconciliation. Finally, however, La Barre reported that the rebellious monks had made a sacrifice of obedience and come to terms with the prelate. "I am overjoyed that this domestic war is finished, although late, nevertheless with good grace."[1]

In this same controversy the intendant, too, had played a part. Offering his services as a mediator, he induced Laval to agree to pay the Récollets 6000 livres if they would relinquish their new site He felt that their ground of resistance to episcopal authority was very ill-chosen, since their presence was "by no means necessary" in Quebec, where there were more churches than were needed for so small a population. "Besides," continued de Meulles, "as Monsieur the Bishop foresees, this would be subsequently a source of perpetual division between the whole clergy and the said Récollets That is what has obliged the said bishop by a veritable motive of peace, as he has assured me, to oppose this new establishment."[2] De Meulles then reasoned with the recalcitrant monks · as their order was not "military," but vowed to poverty and humility, it would become them, without examining their formal rights, to defer to their bishop's desire that they should demolish the belfry. The afore-mentioned reconciliation then took place, and Laval was now free to do his duty by the Récollets according to the intentions of His Majesty.[3]

Although de Meulles, with his characteristic independ-

---

[1] C G, vi, f 244, 341, 354, 365.   [2] Ibid, f. 185.
[3] Ibid., f 399 (Nov. 13, 1684).

ence, had refused to countenance the Récollets when he knew them in the wrong, he sharply criticized the bishop for his obstinate hostility toward them. Their ten or twelve priests dared render no service, although everybody praised them. De Meulles was astonished that the prelate should sacrifice to his ill-will against the Récollets so many wretched people who would otherwise receive good instructions and who died deprived of the sacraments.[1]

From Montreal there came a request for Récollet confessors.[2] De Meulles explained to the minister that, as the Sulpicians were seigneurs of the Island, and were often at variance with some of the inhabitants, many of the latter were thus prevented from going to confession.[3] Indeed, for several years there had been agitation over this matter. In 1677 M. Tronson, with his usual magnanimity, had advised the Sulpicians of Montreal to live " in great harmony with the Récollets if they should come to the Island," while in 1681 he authorized Dolher de Casson to grant them a concession of land, since the people had petitioned to that effect.[4] Although, for the time being, His Majesty refused to allow the Récollets to establish themselves at Villemarie,[5] he vigorously enjoined Mgr. de Laval to employ these zealous monks in missions among the colonists and even in the curacies where the priests of his Seminary thought they could not subsist.[6] In Acadia, too, the religious were needed. A Récollet had gone there in 1675, but during the dispute over the belfry Laval had replaced him by one of his own missionaries.[7] In 1683 the bishop urged Seignelay to establish a curacy at Port Royal with a view to keeping the inhabitants loyal to the king, since they were near the English.[8] Whether the court considered the English peril a reality or a pretext, we cannot say; but the following

---

[1] F 3, II, f. 148. [2] Ibid, f. 95. [3] Ibid, f. 149.
[4] Tronson, vol. ii, pp. 140, 228. [5] B, XI, f. 19 (April 10, 1684).
[6] Ibid, ff. 18, 34. [7] Clair, 1016, f. 493. [8] F 3, IV, f. 73v.

spring the minister informed Laval that some Récollets were to minister to the fishing colony on the coast of Acadia, where "monks who lived on little could serve more usefully than priests on the footing upon which he had placed them." The bishop must not refuse these monks the necessary permits [1]

In 1684 the Récollets prepared a long memorial reviewing the history of their Canadian mission, and setting forth their grievances. Though strongly partisan, and couched in language often bitter and violent, this presentation of the wrongs of the Minor Brothers is in the main worthy of credence. It is an arraignment of Laval and his Seminary. When they arrived the bishop tried to confine them to the life of the cloister, and their convent of Notre Dame des Anges was placed in a solitude, so as to render them useless for the relief of consciences. "The people have no more liberty in Canada than if they lived in a heretic country." The Récollets were under espionage, and Laval would send a priest upon the track of one of their number to discredit his conduct in a given region. He complained of a "difference of maxims" between them and the others. To this accusation they retorted that their ethics were the same in Canada as elsewhere, whereas the "principal chiefs of the illuminees of the Hermitage of Caen, having taken refuge in Canada after being condemned in France, are there establishing their maxims, by which to-day the ecclesiastics conduct the country, and into which the Récollets cannot enter as contrary to the principle of conscience and of the State." [2] By "difference of maxims" the bishop probably meant the difference between Gallicanism and Ultramontanism. With the spirit which characterized the Hermitage of Caen we have dealt in a former section.

In the autumn of 1684, after twenty-five years of consecrated effort, Mgr. de Laval returned to France. The

[1] C.G. vi, f. 244.   [2] Margry, vol. i, pp. 18-33.

following spring, through M. de Meulles, the king warned the Récollets of Canada that he would show them favour only in proportion to their submissive obedience to Laval's successor.[1] The intendant replied that the Abbé de Saint-Vallier was on good terms with the Récollets and employed them extensively in the missions.[2]

Having now dealt with the clergy of Quebec, we turn to the priests of Montreal.

The Sulpicians and the Powers

By this time, in spite of adversities, the seigneury of the Sulpicians had grown into a very considerable domain with good revenues. La Hontan described their Seminary as "a fine, large, and magnificent house of cut stone," and their church was worthy of their dwelling. It was built on the model of St. Sulpice of Paris.

The baron felt quite outraged at the puritanical severity of the Sulpician régime. You could neither have a pleasure party nor play at cards nor see the ladies without the curate being informed of it and preaching about it publicly in the pulpit. "You could not believe how far the authority of these ecclesiastical seigneurs extends I avow they are ridiculous in their way of acting. They excommunicate all the masqueraders, and even run to the places where they are to be found in order to unmask them and overwhelm them with insults." "They forbid and cause to be burned all books which do not treat of devotion." "They are not content to study people's actions; they wish also to ransack their thoughts."[3] The Gascon's verve may exaggerate, but he never lies without reason, and there is no reason why he should lie here.

Be that as it may, M. de la Barre declared that for the

[1] B, XI, f. 18v. [2] C.G., VII, f. 144.
[3] La Hontan, vol 1, pp. 27, 60.

gentlemen of St Sulpice he had "all the consideration imaginable,"[1] and the new minister, Seignelay, was as much their friend as his father had been before him.[2]

Nevertheless, in describing the situation at Montreal in his first letter to Seignelay, the chevalier seemed inclined to minimize the faults of the local governor, Perrot, of whose quarrels with the Sulpicians we have already heard M. Perrot, he said, had been misjudged by Superior Dollier, who was a good man, of very mediocre talent, and easily imposed upon.[3] Apparently La Barre had personal grievances against the Sulpician, as he slighted him in a meeting with the Iroquois ambassadors and sent complaints of him to France.[4] At any rate, the king knew the merits of the Perrot case, and he informed La Barre that if the governor of Montreal could not be reconciled with the seigneurs of the Island, he would have to be replaced. The following year Perrot was sent to Acadia.[5] M. Tronson congratulated his priests of Villemarie on the change of governor: Perrot could "trade at his ease" in Acadia, while Montreal would find his successor, Callières, "a very honest man." Tronson hoped his ecclesiastics would now enjoy the peace and pleasantness which they could not taste under the domination of their persecutor. They had been unjustly blamed for the notorious disturbances in Montreal, whereas the responsibility really lay with the governors, who alone had power to enforce discipline. Nevertheless, this wise and prudent ecclesiastic, bent upon moderating rather than stimulating the zeal of the Seminary of Montreal, concluded thus: "I exhort you . . . to be very reserved in speaking of the Powers . . unless you speak of them in order to justify them. For, when you cannot justify them, silence is the best course you can adopt." Besides, "everything

---

[1] C.G., VI, f. 62v. [2] Tronson, vol ii, pp 177, 246.
[3] C.G., VI, ff. 62, 139. [4] Tronson, vol. ii, p. 269.
[5] B, X, ff. 3, 4; B, XI, f. 5.

is known, and nothing embitters them so much as hearing that people decry them, saying that they carry on commerce, and that they give a bad example " In case of trouble, his priests should write to him,[1] and he would use his influence with the court to see that wrongs were righted.

THE CIVILIZATION OF THE INDIANS

There was one aspect of Sulpician activity which never failed to win the approval of the secular authorities, and that was their method of civilizing the Indians. His Majesty enjoined La Barre to encourage them and the Jesuits in the establishment of strong colonies, which might ultimately bring all the Iroquois to the Faith and under the sovereignty of the king [2] During the Iroquois war the old " General " was delighted with the Indians from the Mountain He said that the Sulpicians were forming good soldiers and good subjects as well as good Christians [3]

It was inevitable that there should be jealousy and competition between the neighbouring missions of the Mountain and of the Sault, but as usual M. de Tronson sought to pour oil upon the troubled waters : " These good (Jesuit) fathers act according to their light and their grace at their vocation, and you according to yours at the work which God entrusts to you " They were all working for the same end, though with " very different views "[4] This difference of views arose over questions of method. The Jesuits believed in the isolation and the Sulpicians in the francization of the savages. It was the latter method which appealed to the intendant as well as to the court of France. De Meulles wrote that the Sulpicians gave religious instruction to the Indians in Latin as well as in their own language, and that they also taught them French, stock-raising, and some

[1] *Tronson*, vol ii, pp 267, 271, 272, 276.   [2] B, viii, f 2v
[3] *Tronson*, vol ii, p 277   [4] *Ibid.*, pp 247, 263.

handicrafts. The Jesuits, on the other hand, though very zealous in spiritual matters, taught the Indians only in their own languages, which did not bring them into communication with the French.[1]

The intendant was equally pleased with the education of Indian girls at Montreal. The young women of the congregation were endeavouring to give them practical instruction. "They are naturally very adroit," said the intendant. He advised a small endowment, which would enable them to clothe themselves in French fashion.[2]

On the other hand, de Meulles held that nothing was more useless than placing the native girls with the Ursulines of Quebec. These nuns taught them only to pray to God and speak French, both of which accomplishments they soon forgot. He advocated the establishment of a manufactory where Indian girls would learn to " live after the fashion of the *villageoises* of France, *i.e.* to spin, sew, knit, and take care of animals." The austerity of the Ursuline convent was incompatible with the savage temperament, and upon leaving it these girls went from one extreme to the other. Only one or two each year married Frenchmen.[3]

Allied with the question of Indian civilization was the controversy over the brandy trade.

The Brandy Trade

The royal instructions to La Barre informed him of the " very considerable difficulty " raised by Laval's reserved case and of the settlement of May 24, 1679. Yet, although the matter had been decided in full knowledge of the facts, there was reason to fear that the bishop might create new difficulties. So His Majesty wished the governor to see to the punctual and integral execution of the aforesaid ordinance.[4]

---

[1] F 3, II, f. 149. [2] C G., VI, f. 193v.
[3] *Ibid.*, 87v, 193v. [4] B, VIII, pt. 3, f. 5.

In the autumn of 1682 La Barre wrote that a difference had indeed arisen between the bishop and the civil administration. The former claimed that he had promised the Archbishop of Paris to suspend his reserved case for one year only, that he had already done so for three years, and that the royal authority must be reconciled with the spiritual. "Nevertheless," continued La Barre, "as I spoke to him . . . with all possible moderation, and represented to him that, since this ordinance, one heard almost no further talk of the disorders among the Indians, he appeared to me to yield. But as he is very adroit, I fear that this was because of the early departure of the vessels. So, I believe, it would be well that the king should write him resolutely that he wishes to be obeyed in this regard." Soon afterwards the bishop promised to follow the exact intentions of His Majesty,[1] and the following summer Louis XIV expressed his pleasure at the harmony which now reigned between the two authorities in Canada. He hoped that "this affair, which has lasted so long, will be at length terminated entirely."[2]

Another portion of La Barre's instructions described the ruin wrought in spite of the law through the wholesale desertion of agriculture by habitants intent upon the fur trade. With a view to bringing them back to their duty, an amnesty had been granted these outlaws, and hereafter the governor and intendant were to give passports for twenty-five canoes annually to visit the distant tribes.[3] This was an acknowledgment of defeat on the part of the home government, which was now trying to retrieve itself by a compromise.

During La Barre's administration the centre of interest in the "fire-water" traffic was Montreal. In 1683 the governor spent the summer there, and his stand against the

[1] G.C , vi, ff 59v, 64, 66v.   [2] B, x, f 3 ; B, xi, f. 9
[3] B, viii, pt 3, f 8v.

liquor trade commended itself to the bishop.¹ The conditions in that town and its neighbourhood were the despair of the Sulpician seigneurs of the Island Superior Tronson wrote the Abbé de Belmont that he could see no remedy ; the remedies proposed by Belmont were vexatious or impracticable Then, recurring to a suggestion formerly made by the Marquis de Tracy and endorsed by the Sovereign Council, he added that the regulation of the quantity of brandy exported to Canada would be the surest and shortest expedient, but the authorities would not bring themselves to that. " As long as they are as convinced as they are at present that these drinks are necessary to commerce and to the maintenance of the colony, we must not hope that they will reduce their quantity It is an evil which God alone can remedy, for to succeed one would have to change both minds and hearts " ²

The Chevalier de la Barre was more sanguine at first, and made a strong effort to destroy this traffic, root and branch However, like all his predecessors, he counted a generous supply of *eau-de-vie* among the necessary provisions in his military expeditions For one crusade against the Iroquois he ordered one hundred barrels of lard, thirty hogsheads of brandy, etc ³ At the Long Sault he was joined by the Iroquois Christians of Sault St. Louis and Montreal. By means of small presents of brandy and tobacco he induced them to take the boats and largest canoes over the rapids. This they accomplished without accident in two days—something Frenchmen could not have done.⁴

La Barre, then, believed in the discreet and cautious use of stimulants in dealing with the Indians, but he resolutely waged war on the commerce carried on at Montreal and in its environs "The people of these quarters," he reported to the Marquis de Seignelay, " are not very sub-

---

¹ F 3, iv, f 73 ² *Tronson*, vol. ii, p. 262 (April 8, 1684).
³ C.G., vi, f 155 ⁴ *Ibid* , f 310 (Oct. 1, 1684)

missive to justice." They do not fear the bailiff of the Seminary. "Drunkenness, with strange excesses, theft, receiving of stolen goods, and desertion are the ordinary things in which two hundred libertines . . . exercise themselves." At Quebec, on the contrary, "obedience is very well established."[1] Montreal, indeed, appeared "rather a hell than a civilized place." La Barre's ordinances proved effective only as long as he was there in person. So, almost in despair, he issued another edict forbidding the cabaretiers to give intoxicating liquors to the Indians either to drink in the tavern or to carry away. They would be fined fifty livres upon the evidence of the first Indian who declared that he had got drink in their house. Corporal punishment was decreed for the second offence. The same ordinance forbade noisy drunkenness among Frenchmen under penalty of a military punishment of one hour upon the wooden horse. La Barre enjoined Callières, governor of Montreal, in consultation with Superior Dollier, to enforce the new decree.[2] Unfortunately for La Barre, his action was *ultra vires*, inasmuch as it was contrary to the royal ordinance of May 24, 1679, which merely forbade Frenchmen to carry liquor to distant tribes. Accordingly the king instructed de Meulles to revoke the governor's decree.[3]

But the intendant also bore witness to the excesses committed at Montreal, and cited as an example a certain Pérotin who, at thirty leagues from Villemarie, so debauched the Indian traders that the whole colony was scandalized. De Meulles confessed that he passed over some such things in silence for fear of "engendering war in the country" because of the protection which, he insinuated, La Barre accorded several of the culprits.[4]

[1] *C G*, vi, f. 138 (Nov. 4, 1683).
[2] F 3, iv, f. 142 (Sept. 28, 1684).
[3] B, xi (March 10, 1685). [4] *C G*, vi, f. 408v (Nov. 1684).

At Montreal, too, we find that even the unruly cabaretiers had their grievances. Certain citizens of Quebec invaded their territory and sold liquor there to the Indians all summer. Deserting the men who had carried them through the winter, the debtors of the cabaretiers would carry their ready cash to the strangers from Quebec. This complaint of the tavern-keepers was endorsed by the Sieur de Tonty in a petition to Seignelay. He pointed out that the intruders from Quebec reaped the profits without bearing the charges of residents (such as the lodging and transporting of troops), whereas in Old France a merchant established in one city could not do business in another. Non-resident merchants should be excluded from Villemarie [1]

Turning from Montreal to the sedentary mission of Sillery, near Quebec, we find that even there the brandy trade has wrought havoc. In 1678 several members of the assembly held in the Château St. Louis had pointed to Sillery as one of the model communities proof against the ravages of alcoholism. In 1683 Father Beschefer reported that the flourishing Algonquin mission of Sillery had been so scourged by intemperance that only a few wretched fragments of the nation remained, and they were scattered in the woods. The new bishop, Saint-Vallier, later described them as living in "frightful disorder." These Algonquins had been replaced by the Abenakis whom the Jesuits led to Sillery.[2]

Among its many duties the Sovereign Council of Quebec counted the regulation of the price of wine. In 1677 the tavern-keepers of that city had petitioned against the provost's ordinance, which, by reducing the price of wine to sixteen sous a jug, threatened them with utter ruin[3] Nevertheless, the next month the general assembly of the citizens, presided over by two councillors, confirmed the

---

[1] *C.G*, vii, f 123 (Oct. 30, 1685).
[2] Rochemonteix, vol iii, p 225 (1), *Estat Présent*, p. 182.
[3] C.S., vol ii, p. 100

said ordinance at least till the arrival of the vessels from France.[1] In 1678 the retail dealers complained again. Alleging that the wholesalers' price was excessive, they begged for liberty to sell their wine at the prices it would command according to its quality. The reply of the Council was that the retailers must obey the ordinance, and that the wholesale merchants must sell a hogshead of wine for 50 livres.[2] For some time there was no further opposition.

Six years later, in the absence of La Barre and de Meulles, the Sovereign Council, with a view to breaking up monopoly and preventing "corners" in the liquor market, again fixed the wholesale prices of wine and brandy. The previous year a merchant of La Rochelle had bought up a whole cargo. This had doubled the wholesale price and rendered illusory the Council's regulations for retailers.[3]

In his dispatch to the Marquis de Seignelay, de Meulles criticized the action of the Council on the ground that hope of profit on liquors was what attracted most of the vessels which came to Canada. For the other merchandise one or two ships would suffice. In 1683 the high price of wine had brought twelve vessels to Quebec—just twice the number of the preceding year. This had resulted in a general reduction of twenty-five per cent. in the cost of other goods—truly a welcome relief to the colony. The Council's decree would prove ruinous, and even the bishop, though present, had not been in sympathy with its attitude.[4]

---

[1] *C.S*, vol ii, p 109   [2] F 3, III, f 69.

[3] F 3, IV, f 131 (Aug. 16, 1684). This merchant paid 48 livres a hogshead for wine. The attorney of the Jesuits secured 56 hogsheads "for them and for some others" at 50 livres a hogshead (*ibid.*, f. 135).

[4] *C G*, vi, f 404 (Nov 12, 1684). Meulles' opinion of the councillors was not flattering most of them were "men of little worth, unlettered and uneducated, having as their sole aim in all their actions a spirit of self-interest." Yet, being so far from the court, if they were not restrained by superior powers they would easily "set up for sovereigns and live in independence" (*ibid*, ff. 404v, 406v) *Cf Journal de Baugy*, p 153 "The best thing about them is their appetite."

M. de la Barre was quite as emphatic as his intendant. He had always found "the mind of the late M. Colbert strongly opposed to these kinds of taxes, having maintained that liberty caused abundance, and abundance, low prices."[1] As was natural, the more substantial merchants raised a clamour in support of the protests of intendant and governor. If liberty of commerce, allowed throughout the Kingdom, were suppressed in Canada, they would be ruined, or rather they would transport their wines to the Isles. The Council had fixed the selling price at 55 livres, whereas their cost price, plus their expenses, amounted to 66 livres.[2]

The king and his advisers concluded that the Council's ordinance had been "prejudicial to the colony," and so annulled it. The sale of liquors was to be free. Moreover, the councillors were forbidden to make regulations of a general character in the absence of the governor and the intendant[3]

In the course of his correspondence on the *eau-de-vie* question, M. de Meulles, like La Salle and several others, accused La Barre of an illicit interest in the fur trade. The governor had said openly that he made a "good fisher in troubled waters." So completely had he reduced Fort Frontenac to the status of a mere warehouse that, after selling their furs, some Iroquois had been able to force and pillage the fort, beat the guardian and his few companions, and drink freely of the brandy which had been prudently refused them[4]

Conclusion

In his avarice, his senile debility, and his inept military policy M. de la Barre recalls his predecessor, Jean de Lauson, although a careful comparison would favour the former. His "shameful peace" with the Iroquois was a determining

---

[1] *C.G.*, vi, f. 367.
[2] *Ibid.*
[3] B, xi, ff. 22, 23, or *C.S.*, vol ii, p. 1021.
[4] *C.G.*, vi, ff. 382v, 384.

factor in his recall,[1] but when we learn that the infirmity of age caused him an intermittent paralysis of the tongue, and that his successor hardly expected him to reach France alive,[2] we may well condone his many weaknesses.

The intendant remained in Canada until 1686 Throughout his four years of office de Meulles' position was somewhat lonely. He had made many enemies, and was rather too independent to make many friends. The intrigues of the former brought him into sudden disrepute with the court, and he had no powerful allies, religious or other, to defend him with vigour. Mother Juchereau said the complaints against him were ill-founded; he had been very equitable, and had performed his duty well, in his time vice dared not show itself[3] La Hontan agreed with the Hospitalière in vindicating the intendant's character. "I am willing to believe that he may have carried on some sort of secret commerce, nevertheless, he did wrong to nobody; on the contrary, he procured bread for a thousand poor people who would have died of hunger without his aid."[4]

It is therefore surprising to learn from the new governor, Denonville, that the retiring intendant was totally discredited, and that his conduct had always been very bad.[5] We can only conjecture that the marquis's impression was gathered from the intendant's adversaries—local judges whose exploitation of litigants he had abridged, councillors whom he had overridden, Jesuits whom he had criticized, and whom M de Denonville followed And this unfavourable impression would be deepened by de Meulles' independent aloofness from his new colleague, as well as by the probable fact that, like other officials, he had supplemented his meagre income by a little trading on the side.

Given abler support and more favourable circumstances, de Meulles would have proved a worthy successor to Talon

---

[1] B, XI, ff. 6, 10v.   [2] C G, VII, f 53 (Aug 1685).
[3] Juchereau, p 289.   [4] La Hontan, vol. 1, p. 72.   [5] C G, VII, f 110.

CHAPTER VIII

A THEOCRATIC REVIVAL

1685-1689

M. DE DENONVILLE

THE Marquis de Denonville came to Canada under the most favourable auspices. "All those who love Canada," wrote M. de Tronson, "are delighted with this choice, for he is a gentleman, wise, gentle, disinterested, and very pious, and there is every reason to hope that he will restore the country" to prosperity.[1] His disinterestedness was hardly called in question,[2] and in that he stands almost alone among the king's representatives in New France. His piety, too, was universally recognized. His orthodoxy was perhaps the more robust that his parents had been Huguenots converted to Catholicism through their own reading and reflection,[3] and after his return to France he seems to have preserved the colony from the intrusion of some "bad doctrine,"[4] possibly Jansenism.

PROTESTANTISM IN NEW FRANCE

The reader will remember that Denonville entered upon his governorship in the year of the revocation of the Edict of Nantes. Since the coming of Champlain the Canadian clergy had been solidly opposed to the toleration of heretics in New France, and Mgr. de Laval had been especially alert

---

[1] *Tronson*, vol. ii, p. 274.　　[2] *C G*, x, f. 92.
[3] *Bernières*, p. 251.　　[4] *Juchereau*, p. 304.

to ward off danger from this quarter. Usually the king's officers co-operated with him. Tracy, Talon, and Courcelle were present at the abjuration of heresy made by Captain Berthier of the Carignan regiment As the captain had embraced His Majesty's religion to the ruin of his domestic affairs, Talon obtained for him a royal grant of 1200 livres. The intendant reported that sixteen Huguenots had been converted within a month, to the glory of God and the king [1] The Jesuits were indefatigable proselytizers, and visited every incoming ship. Their success was commensurate with their persuasiveness and skill [2] As useful auxiliaries they had the Hospitalières On one occasion a stubborn Huguenot, fallen ill, was converted by the ingenuity of a nun who mixed in his drink some pulverized bones of the martyr Brébeuf This intractable heretic became instantly as gentle as an angel and abjured his heresy.[3] In spite of the activity of his allies Laval was still dissatisfied. In a memoir of 1670 he urged that French merchants be forbidden to send Protestant agents to Canada These Huguenots discoursed persuasively, lent books, and assembled themselves together. With New England so near, an increase in their numbers would give occasion to revolutions in the future.[4] In 1676 a royal ordinance forbade Huguenots to winter in Canada without special permission, and prohibited all public exercise of the reformed religion.[5] To encourage conversions to the Faith, the Sovereign Council joined the other forces of Church and State In 1677 it accorded a recent convert the rights and privileges of a citizen of New France upon condition that he cultivated the soil like the other habitants.[6] Colbert, to whom commerce was of supreme importance, alone seemed inclined to favour the Protestant merchants Laval's grand vicar urged the

---

[1] *C G*, II, ff 155, 206
[2] *Journal*, pp. 74, 334.
[3] Juchereau, p 180
[4] *Coll MSS*, vol. 1, p 204.
[5] *C G*, IV, f. 142.
[6] *C S*, vol ii, p 174

English peril once more upon his attention, but with slight result. All the minister would concede was that Huguenots obliged to winter in Canada must present their reasons to the intendant, who might give permits for one year only [1] Such privileges are easily abused, and in 1682 the bishop complained of the infringement of the royal decree. He also protested, though in vain, against a Protestant fishing station in Acadia.[2]

In 1685 his successor, the Abbé de Saint-Vallier, demanded of M. de Denonville that a certain Rochelais family be prevented from passing the winter at Quebec. Although these Huguenots had rendered great service to the country by their commerce, the marquis felt it his duty to comply.[3] The intendant, de Meulles, inquired whether Protestant merchants without families might winter at Quebec "because of the important obligations they may have there."[4] However, the following year Louis XIV expressed the hope that Denonville would strive to bring the heretics of Canada to abjure, like their co-religionaries in France. "Nevertheless, if there be found among them some opinionated persons who refuse to take instruction, he may make use of the soldiers to place garrisons in their houses or have them imprisoned, joining to this rigour the necessary care for their instruction In this he ought to act in concert with the bishop"[5] Naturally inclined to gentle measures, the governor assured the king that there were hardly any more heretics. "If a few remain, we will take care to make them change, and we will not suffer them to exercise their religion . . The Jesuits carry on a mission every day in the ships from France for the sake of new converts."[6] Indeed, we find no record of harsh treatment of Canadian Protestants. There was no need of imprisonment or billetings or dragonnades A handful of Huguenot soldiers or

[1] *Rapport*, pp. c, cxi   [2] *C.G*, vi, ff 94v, 114.   [3] *Ibid.*, vii, f. 101.
[4] *Ibid*, f 140v   [5] B, xii, f 26   [6] *C G.*, viii, f 132.

traders isolated in a solidly Catholic population could seldom escape the network of proselytizing influences which enveloped them

La Hontan [1] regrets that the Protestants affected by the revocation were not sent to Canada. Given assurances of religious liberty, numbers of them would have settled there without difficulty. The reflection of the baron is obviously just. The situation had changed since the days when the cardinal-statesman planned the conversion of a continent by means of a Catholic colony. Since the time of Talon attention had been concentrated upon the French rather than upon the Indian population of America. Under royal direction immigration had been encouraged, but the population was still disappointingly small. Accordingly one might almost expect that an asylum in New France would have been offered the fleeing Huguenots after 1685. What the results, immediate and ultimate, would have been is matter for speculation; but of one thing we are sure, viz. that the whole Canadian clergy would be invincibly hostile to an influx of heretics into Canada. Throughout the century their opposition to Protestant immigration had been energetic and unswerving. Their influence over Denonville and de Meulles' successor, Champigny, would have secured the support of the king's representatives in combating any measure of toleration which might be proposed. Moreover, at this time the power of the Society of Jesus at the court of France was very considerable, and doubtless the Jesuits of the mother country were of one mind with those of the colony on such an important question of general policy.

Governor and Bishop

The administration of Denonville was a halcyon period in the internal politics of Canada. After the eternal squab-

[1] Vol. ii, p. 83.

blings of previous governorships it is restful to peruse the official correspondence of a time when all the heads of Church and State were in complete harmony "It could be wished," wrote the marquis afterwards, "that in all Christendom the clergy were as saintly as it is in all New France." [1]

The Abbé de Saint-Vallier was recommended to Denonville as a "man of exemplary piety," [2] and upon their arrival at Quebec the governor begged the Sovereign Council to show great consideration for a "person of such great merit" [3] There was little danger of trouble with the Council, for Denonville always sought to avoid unnecessary responsibility, and neither he nor the new bishop was "curious to judge lawsuits" [4] When the uncompromising de Meulles was recalled, and M. de Champigny became intendant, the charmed circle was complete. Denonville assured the minister that everybody was pleased with Champigny; that henceforth unity was assured among Council, bishop, intendant, and governor; and that they would work solely for the good of the colony.[5] Champigny fitted perfectly into his new environment. Like Duchesneau before him, he praised all the clergy indiscriminately, and of the Jesuits in particular he reported: "It does not seem to me that they meddle with things other than those that concern their institution." [6] For once in the history of the country we find a governor and an intendant who are both to the liking of the ecclesiastics. "One could not choose," wrote Saint-Vallier, "two men better fitted for the two offices of which His Majesty has judged them worthy" [7] And Mesdames de Denonville and de Champigny were not excluded from the prelate's eulogy.

Had the governor and his lady not been exceptionally submissive to episcopal authority, or plentifully endowed

---

[1] C.G., XI, f. 187 (1690)   [2] B, XI, f. 7   [3] C.G., II, f. 78.
[4] Ibid, VI, f. 60.   [5] Ibid, VIII, f. 129
[6] Ibid, f. 239   [7] Estat, p. 232.

with good humour, one of the bishop's first acts might have irritated them greatly. Rightfully considering himself the guardian of public morals, and alarmed at the luxury and gaiety of Quebec society, he addressed to the governor and *gouvernante* certain counsels "upon their obligation to set a good example to the people." This remarkable document condemned sumptuous repasts, late hours, balls and dancing, comedies and other declamations, costly garments, "nudities of shoulders and throats," and, finally, irreverence in church. It also regulated the social life of the Château, and was especially solicitous for the welfare of Mademoiselle.[1] However, this consecrated aggressiveness seems to have been taken in good part, and the friendship between the civil and the religious heads of Canada continued unbroken to the end.

Nevertheless, when Denonville was looking forward to his great campaign of 1687 against the Senecas, he foresaw trouble with the discouraged habitants, and wished Mgr. de Laval would return in the spring. "Throughout the colony he seems to me to hold so strongly the heart of all the people that his presence here would be very useful to persuade them gently to do with good grace that which one might be obliged to make them do by force."[2] Although Laval himself did not return at once, his grand vicars, Bernières and Ango, rendered the governor effective aid. Finding the people disgusted with the memory of La Barre's fiasco, Denonville issued a manifesto on the motives of the war. To this was joined the grand vicars' charge, which declared that the Church considered this a holy war, since it was "undertaken against the infidels who opposed Christianity most strongly." At mass the priests were to say the orison *contra paganos*, and

---

[1] *Mandements*, pp. 170-4
[2] C.G., VIII, f 163 (1686). Saint-Vallier returned to France to be consecrated in the autumn of 1686, but Denonville evidently expected him back in 1687.

all the curés were to read publicly the governor's manifesto, which would show " the justice of this enterprise and the holiness of this war." In his proclamation Denonville announced his aim as the glory of God " through the humiliation of this infidel nation which contemns the voice of God who is calling it, . . in order to avenge the cause of Jesus Christ, punish the injustices done to our French people, and the infraction of the last peace." The grand vicars exhorted all true sons of the Church to second with all their might the intentions of His Majesty and the enterprises of M. de Denonville The appeal was remarkably successful, and all the people set out on the march "with extreme gaiety." [1]

Meanwhile Saint-Valher had been pleading the cause of his new diocese at the court of France. He dwelt upon the poverty as well as upon the saintliness of the Canadian Church The Seminary was well built, but without revenues, the chapter of seventeen persons had but 2000 livres of income, the bishopric received less than 2000, there was no episcopal residence, although one was available for 15,000 francs.[2] The king's response was prompt and fairly generous He strengthened the bishopric with another abbey; granted Saint-Valher 15,000 francs in order that the bishop might no longer be obliged to live in what Champigny called a " tiny cell of his Seminary "; and gave this Seminary, because of its " great poverty," 2000 livres for the maintenance of its aged missionaries.[3]

The " great poverty " of the Seminary was not due to indolence, for the governor and intendant remarked with approval its saw-mill at the Baie St. Paul, which turned out twenty-five thousand planks per annum.[4] However, its priests were seldom accused of a mercenary spirit, and in a

---

[1] C G , IX, f 21 ; F 3, VI, ff 288, 291 (April 24, 1687)   [2] F, III, f 24.
[3] Estat, p. 226 , C G., VIII, f. 240v ; B, XIII, f. 18.
[4] C G , x, f 8 (Nov. 6, 1688)

A THEOCRATIC REVIVAL

booklet entitled *L'Estat Présent de l'Eglise du Canada*, which Saint-Vallier published in Paris early in 1688, he extolled their " spirit of detachment, which was one of the principal beauties of the newborn Church of Jerusalem in the time of the Apostles "[1] The bishop was doomed to regret his eulogy not only of the Seminary whose bitter adversary he became, but also of Canada in general. Upon his return in the summer of 1688 he seems to have felt disillusioned. In one sermon he blamed the sins of the people for the ills with which the country was overwhelmed. " This discourse," says a contemporary, " only increased the murmurs of his auditors, who attributed them to causes human rather than divine " After this Saint-Vallier felt obliged to suppress the two hundred copies of his panegyric which he had brought over with him.[2]

The Tithes

Before leaving France the first time Saint-Vallier had accepted the court's views on the troublesome question of tithes.[3] In the autumn of 1685 he agreed with governor and intendant to place the minimum salary of the curates at 400 livres, whereas even Frontenac had set it at 500. The tithes amounted to about 6200 livres, and the king contributed 8000 more Thus for 1686 the number of curés was to be raised only from twenty-five to thirty-six, although the court acknowledged that the colony needed fifty-one.[4] Nor was there any hope of a substantial increase in the tithes, which in the opinion of Saint-Vallier, Denonville, and Champigny could not be raised to one-thirteenth without overburdening the habitants[5] One cause of the small yield from the tithes was that Laval had exempted the domains of the Seminary and of the Jesuits because of

[1] P 28   [2] *C.G*, x, f 86   [3] B, xi, f. 8v.
[4] B, xii, f 7.   [5] *C G.*, viii, f. 240.

their services to the infant Church of Canada [1] Even Champigny felt this to be unjust. " The ecclesiastics," he said, " pay no tithes on their lands, and they ought to do so since they possess the finest in the country." [2] A few years later Saint-Vallier complained that it was the example of the Seminary which prevented the Jesuits and the nuns also from paying the tithe.[3] The whole trouble was that, as Champigny reported at the close of the century, the life of the ecclesiastics and the religious orders was " poor and mortified," lacking many of the necessaries of life.[4] The life of the tillers of the soil was at least as hard. In 1700 Callières and Champigny declared that, if His Majesty were to discontinue his annual bounty of 8000 livres, " it would be absolutely impossible to maintain more than eight or nine curés, as the others subsist chiefly through this supplement, since the tithes are not yet considerable." [5]

Sulpicians and Governors

From the outset of his administration Governor Denonville showed his appreciation of the Sulpicians of Montreal. He commended their efforts to develop the Island and fortify it with wind-mills. He would influence his soldiers to settle there rather than elsewhere. As " one could not be worse lodged than the ecclesiastics " were, he approved of their resolution to build themselves a house. The Sulpicians received a still clearer mark of his confidence when he advised that their Seminary should have control of the curacies between Montreal and Sorel because the Seminary of Quebec was so far away.[6] His Majesty left this proposal to the discretion of the bishop.[7]

[1] F, III, ff 68, 70 (1684, 1682).
[2] C.G., XI, f. 265 (1691).
[3] Rapport, 1887, p. liv.
[4] C.G., XVII, f. 66.
[5] Ibid., XVIII (Oct 18, 1700)
[6] Ibid., VII, f. 179v; VIII, ff. 133, 163.
[7] B, XIII, f. 18v.

A THEOCRATIC REVIVAL

During this administration the Sulpicians were enjoying equally harmonious relations with Perrot's successor, M. de Callières, who had restored peace and order throughout the Island. Montreal "had need of such a governor," observed Denonville.[1]

THE RÉCOLLETS

In spite of Le Tac's assertion in his *Histoire Chronologique* · "A bishop, a governor, an intendant act unanimously and work ceaselessly to overthrow, and dash to the ground, these poor religious,"[2] the Minor Brothers of St. Francis seem to have been fairly well treated during this governorship. Denonville had orders to befriend them; Champigny approved them, and Saint-Vallier employed them like the rest.[3] On one occasion only does the governor seem to have aroused their collective resentment, and then, as we shall see, he was impelled by military reasons.

THE CIVILIZATION OF THE INDIANS

As we have observed already, Denonville sympathized and co-operated with bishop and Sulpicians and the religious forces of the colony in general. However, it was in the Jesuits, above all others, that he placed his confidence, especially in Indian affairs. Not long after his arrival he wrote the Marquis de Seignelay upon the old question of how best to civilize the Indians. Here he opposes Louis XIV's pet notions and clearly adopts the Jesuit position. Recalling the old idea that the proximity of the natives to French settlements would aid in Frenchifying and Christianizing them, he continues : " Monseigneur, I perceive that just the opposite has happened For, instead

---

[1] *C G.*, VI, f. 443, VII, ff. 88v, 164. [2] P. 7.
[3] B, XI, f. 8; *C.G.*, VIII, f. 239v; *Estat*, p. 18.

of becoming accustomed to our laws, I assure you that they communicate to us all that is worst about them, and take to themselves only what is bad and vicious in us." The Indians who roamed about the seigneuries caused great injury to the colony, for the sons of the seigneurs imitated their vagabond life and debauched their women. By means of these Indians the habitants could mock at the regulations concerning the fur trade. Finally, drunkenness caused horrible irregularities among them.[1] The following year Denonville reiterated his views. These wandering Indians learned "a thousand nasty tricks" from French libertines; while French children, following Indian example, would learn neither "subjection nor obedience," but strayed aimlessly hither and thither as fancy led them.[2] These extracts suffice to show us that Denonville's opinions on this subject agreed with those long since enunciated by the Jesuits. A memoir summed up their missionary experience thus "It has always been recognized that the neighbourhood of Europeans . has been a great hindrance to the conversion of infidels, and the fruit is always incomparably greater, prompter, and more constant while among Indians and savages there are no Europeans other than the missionaries."[3] Years later their feelings had not changed From Michilimackinac Father Carheil warned Callières: "We must be delivered from the commandants and their garrisons, who, far from being necessary, are on the contrary so pernicious that we can say truthfully that they are the greatest evil of our missions." He wished that all Frenchmen would stay in the French colony and let the Indians carry their furs to them there.[4]

If then Denonville, like the Jesuits, was opposed to the mingling of the two races, what alternative proposal had he to offer for the civilization of the natives? Simply the

[1] *C G.*, VII, f. 90. [2] *Ibid.*, VIII, f. 146.
[3] *Ibid.*, XII, f. 382 (1693). [4] M 204 (1702).

A THEOCRATIC REVIVAL

formation of new *bourgades,* like those of Sillery, Lorette, the Prairie, and the Mountain "Assuredly there is no town or village in France as well regulated as all those places." [1] They contain " a very great number of good Christians who shame us by their zeal and fervour." [2] Denonville did not distinguish between Sulpician methods and Jesuit methods within the bounds of these tiny village states.[3] At the Mountain a priest of St Sulpice taught the Indian boys French, music, trades, and, above all, agriculture.[4] Abbé de Belmont was replacing Indian cabins by French houses, and giving his converts some pigs and poultry. Commenting upon these efforts to gallicize the natives, Denonville remarked that in order to succeed the mission would have to be richer than it was.[5] However, he commended Jesuits and Sulpicians alike, and ignored the rivalry between the Madeleine and the Mountain.

What gratified him most of all was the valorous conduct of the Christian Indians in the campaign against the Senecas " We must have Christian Indians in the war," he wrote, " because if we had none in a certain enterprise, the hostile savages would harass us continually on the wings and at the rear." [6] The Iroquois of the Madeleine had been won for the French from the English by Jesuit patriotism, and Denonville entreated the king to aid in the maintenance of this mission He agreed with Saint-Vallier that the Indian converts were " equally attached to the Christian religion and to the interests of France."

At the same time Intendant Champigny was praising the

[1] *C.G*, VII, f 90.　　　　　　　　[2] *C G*, VIII, f. 146
[3] *Cf* Rochemonteix, vol III, p 389　　[4] *Estat*, p 68.
[5] *C.G*, VII, f 106 (1685). The Mission of the Mountain continued to prosper, and three years later Belmont sent his superior an account of his orchards, poultry, and fountain Tronson replied playfully " Only take care that it does not happen to you as it happened to the Seminary of Autun, which they made so handsome that the ladies of the town chose it for their promenades" (*Tronson,* vol II, p 299)
[6] *C.G.*, IX, f 72v.

mission at Sillery, where, at great cost, the Jesuits had assembled seven hundred Abenakis, enemies of the Iroquois. In the words of a contemporary memoir these Abenakis were " the bravest of all the Indians and the most redoubtable to the English " In the autumn of 1687 Father Bigot, superior of Sillery, journeyed toward Boston with some of his neophytes in order to induce their relatives to join the French forces the following spring. The Abenaki mission was soon moved to St François de Sales. According to Denonville this new mission covered Quebec, and until it was taken Quebec would not be attacked. " The good understanding " existing between him and the Abenakis, thanks to the Jesuits, resulted in the capture of sixteen English forts and the slaughter of two hundred men by these new allies in the summer of 1689.[1] Denonville emphasized the fact that the Iroquois Christians fought unhesitatingly against their relatives from the cantons [2] Four years later, when Frontenac was criticizing the conduct of these same converts under similar circumstances and making insinuations against their Jesuit pastors,[3] Champigny came to their support. Upon the request of the Jesuits, and for the sake of the truth, he certified that since 1684 the Christian Iroquois had combated faithfully against the enemy; that they had even slain some of their own relatives; and that they had lost sixty of their warriors, killed or burned.[4]

In his memoir of 1690 Denonville voiced the sentiment of the intendant as well as his own : " It is of consequence that the Indians be governed only by the missionaries, and that the governor-general and the intendant be always in agreement with them for the general government of the

---

[1] C G., VIII, ff 132, 239v ; IX, ff 3v, 72v, 130v, X, f. 322 ; XI, ff. 185v, 186 ; *Estat*, p. 255. In the margin of the memoir aforesaid the Jesuit policy of " domesticating " the Abenakis at Quebec is criticized · " We believe it much more important to leave them in their ancient residences . . . to make war on the English." This was probably Seignelay's view.

[2] C G., IX, f 65   [3] C.G., XI, ff 233, 236   [4] *Ibid*, f 141, *cf*. f. 258.

country. Otherwise one will be exposed every day to a thousand annoyances into which one is dragged by the interests of individuals who are led by avarice alone "[1] These individuals revealed their avarice most clearly in the fire-water traffic with the Indians.

THE BRANDY TRADE

Nowhere did Denonville and Champigny co-operate more whole-heartedly with the ecclesiastics than in the attempt to control the traders of the Upper Lakes. By order of the governor the merchants possessed of the twenty-five annual *congés* were to choose *canoteurs* who did not trade brandy unlawfully or debauch themselves with Indian women. On leaving Michilimackinac or Sault Ste Marie the commandant of each canoe must bring back a testimonial of life and conduct from M. de la Durantaye, general commandant, or from Father Enjalran, superior of the Ottawa missions. The individual traders must also keep one or both of these men informed as to their whereabouts [2]

A little later the governor assured Seignelay that heretofore the licensed canoes had been freighted not with legitimate merchandise, but almost exclusively with *eau-de-vie*. In defiance of the king's orders the libertines had dared to carry one hundred hogsheads to Michilimackinac in a single year, where they plunged into such excesses that it was a wonder the Indians had not killed them all to guarantee themselves against their violence and to rescue their wives and daughters from them. " All that," he added, " to-

[1] *C.G.*, XI, f. 188v.
[2] F 3, IV, f 243 (Jan 29, 1686) Enjalran was less severe than the other Jesuits in his views of the brandy trade and of the commerce of soldiers with Indian women Broad-minded and tolerant, but out of sympathy with the ideas of the other missionaries, he was recalled in 1688 (Rochemonteix, vol. iii, p 512)

gether with the last war, has won us such great contempt among all the tribes that we ought not to think of retrieving ourselves except by our own effort."¹ In the Ottawa region, said Denonville, the Jesuits needed the protection of the Marquis de Seignelay; they were thwarted by all these libertines, for the Indians saw that Frenchmen did not practise what the missionaries preached²

Like Frontenac before him, the marquis made vigorous war upon these *coureurs de bois*, who mocked at the ordinances prohibiting them from carrying brandy to the Indian tribes When they returned home they gave themselves the airs of noblemen, spent their gains at the cabaret, despised the peasants, and refused to marry their daughters. Their one thought was of plunging again into the forest³ Accordingly, military officers as well as traders, furnished with passports, were authorized to arrest and pillage the deserters, and fire upon them if they resisted. If traders with passports were found with more brandy than ten jugs each at the commencement of their voyage, the officers were to seize it, throw it away, and report the offenders. They were likewise to arrest and pillage foreigners trading without permission on French soil.⁴

While Denonville naturally felt most anxiety over the conditions existing in regions for whose good government he was directly responsible, his interest extended even to Acadia, whence the new bishop, Saint-Vallier, had just returned. There were hardly any Indians left in Acadia; they were dead, for the most part, of debauches of *eau-de-vie*.⁵ So completely had the apprehensions of Father Biard been justified!⁶ The bishop himself was hopeful that the rest of them, in embracing Christianity, would lose their passion for alcohol and repopulate their country.⁷

---

[1] *C G.*, VIII, ff 21, 61v [2] *C.G.*, XI, f. 187v. [3] *Ibid.*, f 188v.
[4] F 3, IV, f 250 [5] *C.G.*, VIII, f. 129v.
[6] *Rel.*, 1611, pp. 14, 15 [7] *Estat*, p 42

A THEOCRATIC REVIVAL

The former intendant, de Meulles, was now in Acadia, and his ordinance issued at Beaubassin, February 1, 1686, throws light upon the situation as he found it. The same abuses flourished there as in the valley of the St Lawrence. The natives, overwhelmed with debts and persecuted by unscrupulous creditors, sometimes went over to the English. De Meulles' ordinance vigorously defended the oppressed Indians, and charged the "honour and conscience" of the settlers not to sell them brandy otherwise than "prudently and with knowledge" of their necessity and the good use they would make of it. The fines were to go to the repair of the parish church.[1] In his memorial of 1690 Denonville observed that the inhabitants of Acadia as well as of Canada had thought more of the beaver and brandy trade than of establishing fisheries, although the latter industry was far better adapted to the real needs of the colony.[2]

We now turn to the sedentary missions within the colony. For a long time Lorette had been a flourishing mission, but the traders succeeded in penetrating its walls of priestly defence, and, "Now," wrote Chaumonot, "the village is very unsettled, soiled with drunkenness and impurity." It appears that after 1690 a reform was wrought through the remarkable personality of Father Michel Germain, who influenced the neophytes to make and keep a vow of abstinence.[3]

Denonville's admiration for the Iroquois mission at the Madeleine was unbounded It was a leaven which might work the conversion of all the nation; but it would have to be withdrawn from Montreal, where intemperance would cause its ruin.[4] In this conclusion the governor endorsed

---

[1] F 3, IV, f. 247   [2] C.G, XI, f 190.
[3] Rochemonteix, vol III, pp. 392-4. In 1686 an Indian from the mission of Lorette, infuriated because a tavern-keeper refused him more brandy, killed him with a spade The Indian deeply regretted his drunken deed, and received a royal pardon for a crime committed in "the heat of *eau-de-vie* and of anger" (B, XV, f 10v).   [4] C.G, XI, f. 186

the Jesuit view that a policy of isolation alone could effect the salvation of the mission Indians.

In spite of their desire to suppress drunken disorders, both colonial and home governments treated intoxicated Indians as practically irresponsible. In 1686 a drunken Indian, related to the Iroquois of the Madeleine, slew a settler. However, the following year he redeemed himself by his courage in slaying an enemy of the French, and, doubtless with a view to encouraging loyalty, Denonville besought for him the royal pardon.[1]

Among the French colonists themselves the ravages of alcohol were sufficiently grave. One great evil was the "infinity of taverns." The trade of cabaretier attracted all the rogues and loungers. The seigneurs ought to appoint or dismiss the tavern-keepers of their villages according to their good or ill behaviour. In some seigneuries with only twenty dwellings more than half of these were taverns. At Three Rivers there were twenty-five houses, and in eighteen or twenty of them drinks were sold. Villemarie and Quebec were on the same footing. Besides all this, there existed in the depths of the forest some wretched cabins where every kind of disorder reigned.[2] The influence of such conditions upon the character of the people was deplorable. For work upon the fortifications masons would have to be brought from France, since the workmen of Canada were "drunkards so inveterate and so lazy that one could not count upon them."[3] The Sovereign Council followed up the governor's suggestion by enacting that no one could keep tavern without permission of judge or seigneur. Only persons of good reputation were to receive permits.[4] Apparently Frontenac's effort in this direction had proved abortive.[5]

[1] C.G., IX, f. 17v; cf. B, XV, f. 10v.
[2] Ibid., f. 92.
[3] C.G., VIII, f. 141.
[4] C.G., X, f. 314 (March 21, 1689).
[5] F 3, II, f. 112.

Turning now to the general discussion of the brandy question which was carried on between Quebec and Versailles during this administration, we observe that upon their departure for Canada both Denonville and Champigny had been warned that, with or without the goodwill of the clergy, the royal ordinance of May 24, 1679, must be enforced.[1] However, three months after his arrival the marquis in a dispatch to Seignelay vigorously denounced the fraud and deceit attendant upon the sale of fire-water to the natives. It had driven an entire Indian village at Chambly to desert to the English and to remain there for fear of the accumulated debts charged against it in Canada by unscrupulous traders. The ordinance of 1679 was ineffective, because the Indians got liquor wholesale in the colony and carried it home; they accomplished with impunity what was forbidden to the French.[2]

In August 1688 Denonville drew up for the minister a "Memorial of one of the greatest woes of the Colony." Indulgence in liquor was so excessive that he foresaw nothing less than the ruin of the country. Twenty years before there had been two thousand Indians, hereditary enemies of the Iroquois, living in the French settlements. Now, one could not gather together thirty of them. Brandy had slain them: he was persuaded of this, because he himself had seen so many die from its effects. Even the white men born in the country did not grow to old age. Hard drinkers, especially the *coureurs de bois*, were broken down before forty. In his voyages Denonville had remarked how the Canadians, fatigued in passing the rapids, would seek to regain strength by taking the neck of the brandy barrel in their mouths, and drinking a pint or sometimes a gallon. After that they felt strong and passed their rapid. Then they went to sleep without eating, having no appetite until evening, when the fumes were dissipated. In all the taverns

[1] B, xi, ff. 10, 14 ; B, xii, f. 5.   [2] C.G., vii, f. 91

the ordinary practice was to drink a pint of brandy after a generous quantity of wine. "What ravages in a poor stomach with these mixtures!" Some of the women get drunk also. The finest regulations failed before the subtleties of buyer and seller. True, *eau-de-vie* was in itself a necessity; but it ought not to be sold to the Indians at all. Even the English governor, Dongan, had forbidden its sale the previous winter under heavy penalties. In closing this memorial Denonville protested to Seignelay that he had not allowed himself to be prejudiced, still less to be governed by any one.[1]

The memorial of the governor was supported by a dispatch of the intendant. He recounted the visit of forty-five canoes of Ottawas for the fur trade: the Indians got drunk and uttered frightful howlings. Assuredly the royal ordinance of 1679 was inadequate. When the Iroquois and other tribes had come to Montreal to treat of peace, Denonville and Champigny had considered it imperative to suspend for a month the right to sell liquor to the Indians. The intendant awaited new orders on this subject.[2]

A little later, in a joint letter to the minister, Denonville and Champigny claimed to have certain knowledge that brandy was the principal cause of all the troubles connected with the fur trade, but unless it were entirely interdicted under heavy penalties they found all remedies impossible.[3]

It is worthy of remark that, when we find a governor and an intendant working together harmoniously and disinterestedly, to the satisfaction of king, minister, and people, these two heads of the colony should incline toward the total suppression of the brandy trade with the natives.

Nevertheless, Seignelay replied courteously but firmly that the king was unwilling to deprive his subjects of this commerce to the advantage of their English rivals. Severe

---

[1] C.G., X, 1.72. [2] Ibid., f. 125 (Aug 8, 1688).
[3] Ibid., f. 12v (Nov. 6, 1688).

punishment would prevent excesses.¹ Champigny promised to obey the king's pleasure ²

Seignelay wrote also to Bishop Saint-Vallier as follows: His Majesty

desires that on your side you prevent the ecclesiastics from troubling consciences by threats of interdiction of the sacraments against those who sell *eau-de-vie* according to regulation. It is certain that if this commerce were forbidden the subjects of His Majesty it would fall at once into the hands of the English, who would thereby entice the Indians, so that the result would be, in absolutely preventing the French from selling, to enrich the English at their expense and to ruin the colony, without stopping the disorder . . ³

In a memoir of this same year, 1689, the attorney-general, Auteuil, though a close friend of the Jesuits, pointed out that the English were dangerous rivals already. They sold their merchandise and their rum very cheap "Otherwise the Indians would prefer to trade with the French, for they like their temper better, and they prefer their *eau-de-vie* to rum arrack." ⁴

Another memoir suggested a new danger. According to law, when English colonial merchants imported brandy from France they were obliged to warehouse it in England —an operation which doubled its cost. But the author of our memoir suspected that some French ships, after making declaration in leaving port that they were bound for Acadia, discharged their cargoes of brandy in the neighbourhood of New England. This brandy, having thus escaped all taxes, could be sold cheaper than the brandy of Quebec, which had to pay an entry duty ⁵ If this suspicion was well founded the illegal commerce was evidently suppressed, for we find no further reference to it

¹ *C G*, x, f. 186, B, xv, f 51v
² *Ibid*, f. 247v.
³ B, xv, f 62v (May 20, 1689).
⁴ *C.G.*, x, f 345
⁵ *C G*, IX, f 150 (1687).

In November 1689 an anonymous writer, apparently a friend of Frontenac, suggested that " those who have been in authority lately in Canada (evidently meaning Denonville) have allowed themselves to be led too much by the ecclesiastics, whose obstinacy is extreme." Those who were going to be in authority would always fear to thwart the clergy, and so Seignelay ought to write strongly to Frontenac, who was returning to Canada, and to Champigny, in order to exculpate them in the eyes of the ecclesiastics. He might even write to the bishop [1] Whether or not he was influenced by this suggestion, in July 1690 the minister wrote Saint-Vallier that all the merchants and most of the habitants were complaining that they were disquieted in their commerce in brandy and even in wine by the " immoderate zeal " of a few ecclesiastics.

> It appears to me to be of great consequence that you take pains to examine very carefully what takes place in this regard . . . in order that you may reduce them to the bounds within which they ought to keep themselves in their ministry, in order not to fall into the mistake of troubling consciences inopportunely. It would even be well for you to observe that their zeal may be excited by private views [2] It is certain that the subjects of the king cannot carry on in Canada any other commerce as useful to the Kingdom as that of wine and of brandy; also that there is none other in which they have such a great advantage over the English and Dutch [3]

At the same time the court sent Frontenac and Champigny instructions which emphasized the necessity rather of protecting the traders than of enforcing the law.[4]

However, Denonville was not easily silenced, and, after his return to France, he prepared another memorial in which he vigorously attacked the trade that he regarded as the peril and curse of Canada. " Avarice alone has made those

---

[1] *C G*., x, f 323 (Nov. 18, 1689).
[2] Vues particulières [3] B, xv, f 16v (July 14, 1690)
[4] *Ibid*., ff 11v, 16 (1690); *cf* f 81v (1689).

say the contrary who thought to enrich themselves by this wretched traffic." And yet recent experience had proven this a vain hope, of late years no one had really become rich thereby. As for its ravages among the Indians, it was "the horror of horrors," the "image of hell." One must have seen it to believe it. Next, Denonville challenged Seignelay's patriotic argument and denied that the Indians would desert to the English "For it is certain that they do not care about drinking as long as they see no brandy, and the most reasonable (of them) wish that there had never been any." The union of the clergy with the governor and intendant was the unique means of governing well a country whose people were not easy to lead [1]

Up to the present we have been treating the liquor question during Denonville's administration in so far as it concerned New France alone But the same question promised to take on something of an international character as well, for the marquis opened up negotiations with Governor Dongan, a co-religionist. In June 1686 he pleaded the cause of the Jesuit missionaries among the Iroquois. "You know better than I what they have borne, the tortures they have suffered, and the fatigues they undergo daily for the name of Jesus Christ . . You are a gentleman who loves religion. Cannot you and I come to an understanding for the maintenance of our missionaries?" English traders injured religion not only when they sold the Iroquois brandy, but also when they sold them fire-arms to make war on New France, the home of the missionaries.[2]

We observe that Denonville's motives were political as well as religious. Toward the end of September he wrote again, asking Dongan to help him to restrain the insolence of these enemies of the Faith. "Do you believe, sir, that religion can make any progress while your merchants give brandy in abundance, which, as you ought to know,

[1] *C G*, XI, f. 186 (Jan. 1690)   [2] *State Papers*, pp 196, 197.

makes (the Iroquois) like demons and their cabins images and spectacles of hell?"[1]

Dongan replied that he had always been a protector of the Jesuit missionaries. Moreover, he had asked the king of England for "priests to preach the Gospel to the natives who are our allies." As to the liquor trade, he observed: "Assuredly our rum does no more harm than *eau-de-vie*, and even in the opinion of the most learned physicians it is more healthful Nevertheless, it is well to conserve those people in temperance and sobriety. Nay, it is a praiseworthy and Christian action. But forbid them all sorts of strong liquors—that would be rather hard on them and very similar to Mahometanism."[2]

This response was probably not entirely satisfactory to Denonville the English governor was merely hedging. At all events, the following summer, when the marquis had arrested in Lake Huron fifty Englishmen whose canoes were charged with merchandise, especially brandy, he wrote to Dongan that he would detain them until suitable assurances were given that the last treaty of neutrality between their two kings would be executed: for Dongan was accused of furnishing the Iroquois with munitions of war.[3] In fact, a letter from a M Riverin accuses Dongan himself of having sent the aforesaid traders up the Lakes "equipped with merchandise and, above all, with brandy, of which they (the English) do not make a case of conscience as we do."[4]

What was the direct effect of Denonville's warning we cannot say, for about the same time Dongan was urged by Peter Schuyler to prohibit the sale of strong drink to the Iroquois for two or three months: they stayed at Schenectady drinking continually, and so incapacitated

[1] *C G*, VIII, f 102 (Sept 29, 1686). [2] *Ibid.*, f. 174v.
[3] *Clair.*, 1016, f. 482 (Aug 22, 1687).
[4] *Ibid.*, f. 485 (Nov. 3, 1687).

themselves for resisting the armed invasion of their cantons by the French.[1]

This argument seems calculated to appeal to Governor Dongan much more forcibly than Denonville's plea for the evangelization of the Iroquois by French Jesuits. However that may be, he did prohibit the sale of brandy to the Iroquois, and this evoked an expression of pleasure from the marquis, who doubtless mistook the motive. "The only thing," he urged, "is to continue on your side as we will do on ours."[2]

In the mind of the French governor, though the religious motive was sincere, it did not obliterate the political reason, and it was the latter which he emphasized in his letters to Seignelay. The only way, he said, to restore peace with the Five Nations was to make them receive the Jesuits amongst them again. Even if the Iroquois cantons did belong to the English, the French monarch alone could send missionaries there, since the king of England had none for that purpose "And with these missionaries (protected by the king of England) we shall govern them But to succeed in this the king must engage the king of England to prohibit, under severe penalties, the sale of any brandy to the Indians," for no missionary could stay with them unless the trade in *eau-de-vie* were absolutely suppressed [3]

In this last sentence, for the first time, we find an adequate proposal for the solution of this whole vexed question. In spite of their intense hostility to the traffic which was ruining their missions, none of the ecclesiastics had grasped the idea of an international agreement. Denonville's plea was the right one, but it was premature. The court was not interested, and the time was not ripe

---

[1] *State Papers* (Sept 2, 1687).   [2] C.G , x, f. 57 (July 5, 1688)
[3] *Ibid* , ff 68v, 104   It was the fire-water traffic which had forced the Jesuits to abandon the strategic post of Pentagouet (f. 105v).

We have quoted Denonville as saying that, with the Jesuits in the cantons, the French could govern the Iroquois. This suggests our next topic, for, even more than his predecessors, the marquis employed the missionaries as political agents.

THE JESUITS AS FRENCH AMBASSADORS

At the governor's call the dauntless sons of Loyola were ever ready for any sacrifice. Father Silvie, with the Chevalier de Troyes, accomplished a hazardous journey into the Hudson Bay region.[1] At Michilimackinac, in collaboration with the Sieur de la Durantaye, the Jesuit Enjalran saved Canada from disaster by preventing the Hurons and Ottawas from allying themselves with the Senecas and trading with the English "Except for Father Enjalran," declared Denonville, "the Iroquois would have been at Michilimackinac long ago."[2]

Unlike Frontenac, Denonville considered the Jesuits the only satisfactory interpreters. With one exception all the professionals were *coureurs de bois*, "not very expert and mostly rogues," who always said too much or too little, and made endless trouble. Accordingly, the governor requested the Jesuit Millet to act as interpreter at Cataraqui and to communicate with Father Lamberville of Onondaga. This step caused indignation among the Récollets, for Father Millet replaced one of their missionaries. Denonville explained to Seignelay that the change was temporary but imperative, because the Récollet, not knowing "two words of the Iroquois language," was "useless for the service of the king." Without the knowledge and skill of Father Millet the negotiations with the cantons would have failed.[3] Although His Majesty approved the governor's act, he

---

[1] C G., VIII, f. 264.   [2] C.G., IX, ff. 21, 22, 65v, *et seq.*
[3] C G., VII, f. 183v, VIII, f. 131.

instructed him to maintain among the religious orders " a sort of equality " so as to avoid jealousies.¹

However, it was right among the Five Nations that the Jesuits accomplished their most effective work as agents of French diplomacy; and it is during this administration that we see most clearly what rôle they really played. Even in the mind of the governor they were first of all evangelists. Counting upon the piety of the king, especially since the revocation of the Edict of Nantes, Denonville sometimes based his whole plea for help upon the religious motive. What His Majesty had done " to annihilate heresy in his states " was an augur of what he would do to the " enemies of the Gospel in this new world." ² These barbarous enemies could be influenced only by force and fear. " Every one in this country is persuaded that the progress of religion among the savages depends absolutely upon the humiliation of the Iroquois." Even Jean de Lamberville conceded so much, in spite of his love for his mission.³

But while Denonville was truly solicitous for the welfare of religion, he never for a moment ceased to play the diplomat. The English and Dutch, he said, regarded the French missionaries as "their cruellest enemies," whom they sought to oust from the Iroquois country. " Even the interest of the civil government in the good of commerce ought to engage us to arrange to have some of them always there, for these uncivilized peoples can be governed only by the missionaries, who alone are capable of keeping them on our side and preventing them from revolting against us every day." ⁴ Even if Louis XIV were to cede the Iroquois to the king of England, the French could still govern them through their Jesuit diplomats.⁵

---

[1] B, XIII, f. 18v.
[2] C.G., x, f. 26.
[3] C G., VIII, ff. 11v, 119, x, f 69
[4] C.G., XI, f. 185.
[5] C.G., x, ff. 68v, 103. At Pentagouet, too, the Jesuits were indispensable. If the fishing company replaced them by other missionaries, the

This was the tenor of Denonville's communications to the French court. Naturally enough he expressed different ideas in his correspondence with the English governor, Dongan, who, though a good Catholic, was a better Englishman. To him he protested that while Jesuit missions among the Iroquois helped to make the cantons French territory, yet the sole aim of the missionaries was the glory of God and the salvation of souls. Frequently he reproached Dongan with his lack of zeal for the true faith, and charged him with encouraging the English merchants who excited the Iroquois against their missionaries. In fact, only the two brothers Lamberville had been able to endure the persecutions instigated by Dongan's "heretic merchants." One of the chief causes of trouble was the brandy trade, in regard to which the rival governors came to no binding agreement.

But while Denonville's language was sometimes peremptory, his Jesuit allies were uniformly tactful and conciliatory in their dealings with the English. On one occasion, with his consent, Superior Dablon wrote Dongan a letter of thanks for what Denonville calls the "cunning protection he had given last summer to the Fathers de Lamberville" whom he wished to expel "adroitly" from among the Iroquois. In this letter Dablon said: "I know that you have tried to save them from a thousand outrages to which they are exposed." The elder Lamberville himself expressed his gratitude for Dongan's "Christian charity" toward the missionaries. Sometimes in their desire to conciliate and perhaps cajole their neighbours, upon whose goodwill the tranquillity of their missions in part depended, the Jesuits used still more flattering language. For example, Father Millet once wrote to Delius, the minister at Albany: "I am a servant of the English, and would give my life to

Indians of the neighbourhood would "give themselves entirely to the English" (*C.G.*, x, f. 104).

be of service to them Father Lamberville . . . says that if the English really knew us they would not mistrust us as they do." Epistles of this kind, when they fell into the hands of adversaries, exposed their authors to charges of disloyalty ; and it was doubtless similar letters to which Frontenac referred in his famous indictment of the clergy in 1677.

However, although Frenchmen might occasionally doubt Jesuit patriotism, the English colonists were only too sure of it. In 1681 inhabitants of Virginia afflicted themselves with "wild and gross apprehensions" of Indian massacre instigated by Canadian Jesuits. Such panics were rare, but English opinion was unanimous in considering the black-robes as agents of French interests In 1687, in a petition to the governor of New York, the commissioners of the town of Albany stated that, under pretence of propagating the Gospel, the French had encroached greatly on their Indian trade and drawn away many of their Indians to Canada. Thus the trade of Albany was diminished and the king's revenue obstructed The remedy was the expulsion of the French priests from the " Indian castles " and the introduction of English priests in their stead. At the time of Phipps's expedition against Quebec the popular feeling in Boston is sufficiently indicated by a letter of Father Michel Germain · " The French (prisoners) in Boston assured us that the design of these heretics was to drive the ecclesiastics and the nuns out of Canada as for the Jesuits, they were to cut off their ears in order to make chaplets of them for the soldiers' bandoliers, and then break their heads " [1]

In 1692, in an address to the king and queen, the Council and House of Representatives of New York affirmed that by the "artifices of Jesuit priests" the French had sought to win the Five Nations to their side. A little later John

[1] A.N., K 1374, no 80.

Nelson warned the Council of Trade at London that the French made themselves "masters of the consciences of the heathen," and so had them always at their devotion.

Thus we see that Governor Dongan merely endorsed the general view when he told the Earl of Sutherland that the French made "religion a stalking-horse to establish their claims." For this reason he had refused the request of Father Vaillant, Denonville's plenipotentiary, that the Jesuits should be restored to their Iroquois missions. Moreover, he flouted the French claim to sovereignty over the Five Nations. France might as well claim Japan, since French priests had resided among the Japanese.

To Denonville he wrote in a similar strain. "You tell me that you have had missionaries among (the Iroquois). I avow the act is extremely charitable, but I . . am very sure that that does not give you any just right or title to the government of these regions." To the pretence of Jesuit singleness of aim Dongan retorted that the Lambervilles were in the cantons "for objects other than the advancement of the Christian religion," as had appeared from letters addressed to them from Canada which by accident had fallen into his hands. In another letter his tone was more aggressive: "I desire that you order M. de Lamberville, as long as he dwells among these peoples, to deal only with affairs which concern his office; and that those of our Indians who are Catholics in Canada be content to live there without trying to debauch the others"

Meanwhile he had appealed to James II for five or six English missionaries. "The French priests," he explained, "will then be obliged to retire to Canada, and the French will lose all claim to the country" Dongan then carried the war into Africa by notifying the Christian Indians of Canada that he would get an English priest for them

Although the Marquis de Denonville was a brave officer, and a man of honour and of religion, yet in his diplomacy deceit played an unusually large part, and occasionally even the end he had in view was not sufficient justification for the means he employed. The treachery practised upon unsuspecting Iroquois at Cataraqui has been condemned by all historians, but Denonville's strategy could victimize friends as well as foes. Jean de Lamberville learned this to his chagrin. No other Jesuit possessed so completely the confidence of the Iroquois, and on more than one occasion he saved Canada from desolating attack. Unlike most of his confrères, he had urged upon successive governors a peace policy. Denonville pretended to acquiesce in his views, and sent him back to quiet the warlike spirit of the Senecas. Meanwhile the governor was secretly preparing to invade that canton in the summer of 1687. Sooner or later the truth was bound to leak out, and to the outraged Iroquois Lamberville would appear a betrayer. Denonville's correspondence with Seignelay proves that he felt uneasy and half guilty over the way in which he was using " this poor father " as a pawn in his military game. He sought to justify himself by an appeal to the reason of state : to withdraw the Jesuit at present would be to bring down immediately upon the feeble colony a devastating horde of infuriated Iroquois. In reply His Majesty, without expressly blaming Denonville, said measures must be taken to prevent the Jesuit from remaining " exposed to the fury of the savages." The devoted missionary's younger brother, Jacques de Lamberville, seems to have been vehement in his indignation. According to a letter from Robert Livingstone to Governor Dongan, this Jesuit was at Cataraqui in the capacity of peace envoy. In conversation with an Iroquois war-party he " exclaimed against the governor of Canada, and said that he and all of his profession had done their best to dissuade him from this war, but in vain."

And so the diplomatic and military duels continued with

varying results. At all events, they threw into clearer relief the twofold part played by the Jesuits as apostles and patriots.[1]

Conclusion

As we saw at the beginning of this chapter, the superior of St. Sulpice attributed to the Marquis de Denonville the qualities of wisdom, gentleness, disinterestedness, and piety. He might have added personal valour, and still the list would have been inadequate. There were lacking the resolute aggressiveness and dynamic energy which alone could have saved New France from the Iroquois scourge. To the end Denonville remained the darling of the clergy, and in his time, seconded as he was by Champigny, the Church regained the position of dominance she had lost under Talon and Frontenac, and in appearance had reached the zenith of her power. Unhappily, this co-operation between the spiritual and the secular authorities, though it gave calm and dignity to the internal life of the colony, did not avail against external dangers. In spite of his wily diplomacy and ephemeral victories, Denonville's military policy was not a success, and his administration ended in the calamitous massacre of Lachine. The governor knew his own limitations: he was neither ambitious nor vain. He confessed that he was unequal to the situation, and that the country had need of an abler man than he.[2]

In this emergency the king turned once more to Frontenac.

[1] B, xiii, f. 20; F 3, ii, f. 168; C.G., viii, ff. 117, 120, 168v, 170; ix, ff. 20v, 23v, 54, 58-60, 92v, 105. *State Papers*, pp. 77, 93, 136, 146, 328, 427, 432, 442, 498, 700, *et seq.*

[2] C.G., x, f. 65v.

CHAPTER IX

DECLINE OF THE THEOCRACY

(1689-1760)

The Return of Frontenac

THE Revolution of 1688 brought to the British throne a formidable adversary of France An open struggle between New France and New England was now inevitable, and Louis XIV could find only one man whose ability and past experience fitted him to grapple with the military situation in America. One of Frontenac's admirers tells us that, with the exception of the Jesuits and some others, the people of Canada were awaiting the count's return " with as much impatience as the Jews await the Messiah " They called him " Redemptor Patriae " [1]

The character of his second administration differed widely from that of the first From 1672 to 1682 internal affairs had been his chief concern ; and here his insistence upon all his prerogatives combined with his impetuous temper to give a discordant and often trivial tone to domestic politics After 1689 the magnitude of external dangers caused internal differences to lose their relative importance. With advancing years the count had gained in self-control ; he was less addicted to violent outbreaks of passion, and less inclined to exaggerate trifles Even his old adversaries in the Sovereign Council now felt his presence indispensable, and their manner was as deferential as circumstances required. Their example was followed by M. de Champigny, although the intendant had cause to regret the departure

[1] La Hontan, vol i, p. 199

of his co-worker, Denonville, and the arrival of an imperious master who treated him, said M de Laval, worse than he had ever treated Duchesneau.[1]

In this period Frontenac's relations with the Church were, on the whole, less troubled and more dignified. True, he had differences from time to time with practically every section of the clergy. He felt that in 1682 he had "succumbed to the artifices and the fury" of the ecclesiastics whose "excessive and abusive authority" he had been in duty bound to repress "My recall," he continued, "which had rendered them masters of the counsels and of the conduct of the government, was followed by all the misfortunes by which this wretched colony has been overwhelmed."[2] He admitted their virtue and piety, but criticized their vehement and immoderate zeal The priests of the Seminary were "persuaded that the Holy Ghost inspired all they thought," and some of the Sulpicians of Montreal were quite as fanatical Even Champigny confessed that one of the latter had been over-zealous.[3] During these years we find M. de Tronson continually admonishing his priests in Montreal to show deference to the civil authorities. "It is of the greatest consequence," he wrote to Belmont, "that you never speak disparagingly of the Powers to any one whomsoever Everything is known and reported So, except toward M Dollier and myself, maintain as an inviolable practice in this regard a profound silence."[4] Meanwhile, the seigneurial justice administered by the Sulpicians had led to their being accused of "excesses, violences, and hardnesses," and had brought them into conflict with the

---

[1] *C.G.*, x, f. 249; xi, f. 266, xii, f. 286   [2] *Ibid.*, xi, f. 230
[3] *Ibid.*, f. 242v, xii, ff. 57, 233 Champigny added that since 1690 all their conduct had been unexceptionable. In this view he was more lenient than their own superior, M de Tronson, who had endless trouble with the "chimerical visions" of some of his "visionaries" at Villemarie (*Tronson*, vol ii, p 308, *et seq*)
[4] *Ibid.*, p 318

Sovereign Council. In 1693 royal justice was established on the Island [1]

THE SUPREMACY OF THE CIVIL GOVERNMENT

The Sulpicians were beginning to feel the increasing prestige of the secular authorities In 1695 Tronson wrote " There is no reason to be astonished if the Powers are so sovereign in Canada ; that belongs to the character with which the king has clothed them. If you do not receive all the help you could wish in your needs unless you pay court to them . . that is not peculiar to Canada." [2] Apparently the bishop had unwittingly rendered the Seminary of Montreal " odious to all the Powers." [3]

However, it was with Saint-Vallier himself that Frontenac had the only serious conflict of his second administration Although he freely bore testimony to the prelate's virtues and immense charities,[4] the governor showed firmness and dignity in steadfastly opposing episcopal pretensions to a control over society such as existed nowhere in the kingdom of France In the long dispute over the famous affair of " Tartuffe " and Mareuil, Frontenac vindicated civil rights, and won the qualified approval of the court.

Although he no longer made slashing attacks on the Jesuits, he refused to approve of their Indian policy, especially in the matter of brandy. In this dispute, as in others, the secular elements were having their way in spite of the Church.

In brief, theocratic power was on the wane. From 1690 onwards the increase of the population, the English peril, and the consequent preponderance of the military element combined to draw the reins of political power more and more into the hands of secular men and to relegate

---

[1] C S , vol. III, pp 576, 635, 664, 760
[2] Tronson, vol. II, p 345.   [3] Ibid., p. 352.
[4] C.G., XII, f. 233 and passim.

ecclesiastics to the performance of exclusively religious duties.[1]

Even by 1720, if we may judge from Charlevoix's description, the theocratic austerity of earlier days had relaxed, and social life had mellowed. From time to time, until 1727, Mgr. de Saint-Vallier intervened in the civil domain, but usually for purposes all could approve. His successor, Dosquet, was neither strong nor disinterested, and when in 1730 he endeavoured to resuscitate Laval's "reserved case" his failure measured the decline of ecclesiastical power. Shortly afterwards, when two Récollets had facilitated the escape of three soldiers condemned to death for mutiny, Louis XV decreed that churchmen guilty of contravening royal commands should be tried by civil judges. This was an infringement upon clerical privilege, but Dosquet's protests were vain. In 1741, when Father Tournois was accused of complicity in fraudulent commerce with Albany, the minister warned the Jesuits of Canada that His Majesty must be obeyed at the Sault St Louis as everywhere else. The governor deported Tournois and his accomplices to France. Seventy years before Jean Talon had received authority to send back to France any one who should offend against the service of the king, but the great intendant never exercised this power against an ecclesiastic, much less against a Jesuit. However, instead of defending themselves after their former manner by plotting the recall of their accusers, the Jesuits of 1741 meekly submitted. They no longer dominated the government at Quebec or at Versailles.

Another proof of the passing of theocracy was the return of Huguenot merchants to Canada. In 1750 Mgr. de

---

[1] This had been foreseen by Colbert. In 1668 he expressed his confidence that "when the country becomes more populous ... the royal authority ... will prevail over the other and will hold it easily within just limits" (*C.G.*, III, f. 13).

Pontbriant demanded the expulsion of the twelve established at Quebec, but the intendant showed how commerce would be thereby injured, and the court refused the bishop's request.[1]

Had Canada remained a province of France she would ultimately have felt the influence of the *Philosophes* and of revolutionary thought. The capture of Quebec isolated French Canada, and, paradoxical as it may seem, under Protestant Britain the Catholic theocracy was re-established.

THE JESUITS AND THE FUR TRADE

We have alluded to the Tournois scandal at the mission of the Sault. This was one of the two most important incidents in the history of the Jesuits and the fur trade after the first administration of Frontenac.

In the last two decades of the seventeenth century the prosperity of Canada continued to depend upon the beaver trade. Champigny summed it up when he said: "In a word, when the peltry fails one year, happy is he who has bread."[2] Accordingly we need not expect to find the Jesuits abstaining from all contact with beaver. The only question is, now as formerly, whether they used the peltry merely as a medium of exchange, or whether they carried on commerce for profit. In his account of his voyage to Hudson Bay the renegade Radisson remarks incidentally that in 1682 he went to see the Jesuits of Paris who were "interested with La Chesnaye in the beaver trade." As Radisson was co-operating with La Chesnaye in the development of commerce with the north, the Jesuits gave him money for his voyage.[3] Evidently there was a business agreement of some kind between the missionaries and Canada's leading merchant.

Still, there was no sign of luxury in the missions. At

[1] Salone, p. 408, etc.   [2] *C.G.*, x, f. 121.   [3] *Rapport*, 1895, p. 1.

Michilimackinac in 1683 La Barre's aide found the Jesuits' fare "very bad." They had neither wine nor bread nor meat, but only sagamite.[1] Five years later Joutel observed that they had "a good and strong establishment" on this island, since it was the principal rendezvous and emporium of the fur country;[2] but he laid at their doors no charge of mercenary conduct. In 1691 we learn that Louvigny, the commandant, had erected there a fort "which placed the house of the Jesuits in surety."[3] As the French village consisted altogether of sixty houses, the lives of the missionaries would be an open book; and if they had traded in a commercial sense we should surely have had precise and frequent news of it.[4]

Meanwhile, the few Jesuits who remained at Quebec seem to have outlived the hardships of early days. In 1684 La Hontan described their monastery thus: "Their house is comfortable in every way . . . These priests have beautiful gardens, with several alleys of trees so thick-spreading that in summer one seems to be in an icehouse rather than in a wood."[5] Frontenac, La Salle, and others declared that this handsome home was due in part to profits from the fur trade. La Hontan himself disagreed with them.

At length in 1706 appeared a document which seemed authoritative and promised to be final. This was a joint letter from Governor Vaudreuil and Intendant Raudot to the minister which vouched for the character of the Canadian Jesuits "The Jesuit fathers, Monseigneur, have never carried on commerce in the Upper Lakes (*en*

---

[1] Baugy, p. 181.   [2] Margry, vol. iii, p 513   [3] C G, xi, f 230.
[4] Cf. Margry, Introd, p lxviii In Acadia the governor, Villebon, and the judge, Goutins, accused the priests of carrying on commerce with the English, of trading illegally in rum, and of designing to appropriate the country (*Coll. MSS*, vol. ii, pp. 15, 306 (1690, 1698)). The governor and the judge made similar accusations against each other.
[5] La Hontan, vol 1, p 19

haut), and assuredly ought to be exempt from this suspicion." Then comes the explanation that the men who journeyed back and forth in the service of the missions had always been accustomed to carry in their canoes merchandise enough to make good their outlay. The annual bounty from the king was not sufficient for the bare maintenance of the missionaries, and they could not possibly pay for the transportation of themselves and their effects, as each canoe would cost them 100 pistoles (1000 francs).[1] For the present, through the support of the civil power, the Jesuits could triumph over their accusers.

But times were changing. The Tournois incident, which we have described already, reveals the fact that toward the end of the French régime a Jesuit was capable of sharing in the profits from a secret and illegal fur trade carried on with the English of Albany by two Frenchwomen.[2]

Allied to and sometimes interwoven with this question of the fur trade is the story of the commerce in *eau-de-vie*.

THE BRANDY TRADE

Frontenac and Champigny

The return of Count Frontenac marked an abrupt change in the relations between the Church and the civil government in the matter of the brandy trade. In his seven years of absence the old soldier had not repented. He still regarded the commerce in liquors as an economic and political necessity. More than that, he meant to encourage it. The result, as we shall see, was a recrudescence of memoirs and petitions emanating directly or indirectly from the ecclesiastical party.

Notwithstanding the new governor's attitude, M. de Champigny continued in the way he had begun. Some

[1] C.G., xxiv, ff 51, 52 (Nov 3, 1706)
[2] Thwaites, vol lxix, p 286.

people tried to find a loophole in the royal ordinance of 1679 by pretending that, though forbidden to carry *eau-de-vie* into the " depths of the forest," they still might carry it to Indians living on the banks of the rivers. The intendant, of course, rejected this specious argument as a quibble on words [1]

Next he attacked the false concessions of distant lands granted by Frontenac to men whose sole aim was to monopolize Indian trade. Champigny advised that actual settlement of these concessions be exacted as a pre-requisite to trading rights.[2] From the tenor of his letters one can see that his preference still lay in the direction of complete prohibition, but meantime he was content to enforce the law, and prevent the persecution of Indians for old debts.[3]

The duties of his intendancy obliged him, on one occasion at least, to sell liquors officially for the benefit of the colonial treasury. After the siege of Quebec by Sir William Phipps the prices of brandy and of wine quadrupled and sextupled respectively.[4] However, the wholesale dealers do not seem to have made fortunes out of the situation, for in October 1692, when Iberville brought home a Spanish vessel freighted with liquors, not a merchant of Quebec was able to buy the cargo So Champigny had to sell it retail.[5]

The following year the intendant came rather sharply into conflict with the governor. In violation of the royal decrees regulating the number of *congés* and the quantity of merchandise the soldiers might carry with them to their posts, Frontenac had sent 146 men to the Ottawa region. Moreover, in contradiction of his own ordinance of 1690, he permitted them to transport brandy in their canoes. Worse than all, some of the men who had the governor's orders to ascend to the Ottawas sold them publicly like *congés*

[1] C G, XI, f 255 [2] Ibid, f. 264 [3] Ibid., f 286v (Oct 1691).
[4] F 3, IV, f 384 [5] C G., XII, f. 82.

DECLINE OF THE THEOCRACY

for 1000 livres and more. Frontenac said to the intendant's secretary that he wished they could be sold for 40,000 livres. When Champigny posted up an ordinance insisting upon the observance of the king's decrees, the governor covered it with a sentinel until he had drawn up a contradictory ordinance of his own. Laden with goods, fifty-five canoes set out. Courtemanche de Repentigny said openly that he had 6000 livres' worth of merchandise. Besides, the Indian canoes were loaded with brandy, although in his own edict Frontenac professed to have at heart the prevention of disorder.

As for the regular *congés*, he distributed them to favourites, to the detriment of the poor, and his secretary was thought to traffic in them. With the pretext of maintaining harmony among the tribes Frontenac sent men up the Lakes to trade; and his orders differed from *congés* only in the fact that the intendant had no right to examine them. Though he pretended to be sending them to man Fort Michilimackinac, all these voyageurs scattered off into the woods by twos and threes, and arrived at the fort when they had finished trading. Louvigny was in command there, and when lately he had opposed the brandy trade a sedition broke out, and one man threatened him with his musket. These traders made scandalous profits, the ordinary price of brandy being 50 livres a jug [1]

Even His Majesty's presents to the Ottawa tribes were evidently tampered with at times, for Champigny now issued a decree that the distribution of the royal gifts should take place in presence of the missionaries, or of the principal residents above suspicion of collusion [2] The intendant still held to Denonville's policy of hearty co-operation with the clergy both within and without the colony.

In Frontenac's second administration his attention was

[1] *C.G.*, XII, f. 282 (Nov. 4, 1693).   [2] *Ibid.*, f. 262v.

given mainly to military affairs. Consequently his quarrels with the Church were less constant than during his first government. Nevertheless, as his views and actions in the matter of the liquor trade remained practically the same, he could not command the approbation of the ecclesiastics. Sometimes he made what they would concede was a legitimate use of liquors in negotiating with the natives. On one such occasion, in order to assure himself of the help of the Ottawas against an impending Iroquois attack, he engaged them to remain at Quebec by offering them a "solemn feast" of two oxen, six large dogs, prunes, tobacco, and two hogsheads of wine.[1] But a little later, in an address to the same tribe, the governor appeared in the rôle of general agent for the French brandy interests.

Do to the Iroquois what he has done to you . . . and to the Englishman what he wants to do to you, taking the part of your veritable father, who will never abandon you. Must his (the Englishman's) brandy, which has slain you in your cabin, attract you so strongly as to put you in the Iroquois kettle? And mine, which has never caused your death, which has always given you strength,—is it not better?[2]

Evidently Frontenac felt English competition a real menace even to trade with the Ottawas. Hence his bold advocacy of French brandy, the one article whose superior quality gave an advantage to the Canadian merchant over his English rival. Yet this did not prevent his promising

---

[1] C.G., XI, f. 25.

[2] Ibid, f. 133. Contrast the attitude of Governor Fletcher on this question. In 1693 four sachems beg him to prohibit the sale of rum as long as the war lasts against New France. He promises to do so. Later on he says in substance to the Five Nations: The enemy cannot harm you unless you are careless and enfeeble yourselves by intemperance. Drunkenness is the worst vice of martial men; so be sober and vigilant (State Papers, p. 50).

Of course, the situation was somewhat different in the two cases. Fletcher wanted the Iroquois to keep away from English towns and defend their own cantons; Frontenac wanted the Ottawas to remain at Quebec and defend the French fortress.

the minister in 1692 that he would do his best to cure the disorders which, he finally confessed, "intoxicating drinks cause sometimes." In fact, the governor protested that nobody was more an "enemy of drunkards" than he, and that he punished them severely when the occasion presented itself.[1]

The Ottawa Missions

We have seen how in November 1693 the intendant accused Frontenac of issuing numerous orders to visit the Indian tribes—orders which were in reality permits. He also alleged that in the summer of 1693 the governor had allowed his supposed envoys to carry as much merchandise and brandy as they desired, and that Courtemanche de Repentigny had claimed to have 6000 livres' worth. A journal kept by Courtemanche on a similar expedition in 1691 shows that the abuses later denounced by Champigny were already creeping in. But as yet the head of the expedition did no trading himself. Courtemanche assured the Ottawa chiefs that he had come not to sell brandy, but to tell them of the victories won by Onontio over their common enemies. He had brandy only for his own provision, but he would invite them to drink with him. Very soon the Jesuits and Louvigny appeared uneasy; they had learned that his followers had "a little in reserve, out of which they were hoping to make a little beaver." As the missionaries had received an order from Saint-Vallier to refuse the sacraments to sellers of brandy, Courtemanche admonished his followers to take every precaution against disturbances. One man disposed of a small keg during the night. In the morning the reverend fathers came to say that everything was on fire in the village of the Hurons. Courtemanche and some of his men hastened to the rescue, but they were "extremely surprised" to find nothing but

[1] *C G*, XII, f 233v.

a little hilarious gaiety. However, Louvigny and the Jesuits obliged him to promise not to trade any brandy.

I kept my word to them. But my men did it four days and four nights without any one knowing that they had given a drop. We prepared for our return; and I was content with the fathers, if they were satisfied with my conduct. They eulogized me, making a hundred obliging remarks on the subject of brandy. After they had given me plenty of praise for the reserve I had maintained, I told them that my men had been trading for four days and four nights without their noticing it. That surprised them extremely, and they spoke to me never a word.[1]

The implication is, of course, that the Jesuits' reports of Indian excesses were exaggerated or unfounded. But for us the immediate significance of this story is the confession it involves that as early as May 1691 a so-called political mission was to some extent a trading expedition. Apart altogether from Champigny's usual veracity, it is easy to credit his statement that in 1693 the commercial character of these embassies entirely overshadowed their political function. As for Courtemanche himself, he had always been a friend to the king's representatives, and he now enjoyed Frontenac's protection.[2]

We also observe that the Ottawas (who were declared by several members of the assembly held at the Château St. Louis in 1678 to be ignorant of the use of strong drink) had become, within a few years, regular customers of the brandy traders. What is more, they were so enamoured of this strange stimulant that they had attracted venturesome Englishmen into their country with canoe-loads of liquor, and Frontenac feared New France might lose their patronage.[3]

---

[1] *C.G.*, xi, f. 206 (June 18, 1691). [2] *Ibid.*, f. 244
[3] The Abbé de Belmont remarks this change in his history of brandy cited *infra*.

DECLINE OF THE THEOCRACY 273

Shortly after this visit of Courtemanche a missionary among the Ottawas addressed to the governor a letter, the tone of which was frank almost to severity. "If you want to contribute to the service of God and the king, to the establishment of commerce, . . . and, finally, to assure your own eternal salvation as well as that of the French and of the peoples who trade with them, you will not permit the transportation of this wretched drink, and you will execute the orders of the king, who expressly forbids the carrying of it into the depths of the forest" The Ottawas have held a great council. They have sent word to Frontenac that they regard this commerce as a public pillage If he still allows it, then he and the bishop and the missionaries must be in concert for the plunder of the Ottawas Or, if the missionaries have done their duty by conveying to Onontio the pitiful complaints of the Indian elders, and if he pay no heed, then he alone neglects his duty, and they will no longer recognize him as their father [1]

Jesuit Memoirs

To warnings of this kind Frontenac turned a deaf ear; he distrusted the Jesuits and he knew his own mind. The missionaries therefore, despairing of the governor, turned to the minister, de Pontchartrain. To him in 1692 they addressed a collective memorial, in which they summed up all the available arguments against the continuation of the traffic [2] It would drive the Indian allies out of the colony, and Canada would be thus deprived of their services against the Iroquois, whom they alone could reach in the woods. In urging Pontchartrain to put an end to the evil, the

---

[1] C G, XII, f 140 (June 30, 1691)
[2] This memoir speaks of the "Indiens, qu'on appelle sauvages" This is the first instance we have observed in missionary writings of the employment of the word *Indiens*

memoir made the rather surprising statement that the sale of brandy to the Indians did not amount to more than fifty hogsheads out of over six thousand imported annually into Canada.

By way of remedy the Jesuits proposed nothing new—merely the enforcement of existing ordinances. They urged the repression of the *coureurs de bois*. The " *élite* of the Canadian youth " plunged into the woods, partly to avoid the war with the Iroquois, partly to escape the tilling of the soil, and by visiting the tribes in such numbers they prevented the Indians from coming down to the colony to trade with the real settlers.[1] Attached to this memorial were an extract from the laws of Boston and certain letters. One of these was from the famous Captain Duluth, who testified that in all his ten years' experience he had never seen any commerce in brandy which was not followed by great disorders. It was morally impossible to avoid them.[2] Another letter, from a Jesuit at Michilimackinac, told of the return of their Indians from Montreal with over one hundred barrels of brandy. For six weeks Hurons and Ottawas got drunk alternate days, and pandemonium reigned. Louvigny could not hold council with the chiefs, and so this protracted debauch prevented the Indians from going to the aid of the French against the Iroquois. An indirect result had been the massacre of La Chine.[3]

We find an anonymous memorial of 1693, drawn up perhaps by the Jesuits of France. In addition to the stock arguments, it said : " It has always been recognized that the neighbourhood of Europeans, in the matter both of drink and of morals, has been a great hindrance to the conversion of the infidels." The best results were obtained when no Europeans except missionaries lived among the natives. Brandy had worked havoc among the Indians :

[1] *C G*, XII, f. 125 (Feb. 1692). [2] *Ibid.*, f. 131.
[3] *Ibid*, f. 132 (May 27, 1692).

their dead bodies had been found in the water, in the woods, and on the river-banks, with their barrels of brandy beside them Intoxicated savages had set fire to the houses of settlers or " defiled them with the most abominable lewdness "; in the very churches Indian women, drunken and nude, had danced and fought

The French traders themselves met with disaster: continual poverty, horrible deaths, suicide, apostasy (some had turned Huguenot) Some who had "gloried in having debauched with their brandy more than two hundred Indian women or girls" had been found, their "bodies a prey to birds, and food for wild beasts." In 1692 at Quebec " savage men and women, drunken and naked, dragged each other into the streets, where, in the sight and to the great scandal of everybody, they did publicly, like brute beasts, things shameful and infamous . . . that decency does not permit " the author to recount [1]

The testimony of La Chesnaye corroborates that of the missionaries "I tell you in all conscience, Monsieur, that one cannot better represent hell than by the view of Indians and squaws intoxicated "[2]

Saint-Vallier and the Traffic

The zeal of the Jesuits had not abated, and they were seconded by Saint-Vallier as they had been led by Laval Nevertheless, for a time the new prelate and Frontenac were on friendly terms. Indeed, there were people who wished the understanding between governor, intendant, and bishop were not so great [3] " The great zeal of Monsieur the Bishop," said Frontenac, " sometimes causes him chagrin when he sees that the king's order touching drinks is being executed " The bishop's grievance was, of course, that it was

---

[1] C G., XII, ff 382, 384 [2] Ibid, f 380 (Oct. 24, 1693)
[3] C.G., XI, f. 98 (Nov. 12, 1690).

not being executed. "But," continued the governor, "I let his bad humour pass, and I afterwards oblige him to embrace me as heartily as usual His ecclesiastics, principally those of Montreal, . . . also greatly trouble consciences on this article and on other bagatelles of coiffures and of laces, which are so extraordinary that they cause much murmuring"[1]

The minister's reply assured Frontenac that with Champigny's help, and with amiable remonstrances, he could restrain the bishop when his zeal or the suggestion of prejudiced (*passionés*) or covetous (*intéressés*) ecclesiastics might cause trouble.[2]

But his personal sympathy with Frontenac did not prevent Saint-Vallier from criticizing him, by implication, in a pastoral letter addressed about this time to the inhabitants of Montreal Having reproved their greed of gain, which led them to intoxicate the Indians contrary to the "public and private opinion" of Count Frontenac, he warned them that if the temporal power could do nothing, God would recognize and punish the guilty. "Nothing can equal the bitterness of heart in which I am to see that my presence has been so little capable of preventing you from satisfying this mad passion of interests."[3]

In 1693 the count again wrote appreciatively of Saint-Vallier. he had exhausted his resources in succouring the poor of the general hospital; why not levy an extra import duty of fifteen sous a hogshead of wine, and thirty sous a hogshead of brandy, payable to the administrators of the hospital for twenty years?[4] It is just conceivable that, coupled with Frontenac's desire to aid the hospital, was a half-humorous resolve to make the bishop feel that the liquor trade was not an unmixed evil.[5] However that may

---

[1] *C.G.* XI, f. 98 (Nov 12, 1690).   [2] B, XVI, f. 32 (April 7, 1691).
[3] *Mandements*, p. 287   [4] *C.G.*, XII, f. 233v.
[5] After 1693 we cease to follow the official correspondence closely, and we refer to outstanding documents only.

be, in April 1696 we find another deliberation in the Sorbonne instituted at the request of Saint-Vallier. Tired of ineffectual struggles with the unruly habitants, he had fixed his attention upon the wholesale merchants. Could these great merchants conscientiously sell to lesser merchants liquors with which the latter intoxicated the Indians? On their behalf it was urged that they sold liquor for the needs of the colony and to make money, and, as it was not " the part of a good Christian to judge ill of his neighbour," they did not believe the retailers would make bad use of it. In contradiction of this claim it was argued that the wholesalers imported more brandy than the colony needed, and that they kept it for the time when the voyageurs set out for the Indian tribes, or when the Indians came down to the settlements. Hence they shared the guilt of the retailers. The Sorbonne's response was as follows: " It is against the charity one owes his neighbour to furnish him matter or an occasion to offend God mortally, even if the thing is indifferent in itself, when one knows that he will misuse it, because in this case one is judged to be co-operating in the sin of another." Again, the suppression of the sale of brandy would not be a " public calamity but a simple loss to individuals." The conclusion was that the sale must be limited: the petty merchants must receive from the wholesalers only the exact quantity necessary for their personal use on their voyages; they must be sold none at all when the Indians come down to the colony.[1] This decision of the Sorbonne was read from the pulpit by the order and in the presence of Mgr. de Saint-Vallier in July 1698.[2]

The Sulpicians

In one of Frontenac's dispatches which we have quoted he accused the Sulpicians in particular of excessive zeal.

---

[1] *Mandements*, p. 354.   [2] *Fds. Fr.*, 13,516, f. 62v.

The broad-minded and tactful M. de Tronson sometimes appeared inclined to the same opinion.

Though Tronson had a particular esteem for the Abbé de Belmont, Superior of the Mountain, he gently expostulated with him "Your abject life causes you to be decried everywhere . . . among your (Indian) pupils and drunkards, to whom you are terrible."[1]

In 1692 Tronson admitted that the Faith would flourish only if intemperance were absolutely banished from Montreal, but meantime Belmont would have to imitate the curés in France, who had many drunkards in their parishes They did not "cry out against the Powers" who tolerated strong drink, but declaimed rather against vice itself, and made use of the means which God had put in their hands "without wishing to usurp an authority in the judgment-seat of men (*for extérieur*) which does not belong to them." "I only wish that those who have clamoured too much would reflect upon the past and could convince themselves that these cries, raised inopportunely, have no other effect than to embitter the Powers and to raise up obstacles to the good one would do" They ought to cry "only when it is useful to cry."[2]

M. Dollier was superior of the Seminary at Montreal. In 1691 he was as fervid in his denunciation of the "detestable misuse" of liquor as he had been twenty years earlier when he composed his history of Montreal. In a letter to a fellow-priest returning to France he exclaimed "There is only this accursed drunkenness, which is to them (the Indians) a damnable reef." "Emissaries of the Demon" mislead our "incomparable monarch" If the "sweetness of Christianity" were not diluted here, even more than among the heretics, with the "gall of strong drink," the French would be the "charm of all the savage nations," and all the Iroquois would have come to their missions.

[1] *Tronson*, vol. ii, p. 259.   [2] *Ibid.*, p. 317

On this point the professional interpreters falsified the sentiments of the Indians to please the partisans of the traffic. Dollier had once heard an Algonquin squaw "scream in tones infernal against the 'intoxicators' of the savages." After her drunkenness, when she saw herself stripped of everything, she said to Dollier: "Ah! would God I might see them plunged in the midst of hell!" In conclusion, the superior exhorted his friend " to put in motion every spring and machine to obtain from the piety of our prince the abolition of this disorder "[1]

Some of the Sulpicians so dreaded the effects of strong drink upon their neophytes that they proposed to remove the Mission of the Mountain far from Montreal This would have been a concession to the Jesuit policy of isolation Tronson pointed out the advantages of the present situation, and advised a careful examination of the question from all sides.[2]

Belmont's Sermon

Passing over the activities of the Sulpicians in the next few years we come to the record of a sermon which internal evidence would seem to indicate was delivered about the end of the century, and very probably by the Abbé de Belmont The preacher makes a slashing attack upon the tavern-keepers of Montreal "Their house is not only a cave of robbers, but a very sink of prostitution and of all uncleanness." They cheat the Indians by having ice or grease in the measures.[3] In the confessional they say: " Sir, I received from God this talent for selling brandy, but I conduct myself therein with such prudence that . . . I am sure I ward off many evils by following this trade. Every one is not as scrupulous as I."

---

[1] C.G., xi, f 220   [2] *Tronson*, vol ii, p. 321.
[3] The Seminary instituted a system of verification of weights and measures to prevent frauds (Faillon, vol iii, p 406)

Then, in alluding to the horrible massacre of La Chine, the sacred orator cried · " Cecidit, cecidit Babylon Illa parva, quae de vino prostitutionis suae potavit omnem terram."

Addressing the brandy traders he exclaimed : " Alas, wretched men ! If an army of Iroquois smeared with blood and charcoal, howling and running naked, sword in hand, is able to freeze your heart, what will you do when you hear this horrible *sakakoua* of the demons on your arrival in hell ?—they who infinitely surpass the Iroquois in number, in cruelty, in strength, and in hatred."

The priest was astonished that in " so large a town there is no one to be the man of God, the attorney of God, to oppose the torrent " of intemperance. To the citizens he says accusingly : " The moose and the beaver are the gods which brought you from France." He warns the merchants, " men full of merit and esteem," that God " well knows how to engulf these diabolical cargoes of brandy. It is this baleful ballast that sinks them to the bottom of the sea, and draws the Jamaican filibusters to deliver Canada from this merchandise of hell " The good people ought to demand of the authorities the execution of their own ordinances which are " rotting uselessly at the bottom of the archives." Even the confessors are blameworthy, for the traders (public pests, " serpents and mad dogs " that they are) are able to obtain absolution without the restitution of profits required by the bishop

In conclusion the preacher bemoans " the execration and disrepute in which the name of Montreal is found, not only here, among all the neighbouring peoples, but also in Europe." Montreal is the " stumbling-block of the country." [1]

With his fearlessness and his violent imagination the author of this sermon has painted the condition of Montreal

[1] *Fds. Fr*., 13,516, ff. 123-62.

in sombre hues. But his picture is almost equalled by that of another contemporary observer of a very different character, the Baron de Longueuil : Libertinism has not been punished for several years The establishment of special cabarets for the Indians has not prevented their roaming the streets and misbehaving, for after intoxicating them the cabaretiers throw them out These taverns cheat the merchants who make advances of goods to the Indians, and so, for several years, the majority of the merchants, by building stores along the river-banks, have forestalled the commerce of the town. In Montreal disorder is everywhere ; carriages travel at a hard gallop, causing numerous accidents ; bands of lawless youths terrorize the citizens at night. "There is no kind of insolence they do not commit, banding themselves together with the cabmen, who, after getting drunk, swear and blaspheme and fight at the church-doors during divine service," to the scandal of the Indian converts.[1]

The attorney Raimbault added his testimony. He had learned from a Sulpician missionary that many inhabitants of the upper end of the Island were selling brandy to the Indians and thus hurting the mission of the Lake of Two Mountains. Raimbault conjectured that most of this brandy was kept for the voyageurs, who loaded their canoes with it here, thus outwitting the inspectors at La Chine It had always been very difficult to secure sufficient evidence to convict the brandy traders, since sellers and buyers were alike very cautious At present the difficulty was greater than ever, for the liquor was sold in kegs and bottles to the Indians, who carried it off and drank it outside the town, open on all sides Even the former practice of arresting and questioning drunken Indians had brought little satisfaction, for they used to name several persons successively, and thus leave the true culprits unknown and unpunished.

[1] F 3, II, f 273

The repression of this offence would require patrols all night. A fine was powerless against those who were in a condition to pay it; and there were many of them.[1]

A History of Eau-de-Vie

Such, then, was the state of affairs in Montreal at the end of the seventeenth century. About 1719 the Abbé de Belmont—that indefatigable foe of the brandy trade—produced his "Histoire de l'Eau-de-Vie."[2] By far the greater part of this history consists of material with which the reader is already familiar. The style of composition is loose and unscientific, and the whole production partakes of the nature rather of a sermon than of a history. Accordingly, instead of giving a résumé of the author's facts and findings, we shall point merely to those which may offer some fresh interest. At the outset he insists upon the fact that the intemperance of the Indians is different in nature from that of all other men. They do not take brandy as a "beverage agreeable or useful to their life . . . (most of them have a horror of it), but as a potion." It warms up their "natural coldness." Formerly they used to intoxicate themselves with tobacco.

Now comes a *digression physique* upon the nature of brandy:

Physicians remark very justly that brandy is a remedy, but not an aliment, . . . and that it is all composed of parts sulphurous, oily, inflammable, and spirituous. Taken, they say, in small quantities and not too often, brandy produces three good effects. For in pricking and spurring by the points of its parts the orifice of the stomach, it draws spirits there. These spirits give strength and joy, that is to say, vigour to the heart; they aid in the proper distribution of nutriment; they dissipate and exhale viscous vapours.

---

[1] F 3, II, f. 275v.   [2] *Fds. Fr.*, 13,516, ff. 45-93.

After this little disquisition, reminiscent of mediæval physics, the abbé enumerates the evils attendant upon excessive drinking Most of his observations are fairly accurate, almost modern in character ; but he returns inevitably to the pseudo-science of his time brandy " harms by its fumes, which rise in whirling rounds and cause dizziness, whence it comes that drunkards walk in a ring These fumes ascend to the brain, principal of the nerves, and take possession of the channels of the spirits which animate the movements of the muscles of the whole body " When the Indians begin to feel the fumes, they rejoice : " Good ! Good ! There's my head going round ! " Then they commence their death-song

Belmont [1] relates an incident, of which, however authentic, we have found no record. Major Andros, governor of Orange and Manhattan, had proposed to the governor of Canada that they forbid, each in his own government, the sale of brandy to the natives [2] His suggestion was not heeded, and since then the French had extended the reign of brandy even to the Ottawas, who formerly hated this drink because of its bitterness, but were now become passionately fond of it The traders victimized their Indian customers in every way Some mingled salt water with the brandy. Belmont knew one man who had made an Indian believe " that he had drunk fifty moose-skins in one night "

In the time of Laval this quarrel had " divided the Church and the World " The University of Toulouse was consulted, but its decision favoured the traffic.[3] " All that was surely

---

[1] *Fds. Fr*, 13,516, f 58.

[2] Early in 1679 Bishop Laval had stated that two years previously Governor Andros had absolutely forbidden the sale of intoxicating liquors to the Indians. " Il ne leva cette défense que lorsqu'il eût appris que les Français leur en traitaient" (*Fds. Fr.*, 13,516, f 102). Perhaps Belmont's memory is at fault.

[3] Perhaps that is why we have found no contemporary record of it.

obtained underhand"; the Company of the Occident took an interest in the question, for it coveted the big import duties. However, the decisions of the Sorbonne were favourable to the contention of the clergy. After the death of Frontenac the Council wished to renew the ordinances, the execution of which he had prevented, but the conflict between the authorities concerning their respective jurisdictions had allowed the tavern-keepers to continue "with an extreme impudence . . . to triumph over the Church and the cause of God."[1]

When their Indian customers became intoxicated "they rushed naked through the town . . . and rejoiced to see women and children flee before them, as if they had become masters of the world. That is what is often seen at Montreal." It was one of those orgies which in 1694 caused the fire that destroyed the Mission of the Mountain.

In the massacre of La Chine (1689) women had been impaled, children roasted, and ninety persons led captive. The majority of these were "burned cruelly and immolated to the vengeance of the Iroquois, or rather to that of God, who made use of the Iroquois as ministers of His justice, because this parish of La Chine had been, and still is, the most famous theatre of Indian drunkenness." In that crisis God seemed to deprive the French of the "spirit of strength and counsel"; they were "shamefully vanquished, insulted, mocked" by the Iroquois. But this was only the crowning calamity; others had preceded · pestilence and famine. Moreover, in 1690, the morning after a famous debauch of Ottawas and Hurons, the fine wheat was found all rusted with the fog. "One must be blind not to attribute the other distresses (also) which have overwhelmed this country to the brandy trouble."

Not only the Mountain but even the Madeleine had at

[1] In the original this reference to Frontenac, etc., is struck out. Probably it was considered imprudent.

last been invaded by drunkenness.¹ The abbé estimated at 100 hogsheads the annual consumption of brandy by Indians ² This yielded a duty of 2000 francs, but the loss in furs through the demoralization and death of the native hunters was much greater "The king has no need to profane his coffers by a gain so filthy and so insulting to God"—a gain from "tolerated brigandage"

In conclusion, the Abbé de Belmont proposed certain regulations but no thoroughgoing remedy The cabaretiers ought to hold a certificate from the curé and be approved by governor or magistrate, no tavern should be tolerated outside the three towns of Canada; informers and witnesses should share in the fines; existing laws should be enforced

The documents from which we have just quoted show clearly the stand taken by the Sulpicians of Montreal in this endless dispute between "the Church and the World." We have likewise discussed at length the part taken by the Jesuits and by the Seminary of Quebec in the controversy. It remains to interpret the attitude of the Récollets

The Attitude of the Récollets

Of these Minor Brothers of St Francis there is little to say in this connection. Returning to New France under the especial protection of the secular power, for the express purpose of affording relief to oppressed consciences, and finding themselves somewhat isolated from the rest of the clergy, the Récollets at first stood aside from the struggle. Nevertheless, after his missionary experiences in Gaspesia their chief historian, Father Le Clercq, attacked the liquor traffic as bitterly as any of his confrères Recounting the enormities of which it was the fertile source, he told of one young libertine "who boasted that he could do more evil with a bottle of brandy than the missionaries could do good

¹ *Fds Fr*, 13,516, f 74   ² *Ibid*, f. 79v.

with a bottle of holy water "¹ Then, with the partisan jealousy which not infrequently marred his writing, he relegated the Jesuits to obscurity when he wished " to justify the zeal of Mgr. the Bishop of Quebec, the Récollets, and the other missionaries who have declared themselves strongly against these disorders " ²

Upon the death of Frontenac the Récollet father who pronounced his funeral oration merely pleaded extenuating circumstances. Though the king had forbidden the sale of brandy to the Indians, Count Frontenac, who regarded it as necessary to the growth of the fur trade, had appeared to favour it.

But at length, feeling this fatal moment draw near when truth ordinarily reveals itself to the mind in its full light, he recognized that the transportation of this liquor had caused very great ills to this infant Church and to the colony. Vexed at having in this matter committed his authority to men who had abused it, he protested that if God did not withdraw him from this world he would act with more circumspection ³

Though there is little likelihood that this death-bed repentance indicated a true intellectual conversion, it may possibly have been used in such a way as to influence the views of the court. At any rate, on March 30, 1699, before the news had reached Paris, M. de Tronson admitted to the Jesuit Bruyas that brandy was the great obstacle to the conversion of the Indians, but, he added, " the difficulty is to convince the court, after what took place in the time of M. Colbert, (who was) well enough intentioned." ⁴ Yet two months later instructions were issued for Callières, which would almost suggest that the court had been convinced. Instead of harping upon the necessity of resisting the encroachment of the Church on the domain of the State, his

---

¹ *Gaspésie*, vol. i, pp. 425-37.   ² *Ibid.*, p 432.
³ *Fds Fr*, 13,516, f 175 (Dec. 19, 1698).
⁴ *Tronson*, vol. ii, p 383.

orders described intoxicating drinks as " the source of the greatest crimes committed in the colony," and His Majesty commanded him " to reform all the abuses and the disturbances which these drinks have caused."[1]

However, as Belmont has informed us, the appointment of a new governor failed to mark the dawn of a new era, and at the opening of the eighteenth century the outlook for the aboriginal races was dark indeed. If further proof were needed, we could quote from the Baron de la Hontan, whom no one will accuse of feeble acquiescence in clerical views :

> Brandy causes terrible ravages among the peoples of Canada. . . This drink, which is murderous in itself, . . . consumes them so that one must have seen its baneful effects in order to believe it. It extinguishes their natural heat and makes nearly all of them fall into this languor called consumption. You see them pale, livid, and frightful as skeletons[2]

Mercenary Motives ?

Before summing up the results of our study we must draw attention to a question we have not hitherto discussed.

At times there were vague rumours afloat that the ecclesiastics were not entirely disinterested in their opposition to the sale of brandy to the natives. Even the Marquis de Seignelay suggested the possibility not only of prejudice, but also of covetousness, of *vues particulières* on the part of the most zealous opponents of the traffic. The minister, however, made no accusation, but merely threw out a hint, a question. Some critics were more outspoken, among them certain of the Récollets, who in 1681 were firmly convinced that Laval and the Jesuits sought to

[1] *Coll. MSS.*, vol ii, p 322.
[2] La Hontan, vol ii, p 145. The Jesuit *Relations* sometimes allude to a " sickness common enough among the savages," which was evidently tuberculosis, *e.g. Rel.*, 1643, p. 41 ; 1658, p 24 ; 1671, p. 29.

monopolize the brandy trade for themselves.[1] In estimating the importance to be attached to this Récollet conviction one must remember that in 1681 these monks were the allies and protégés of Frontenac and the friends of La Salle, with very slight personal knowledge of the Indian missions. Considering how closely the bishop confined them to their monastery, it is fair to surmise that the afore-mentioned accusation was based on hearsay from the party interested in the sale of brandy. Moreover, as we have shown, the Récollets themselves abandoned their early attitude on this subject. And the Sulpicians, who were equally prone to criticize the Jesuits, found no fault with their conduct in the fire-water controversy.

In the latter part of the century several laymen made direct charges. Governor Mésy accused bishop and Jesuits of enriching themselves by trafficking in furs and brandy, but on his death-bed he appeared to retract. In 1671 Dumesnil, after his brief and stormy experience of Canadian politics, charged Laval and Father Ragueneau with trading in liquor through an employee.[2] La Salle multiplied his attacks upon the monks, of whose Company he had once been a member. His assertions were particularized and direct. Though the Jesuits concealed their commerce, he himself had surprised them at it.[3] In 1676 Frontenac, who was in close touch with La Salle, assured Colbert that the Jesuits exaggerated the disturbances caused by brandy, and that they easily convinced people "who do not know the interested motives which had led them to harp continually on this string for more than forty years."[4] The following year the count informed the minister that the Jesuits were planning to have the commerce in brandy put *en parti*. "But," he continued, "my mind is at rest on that point, because I know that your insight will discover clearly enough

---

[1] Chapais, p. 322, note.
[2] *O R*, ch. xxi.
[3] Margry, vol. i, pp. 345-402.
[4] *O R*, ch. xxi.

its impropriety (*inconvénients*) and consequences." [1] The implication is that the Jesuits would profit by the proposed arrangement.

Unhappily, we have been unable to find any of the alleged proofs upon which these several accusations are based. Owing to the closeness of their associations Frontenac, La Salle, and the Récollets can scarcely be considered independent witnesses. Moreover, they share with Mésy and Dumesnil a proneness to violence and exaggeration; and, although for the most part sincere, their uncorroborated testimony is insufficient to establish their charges.

Is there, then, some indirect or presumptive evidence of a more conclusive character?

We happened upon Father Pierron's winter supply of brandy and wine, and we exonerated him from any suspicion of mercantile projects. We have not found the inventory of any other Jesuit's private supply of liquors, but we have seen that they considered a certain amount of brandy as a necessity on long journeys and for medicinal purposes. It is therefore probable that many missionaries were seen giving small quantities of brandy to Indians in need. It is just possible that some of them accepted presents in return, but of this we have no proof. But if we are ignorant of the conduct of individual missionaries, have we any knowledge of the policy of the Jesuit order in Canada?

In 1681 the ecclesiastical communities of New France petitioned the king for exemption from entry duties on 39 hogsheads of wine and 10 of brandy annually, which was equivalent to an allowance of 2000 livres. During the time of their lease the farmers of the Company of the Occident had accorded them this present in money, and it was only since the king had taken over their domain that the communities had lost their special privilege.[2] Two years later

[1] *Clair*, 1016, f. 43.   [2] *C G*, v, ff 373-5

Bishop Laval urged that this exemption be granted in perpetuity, and added that the present farmers-general were already according it spontaneously.[1] Apparently they continued their custom of paying the 2000 livres in cash until 1693, when Champigny reported that they had ordered its discontinuance; thenceforth the communities would enjoy the indemnity only on the wines and brandies they actually imported within the limit assigned. The intendant protested that the Récollets would be losers by this change, as it did not suit them to import liquors; the other communities would take the precaution to import the requisite amount, and so the farmers would gain nothing. "It would be more expedient to continue the payment of this exemption in money, because the communities are poor."[2]

It is clear, then, that the religious orders had not been importing their allotted hogsheads of wine and brandy. Their stewards doubtless secured their supplies from local merchants. On one occasion,[3] as we have noticed, the steward of the Jesuits bought fifty-six casks of wine for them and for some others at a relatively low price. The others were perhaps the remaining communities and certain of their lay friends. When Duchesneau imported a large quantity of liquors[4] it is just possible that part of it was for the use of the religious groups with whom he was on good terms, but we have discovered no record of the amount of brandy actually bought by the Jesuits for themselves.

Accordingly, whether regarding them collectively or individually, we have found no conclusive evidence to show that Jesuits or other members of the clergy trafficked in brandy either for the good of their missions or for filthy lucre.

[1] F 3, IV, f. 73v (Nov. 10, 1683).   [2] C.G., XII, f. 278.
[3] F 3, IV, f. 135.   [4] C.G., V, f. 361.

General Conclusions

In conclusion :

From the standpoint of the aborigines the brandy trade was an unmitigated curse. The attitude of the Church and its supporters has been approved by subsequent experience, and endorsed by the more humane governments of civilized countries.[1]

It is quite impossible to estimate, with any approximation to accuracy, the quantity of French brandy actually consumed by the Indians. Now and then from Fort Frontenac or Michilimackinac comes a report of the arrival, in a single year, of 40, 80, or 100 hogsheads of brandy, causing consternation to the missionaries. Nevertheless, the Jesuit memoir of 1692 estimates the annual consumption of French brandy by the Indians at 50 hogsheads out of a total of over 6000 hogsheads of liquors of all kinds imported annually into New France. But it must be noted that the object of this estimate was to impress Pontchartrain with the economic insignificance of the Indian brandy trade in comparison with the aggregate of Canadian commerce. Some years later the Abbé de Belmont, though with a similar aim, raised the estimate to 100 hogsheads. But whether the number of hogsheads was greater or less, we know that the immediate effects upon the native races were utterly demoralizing, while indirectly it rendered them more susceptible to consumption and other diseases.

The other side of the problem concerns colonial prosperity. Here the situation is more complex. Clearly, the immediate profits from the fur trade were greater when brandy was used as an article of barter, inasmuch as it rendered possible a scandalous exploitation of the Indian.

On the other hand, the reflex influence of the traffic upon

[1] Witness, *e g*, the Indian Act of Canada, 1906, sections 135-46.

the traders was baneful in the extreme. Their exorbitant profits were dissipated in debauchery, and seldom represented a real increase in the wealth of the colony Furthermore, brandy was the chief stimulus to the exodus of hundreds of young men from the colony into the wilderness, lured by the hope of extravagant gains and sensual indulgence. This wholesale desertion of the settlements arrested the agricultural development of Canada for many decades. To some slight extent this economic loss was offset by a gain to which Intendant de Meulles calls attention, viz. a reduction in the price of general merchandise caused by the visit of vessels attracted to Quebec by the prospect of large profits in the wholesale liquor trade.

On the whole, we may safely say that the Indian liquor traffic was bad even for the French colony; but royal edicts, governors' ordinances, and ecclesiastical excommunications were alike powerless to control it—the more so because (as the assembly of 1678 clearly showed) the majority of the inhabitants were convinced that successful repression of the brandy trade in New France would involve the deflection of the fur trade to New England.

Hence we are forced to the conclusion that the solution of the problem could be achieved only by a more radical measure—viz an international agreement between France and England for the limitation of the export of spirituous liquors to the minimum required by the colonists themselves. Denonville alone seems to have suggested the feasibility of such a far-reaching measure

The Closing Decades of French Rule

With the close of the seventeenth century our period of special study ends, and of the remaining decades of French rule in Canada we have but little to say No fundamental change seems to have taken place in the course of the liquor

DECLINE OF THE THEOCRACY

trade between Europeans and natives. The sedentary missions founded by the Jesuits succumbed to the virus of alcoholism or expelled it temporarily—according to time and circumstances and the personality of their pastors.[1] In 1724 the learned Jesuit Lafitau exclaimed: "And would to God that the Europeans had never acquainted (the aborigines) with these unhappy beverages, which serve only to destroy them!"[2] In 1730 Father Laure wrote with admiration of an exceptional tribe along the lower St. Lawrence which was not addicted to alcohol. Five years later Father Nau of the Sault St. Louis confessed: "Our Indians find all the fire-water they want, and as soon as they are drunk they are capable of any crime", and again "Drunkenness is the great vice of the Indian"[3] In 1730, also, a charge of Bishop Dosquet to his clergy forbade them to absolve those who contributed to the intoxication of the Indians. But this measure aroused a storm of protest and accomplished nothing.[4]

According to Latour, liquor prevented the Micmacs and the Ottawas from performing their duty in the wars with the English,[5] but towards the close of the French period the "furore for brandy diminished a little," as the Indians became accustomed to it.[6] However, Latour's range of observation must have been limited, for Bonnefons in his ten years (1751-61) of Canadian travel found that, apart from the sedentary missions along the river, the natives were still passionately fond of alcohol. In 1757 Montcalm described the conduct of the Indians who had been given brandy at La Chine: "They swam in barrelfuls of this liquor, and did not quit the barrel until they fell dead-drunk. According to them, to die of inebriation would be

---

[1] Rochemonteix, vol. III, pp 395-400.
[2] Lafitau, p 125
[3] Jones, vol I, p. 36, vol II, pp 59, 60
[4] *Mandements*, vol. i, p 535.   [5] Latour (1761), p. 77.
[6] *Ibid*, p 87.

a glorious death; their paradise is to drink."[1] And French officers and French historians affirm that rum was the cause of the terrible massacre of Fort William Henry—the darkest blot upon French military honour.[2]

[1] *Voyage au Canada*, p 144, *et seq*, *Journal du Marquis de Montcalm*, p. 299, both cited by Salone, *Sauvages du Canada*, 1907, p 15.

[2] E.g. Casgrain, *Montcalm et Lévis*, p. 112; *cf.* Kingsford, vol. iv, pp. 64, 66.

BIBLIOGRAPHY

A. PRINTED SOURCES

I. Contemporary Records

AUTHOR AND TITLE	ABBREVIATION.
Factum du procès entre Jean de Biencourt et les Pères Biard et Massé, Jésuites. (Paris, 1614. Reprinted, 1887, by Maisonneuve et Leclercq)	*Factum*
Jean de Laet: *L'Histoire du Nouveau Monde* (Leyde, 1640, in fol) *Cf.* p. 63 for account of quarrel between Poutrincourt and Jesuits.	
Lescarbot: *Histoire de la Nouvelle France.* (Paris, 1609, 1611 Republished, 1866, by Tross) English version, annotated edition, *History of New France,* Toronto, 1911 Biggar and Grant.	Lescarbot.
Père Biard, S J.: *Relation de la Nouvelle France.* (Lyon, 1616, in 12mo)	
Relations des Jésuites dans la Nouvelle France (Quebec, 1858, 3 vols)	*Rel.*
Thwaites *The Relations of the Jesuits* (Cleveland, 70 vols. in 4to)	Thwaites
Carayon: *Première Mission des Jésuites au Canada: Lettres et Documents Inédits.* (Paris, 1864)	Carayon.
Mission du Canada: Relations inédites des Jésuites, 1672-1680. (Paris, Duniol, 2 vols.)	*Rel. inéd.*
Laverdière et Casgrain: *Le Journal des Jésuites,* 1645 to 1668. (Quebec, 1871)	*Journal.*
Avis au Roi sur la Nouvelle France. (Paris, 1626, in 8vo)	*Avis au Roi.*

Author and Title	Abbreviation
Champlain: *Les Voyages de la Nouvelle France Occidentale*, 1603-1629. (Paris, 1632, in 4to) . Accounts of Champlain's voyages were published in 1613, 1619, 1620, and 1627. In 1830 they were republished at the expense of the French Government	Champlain, 1632.
Laverdière: *Œuvres de Champlain*. (Second edition, Quebec, 1870, 6 tomes)	*Œuvres de Champlain.*
Sagard. *Le Grand Voyage du pays des Hurons.* (Paris, 1632, in 8vo)	*Grand Voyage.*
Sagard: *Histoire du Canada.* (Paris, 1636. Republished at Arras, 1865, in 3 vols.) . .	Sagard.
Le Clercq *Premier Etablissement de la Foi* (Paris, 1691, 2 vols.)	Le Clercq.
Le Clercq: *Nouvelle Relation de la Gaspésie.* (Paris, 1691) . . . . Translated and published at Toronto, 1911, by Ganong as *New Relation of Gaspesia*	*Gaspésie.*
Claude Martin *Lettres de la Vénérable Mère Marie de l'Incarnation*. (Paris, 1681, in 4to) . .	*Lettres.*
Mère Juchereau: *Histoire de l'Hôtel-Dieu de Québec*, 1639-1716. (Montauban, 1751, in 12mo) Republished by Abbé Casgrain, Montreal, 1888.	Juchereau.
Antoine Arnauld. *Œuvres Complètes.* (Paris, 1775-1783, 38 vols.) Vol. xxxiv contains the memoir of M. d'Allet	Arnauld.
Bressani: *Relation abrégée de quelques missions des Pères de la Compagnie de Jésus.* Translated by R. P. Martin. (Montreal, 1852, in 8vo) . .	Bressani.
Dollier de Casson: *Histoire de Montréal*, 1640-1672. (Montreal, 1868)	*Montréal.*
Les Véritables Motifs de Messieurs et Dames de la Société de N.D. de Montréal pour la Conversion des Sauvages de la Nouvelle France. (Paris, 1643, in 4to)	*Véritables Motifs.*

BIBLIOGRAPHY

AUTHOR AND TITLE.	ABBREVIATION.
Lefebvre : *Histoire Chronologique de la Province des Récollets de Paris.* (Paris, 1677.)	
Pierre Boucher: *Histoire Véritable et Naturelle du Canada.* (Paris, 1663 ; Montreal, 1882).	*Hist. Vér.*
Evêque de Québec; *Estat Présent de l'Eglise et de la Colonie Française dans la Nouvelle France.* (Paris, 1688, in 8vo) Reprinted at Quebec, 1856.	*Estat.*
Asseline · *Les Antiquités et Chroniques de Dieppe.* (Dieppe, 1874, 2 vols. in 8vo. Apparently written about 1682)	Asseline.
Daval : *Histoire de la Réformation à Dieppe*, 1557-1657. (Rouen, 1879, 2 vols. in 4to)	Daval.
Abbé de Latour: *Mémoire sur la vie de M. de Laval.* (Paris, 1761, in 12mo)	Latour.
Père Ragueneau: *La Vie de la Mère Catherine de Saint-Augustin.* (Paris, 1671.)	
Père d'Orléans, S.J. : *La Vie du Père Pierre Coton ... Confesseur des Rois Henri IV et Louis XIII.* (Paris, 1688, in 4to)	*Vie de Coton*
La Hontan · *Nouveaux Voyages de M. le Baron de la Hontan dans l'Amérique Septentrionale.* (La Haye, 1703, 2 vols in 12mo ; Amsterdam, 1728).	La Hontan
Hennepin · *Nouvelle Découverte d'un très grand Pays.* (Utrecht, 1697). English edition, Chicago, 1903, in 2 vols., edited by R. G. Thwaites.	Hennepin
Chevalier de Baugy: *Journal d'une expédition contre les Iroquois en 1687.* (Paris, 1883, in 8vo)	Baugy.
Bacqueville de la Potherie : *Histoire de l'Amérique Septentrionale*, 1534-1701. (Paris, 1722, 4 vols. in 12mo) Republished in 1753, and in Amsterdam in 1723.	Potherie.

| AUTHOR AND TITLE. | ABBREVIATION. |

Père Lafitau, S.J.: *Mœurs des Sauvages Américains.* (Paris, 1724) . . . . . . *Lafitau.*

Bertrand: *Correspondance de M. Tronson* (Paris, 1904, 3 vols. in 8vo) . . . . . *Tronson.*

Margry: *Mémoires et Documents des Origines Françaises des pays d'Outre-Mer.* (Paris, 1879, 6 vols. in 8vo) . . . . . . *Margry.*

Margry: *Relations et Mémoires inédits.* (Paris, 1867, 1 vol.) . . . . . . *Margry, Relations.*

A. E. Jones, S.J.: *Documents Rares ou Inédits.* (Montreal) *Recueil de pièces sur la négociation entre la Nouvelle France et la Nouvelle Angleterre ès années 1648 et suivantes.* (New York, 1866, in 8vo.) Contains an account of Père Druillettes' famous journey . . . . *Recueil.*

Collection de Mémoires et de relations sur l'histoire ancienne du Canada. (Quebec, 1840, in 8vo.) Contains Belmont's "History of Canada" and a "Histoire de l'eau-de-vie."

Alfred de Ramé: *Documents inédits sur le Canada* Second Series. (Paris, 1867, in 8vo) . . *Doc. inéd.*

Collection de mss. contenant lettres, mémoires et autres documents historiques, relatifs à la Nouvelle France (Quebec, 1883-85, 4 vols. in 4to.) Vol. i contains an important memoir of La Chesnaye, some correspondence of Talon, etc.. . . *Coll. MSS.*

Nouvelle France, Documents Historiques. (Quebec, vol. i, 1893) This volume is to be found in the Parliamentary Library of Quebec . . *Nouvelle France.*

Edits et Ordonnances Royaux. (Quebec, 1854) . *Edits.*

Mandements . . . des Evêques de Québec. (Quebec, 1887, 5 vols.) . . . . . . *Mandements.*

Jugements et Délibérations du Conseil Souverain de Québec. (Quebec, 1885-91, 6 vols.) . . *C.S.*

Procès-Verbaux des Assemblées-Générales du Clergé de France. (Paris, 1770) . . . . *Procès-Verbaux.*

BIBLIOGRAPHY

AUTHOR AND TITLE.	ABBREVIATION.
Le Mercure François. (Paris, annual volumes throughout seventeenth century, in 8vo).	*Mercure.*
Rapports sur les Archives du Canada (Ottawa, in 4to)	*Rapport.*
Calendar of State Papers. (The copy used is in the Bibliothèque Nationale in Paris)	*State Papers.*

II. MODERN PUBLICATIONS

Publications of the Royal Society of Canada . Royal Society

Ferland : *Notes sur les registres de Notre Dame de Québec.* (Quebec, 1863, in 4to.)

Faillon : *Histoire de la Colonisation Française en Canada.* (Paris, 1865, 3 vols. in 4to) . . Faillon.

R. P. de Ravignan : *De l'Existence et de l'Institut des Jésuites* (Paris, 1862, in 8vo) . . . Ravignan

P. Camille de Rochemonteix. *Les Jésuites et la Nouvelle France au dix-septième siècle.* (Paris, 1897, 3 vols.) . . . . . Rochemonteix.

Allier : *La Cabale des Dévots.* (Paris, 1902, in 8vo) Allier.

Parkman : *Old Régime,* etc. O.R.

H. P. Biggar : *The Early Trading Companies of New France.* (Toronto, 1901, in 8vo.)

Abbé Auguste Gosselin : *La Vie du Vénérable François de Montmorency-Laval* (Quebec, 1890, 2 vols. in 8vo) . . . . . Gosselin.

Gosselin *Henri de Bernières.* (Quebec, 1902) . *Bernières.*

Chapais : *Jean Talon, intendant de la Nouvelle France.* (Quebec, 1904, in 8vo) . . . Chapais.

Léon de la Sicotière : *L'Emigration percheronne au Canada pendant le XVII· Siècle* (Alençon, 1887) . . . . Sicotière.

Salone : *La Colonisation de la Nouvelle France.* (Paris, Guilmoto, in 8vo) . . . . Salone.

Salone : *Sauvages du Canada.* (Paris, 1907.)

B. MANUSCRIPT SOURCES

I. Paris

	ABBREVIATION.
(a) Bibliothèque Nationale	B.N.
(1) Mélanges de Colbert	*Mélanges.*
(2) Les Cinq Cents de Colbert	*Cinq Cents.*
(3) Fonds Français	*Fds. Fr.*
(4) Supplément Français	*Supp. Fr.*
(5) Ancien Fonds	*Ancien Fds.*
(6) Collection Moreau	*Moreau.*
(7) Fonds Clairambault	*Clair.*
(8) Nouvelles Acquisitions Françaises.	

(b) Ministère des Affaires Etrangères . . . A E.
   (1) Fonds Amérique . . . . . *Am.*
   (2) France.
   (3) Correspondance d'Angleterre . . *Angleterre.*

(c) Archives Nationales . . . . . A N.

   (1) Series C (C¹¹ Colonies). This is the Correspondance Générale du Canada, the most important of our sources. Many of the documents credited to the Affaires Etrangères are duplicated here (While the Colonial archives were being transferred from the Pavillon de Flore to the Palais Soubise, we were obliged to work in the archives of the Foreign Office) . *C.G.*

   (2) Series B. *Lettres envoyées.* Royal dispatches to Canada . . . . B.

   (3) Series F 3. Collection Moreau Saint-Méry. Many of its documents are copies or summaries of the originals in the Correspondance Générale . . F 3.

   (4) Series F. *Missions religieuses,* vols. 2, 3 . F.

   (5) C 13 (Colonies), series 3, vol. iii : La Salle's enterprises . . . . C 13.

BIBLIOGRAPHY

ABBREVIATION.

(6) Colonies en Général, Carton F 78 contains, among other things, Laval's factum against Mésy . . . . *Colonies.*

(7) Cartons M 242, M 247, K 1374

II. QUEBEC

Provincial Archives, in the Parliament Building "Documents." Vol. i contains documents pertaining to the early history of Montreal . . *Doo.*

III. MONTREAL

Archives of St Mary's College. Through the courtesy of Rev. A E. Jones, S.J , archivist, we were able to consult the rich collection of materials in the Fonds Rochemonteix . . *Fds. Roche*

IV. OTTAWA

The Dominion Archives . . . . . Dom. Arch.

VITA

Mack Eastman was born in Oshawa, Ontario, November 18, 1883. In 1904, after three years of teaching in the public schools, he entered the University of Toronto. In 1907 he graduated with first class honors in the English and History course, (classical option) and was awarded the Mackenzie Fellowship in history. During the following year he acted as locum tenens for the professor of English in the Western University, London, Ontario. The next three years (1908-1911) were spent in Paris. Here Mr. Eastman devoted most of his time to research work in early Canadian history, but he also took courses in modern European history and social economy at the Sorbonne, the Ecole des Hautes Etudes Sociales and elsewhere. Among the professors whose lectures he followed, were Messieurs Seignobos, Emile Bourgeois, Debidour, Aulard, Charles Gide, Bougle and Lagardelle.

For the academic year 1911-1912, Mr. Eastman was appointed George William Curtis Fellow in Columbia University. At Columbia he took a seminar in English industrial history with Professor Shotwell and another in economics with Professor Seager. He also followed courses given by Professors Robinson, Sloane, Dunning, Shotwell and Simkhovitch.

From October, 1912, to May, 1915, Mr Eastman taught history in Calgary College, Calgary, Alberta. During his vacations he carried on some researches in Quebec Province and prepared his dissertation for the press.

CPSIA information can be obtained
at www.ICGtesting.com
Printed in the USA
LVHW081928250123
737953LV00004B/13